Explaining our world
An approach to the art of
Environmental Interpretation

Explaining our world

An approach to the art of Environmental Interpretation

Andrew Pierssené

E & FN SPON

An Imprint of Routledge
London and New York

Published by E & FN Spon
an imprint of Routledge
11 New Fetter Lane
London EC4P 4EE

Simultaneously published in the USA
and Canada
by Routledge
29 West 35th Street
New York
NY 10001

First edition 1999

Edited and designed by
Jane Havell Associates, London

Printed in Great Britain by
The Bath Press

Frontispiece: near Hay Bluff, border of
Powys (Wales) and Herefordshire
(England).
Photograph: Andrew Pierssené

*British Library Cataloguing in
Publication Data*
A catalogue record for this book is
available from the British Library

*Library of Congress Cataloging in
Publication Data*
A catalogue record for this book has
been requested

ISBN 0 419 21940 4

Contents

Dedication

To two 'anonymous' interpreters from opposite sides of the world – one who interpreted language in Moscow's Kremlin, and the other the environment of the Grand Canyon in Colorado – both of whom have influenced the form of this book. They are portrayed at work in chapter 1.

Foreword

The designers of China's gardens, whether private or public, based their work on a traditional philosophy, with which I find myself in total sympathy. Expressed in its simplest form, it held that a visitor to a garden was a central feature of its composition. The garden had two essential and closely interlinked elements: the design itself, and the people who came to enjoy it and to obtain inspiration and comfort from it. That the visitors and the garden were separate from one another was a completely alien and incomprehensible concept: the visitors were part of the garden. One interacted with the other and gave meaning and purpose to the whole.

For a long time, and greatly to our disadvantage, our Western attitude to any kind of exhibition has been markedly confrontational. We have looked at gardens, museum exhibits and zoo animals, but always as spectators. We have not been regarded, or regarded ourselves, as an integral part of the total scene.

In my own work, the museum field, I have become increasingly impatient with the notion that museums are essentially places where interesting material can be brought together, conserved and displayed – i.e. institutions to be visited. More and more I have come to regard every street, farm and river as a 'museum', interlocking and mutually supporting one another to form the Great London Museum, the Great British Museum or whatever the chosen unit may be. These units become progressively bigger, and eventually add up, in our case, to the Great European Museum.

A Great Museum, whatever its size, is one that one cannot avoid visiting, because one lives in it and sees part of it every day. There is nothing elitist or selective about it: the people who use it look at it day by day. Whether they are aware of what they are looking at is another matter, and this is why Andrew Pierssené's book is so welcome. I particularly like his declaration that 'the process of interpretation requires a threesome'. In Environmental Interpretation, he says 'the trio consists of the Feature, the Visitor and the Interpreter' – which means, in effect, that people, whether residents or tourists, have to be given eyes with which to see and attitudes with which to understand. Given such guidance and encouragement, they become sharers of the landscape, urban or rural. They have been made sensitive to what is exposed to their view and, as a result, their range of interests and their concern for proper conservation has been enormously enlarged.

It is more than twenty years since Andrew Pierssené and I became aware that we were on the same wavelength. I owe him a great debt of gratitude for laying the foundations of my present conviction that the environment, both natural and man-made, has to be regarded and understood as a whole, and that a series of partial approaches is both sterile and a great waste of opportunity. Environmental Interpretation is a jigsaw, in which all the pieces are of equal value and importance, and in which final satisfaction comes from seeing all the bits in place.

I am convinced that this book – with its courage, its freshness of approach and its complete freedom from intellectual clichés – is one of the three or four most valuable works on the subject to have been produced during the past fifty chaotic years. It deserves a wide readership and all possible success.

Kenneth Hudson
Director of the European Museums Forum

Preface and acknowledgements

This book is not intended to be an academic review of the art and craft of Interpretation, nor a DIY handbook for Interpreters. An academic review would no doubt be worthwhile to write and interesting to read, but another handbook might unwittingly do as much harm as good.[1] To those who have already thoroughly absorbed the aims and principles of Interpretation, a how-to-do-it handbook can indeed provide useful ideas, but for others less well grounded it can reinforce the misconception that Interpretation may be achieved mechanically (rather as if a work of art might result from painting by numbers). Imagination, perception and inspiration are important elements in good Interpretation, which also depends upon an understanding of a wide range of social, psychological and educational principles – beware of anyone offering a formula that promises automatic and instant success.

Instead, here is a discussion (opinionated, no doubt) of many of the principles that seem to me to be important. Virtually all the ideas and instances come from my own observation and experience. Although I am aware how much I owe to what fellow-Interpreters have done, said and written, I have tried to make my own assessments rather than to rely on the conclusions of others. Since, therefore, this is in a sense a personal book, I have not hesitated to write in the first person when it seemed natural to do so. But because I and other Interpreters are also members of the general public and thus frequent visitors to places of interest, the personal pronouns may refer both to people in their capacity as providers of Interpretation, and also in their capacity as receivers or consumers of it.

Interpretation, both in its antecedents and in its current form, is an international phenomenon, and deserves to be practised intelligently and effectively throughout the world. It would be satisfying to think that this book was written in terms that were equally applicable to every nation. The snag, I have discovered, is that much of the actual practice of Interpretation is governed by the institutions, traditions and circumstances peculiar to each country. I have therefore framed my ideas in terms of Britain, the culture I know best – but those who are skilled in reading between the lines will not find it difficult to translate the principles, and even some

1. Though there are several good ones available, some published first in USA and others in Britain.

of the specific examples, into terms familiar to them from their own experience.

I have cited certain Interpretation schemes for what seems to me their high quality and others for their weaknesses, but I do not always name them. The reasons for not putting names to poor practice are obvious; even good schemes may have weaknesses, and it would be unfair to identify them and risk spoiling the reputation they deserve for their best work. The main reason for being cautious about naming the good is the inevitable (and very proper) transitoriness of most Interpretation. Where I do show enthusiasm for good or interesting practice, readers must remember that what I describe may no longer exist in the same form, or at all, so please do not rush off to see it! Because of the short shelf-life of most Interpretation, many of the photographs in this book may be considered to be in the category of archival interest rather than reportage.

The main aim of the book is to help anyone who attempts Interpretation, professional or amateur, to think more clearly about what he or she is doing, and why. There is now quite a substantial body of literature about the subject, ranging from manuals to conference reports, from interpretive plans to papers in learned journals. It is not easily accessible, but anyone who studies this material will soon become aware that the ideas and practices that developed in the National Parks of the USA over many decades[2] have, as they spread, found new contexts and new motivations, and generated new terminology and definitions. As a result there can be confusion and contradiction about what Interpretation really is or should be, and what it is for. There is therefore a need to provide Interpretation with a revised *raison d'être*.

Where I seem dogmatic, this is not so much in order to refute others as the result of the search for reconciliation. It is the underlying principles of Interpretation and its ultimate motivation that I have tried to identify: it is, as I have found myself in practice, much easier to see what needs to be done in a specific situation once the principles are identified and held clearly in mind. Firm principles should help to guide Interpreters as they freely use their imaginations in their creative work.

The book will, I hope, prove useful to teachers and planners, naturalists, archaeologists and historians, heritage managers, tourism officers and general environmentalists, as well as to those who already see themselves as Interpreters. I hope the occasional copy might fall into the hands of members of the public. It would be good for Interpretation if our consumers or visitors were encouraged to develop a critical attitude to what we offer them: a critical attitude towards all aspects of the world about us is what Interpretation seeks to stimulate.[3]

All who are involved in Environmental Interpretation will be

2. Reviewed and, to a certain extent, formulated in 1957 by Freeman Tilden in his seminal book *Interpreting our Heritage*, University of North Carolina Press, 1957.

3. For a definition of 'criticism' in this context, see the list of terms at the end of chapter 1 (page 7).

aware of their debt to Freeman Tilden, whose book *Interpreting our Heritage* was the first substantial publication on the subject. Fairly short and immensely readable, it is still in print, and its contents are as relevant and inspiring as ever. British Interpreters must be grateful that in 1966 Don Aldridge, then the recently appointed Information Officer for the Peak District National Park, was granted a Churchill Scholarship to study Interpretation in the USA, and was able to bring back his experience and enthusiasm and communicate it to those ready to do comparable work in Britain.

My own work experience includes full-time youth work; training youth leaders; freelance printing and design; work on a regional Interpretation project for the Carnegie United Kingdom Trust (in the course of which I was privileged to learn the principles of Interpretation from Don Aldridge and others advising the Trust); practical Interpretation work and consultancy over many years; part-time adult education; and part-time tutoring in Interpretation at a college in East Anglia. I owe a great deal to my colleagues in all these various phases of my career: much of what I have learned from and with them has found its way into this book.

Several friends and colleagues have kindly read and commented on individual chapters, and have been able to save me from a number of errors of fact and ambiguities of expression. Without their generous help the book would be the poorer; but I am well aware that they do not all necessarily approve of everything I have to say, nor the way I say it. I take full responsibility both for the opinions I express, and for factual accuracy.

Among those who have helped me in this way I must particularly thank Don Aldridge, Gillian Binks, James Carter, Michael Glen, Jo Hammond, Cynthia Harrell, Richard Harrison, John Iddon, Ken Jackson, Phil Jayne, Andrew Jenkinson, Gerry Pocock, Roger Whittaker and Sally Wright. Others have helped in other ways, such as providing information or illustrative material: Harold Hendriks, Bartosz Jacyma, Marista Leishman, my wife Avril Pierssené, Dr Oliver Rackham, the respondents to my pilot survey on enthusiasms (see chapter 15), and the various institutions, organisations and individuals who have generously lent their photographs.

I must thank also my old friend David Elliston Allen and his publisher Penguin Books for allowing me to quote passages from his book *The Naturalist in Britain*; Penguin Books also for permission to quote from Robert Arvill's *Man and Environment*; Faber and Faber Ltd for permission to quote from T. S. Eliot's Chorus I from 'The Rock' in his *Collected Poems 1909–1962*; Peters, Fraser and Dunlop for permission to quote from *The Best of Beachcomber* by J. B. Morton, and the National Geographic Society for permission to quote from Bruce Babbitt's introduction to 'Our National Parks' in the *National Geographic* for October 1994. I am particularly appreciative of the kindness of Kenneth Hudson, Director of the European Museum Forum, whose writing on a wide range of topics I have always admired, in agreeing to write a Foreword for this book. To my publishers I must express thanks for their advice and patience.

My efforts to identify and make contact with the two anonymous dedicatees of this book have been only partially successful. I discovered to my delight that the Park Ranger on the rim of the Grand Canyon (see page 6) was Cynthia Harrell, with whom I have since been able to correspond, and to whom I am grateful not only for the Interpretation she provided one day in October 1990, but for her gracious acceptance of the dedication. My attempts to get in touch with the other dedicatee have so far proved unsuccessful – but I will go on trying.

Andrew Pierssené
1998

Environmental interpretation
What is it? Some key concepts

We English-speakers have, so the dictionaries tell us, been 'interpreting' language since the middle ages; we have 'interpreted' observed phenomena since the 1700s; and performers have offered their 'interpretations' of musical works since 1880. But this useful word has recently been called into fresh service, with another connotation so recent that the second edition of the Oxford English Dictionary, published in 1989, does not record it. There is now a whole range of activity (virtually a profession) known as 'interpreting the environment' – sharing our understanding of how the world works. For those of you too impatient to wait another sixty years for the OED's third edition, I offer here a provisional definition of this new usage, together with a couple of dated examples:

> **interpretation** (n). (i) The skills, practice or profession of explaining to the general public features of our natural, historical or cultural environment; (ii) the educational process or experience of enlightenment resulting from such explanation. Examples: Freeman Tilden, *Interpreting Our Heritage* (book title), 1957; Centre for Environmental Interpretation (former institution within Manchester Metropolitan University, 1980–1997).

In current practice, this is an activity largely directed towards tourists – not just visitors travelling abroad, but any of us as we move about our own country. There are nature reserves, national parks, stately homes, industrial monuments, archaeological sites, museums and, more recently, purpose-built visitor centres, discovery parks and 'experiences'. All are anxious to give us explanations of what they offer, and most of us are happy to learn more about what we have come to know as our heritage. The past two decades have seen a burgeoning of such provision, and connoisseurs will probably agree that much of it is better presented than it used to be. The more cynical may comment that we could do with less of it, while the discerning will also be aware of the rubbish that sometimes masquerades as interpretation, and will recognise how counter-productive second-rate work can be.

What at first sight may seem, from my proposed dictionary definition, to be a simple and straightforward concept deserves to be

A useful explanation of the term is offered on the letter paper of the Society for the Interpretation of Britain's Heritage: 'Interpretation is the process of communicating to people the significance of a place or object so that they may enjoy it more, understand their heritage and environment better, and develop a positive attitude to conservation.'

2   Environmental
     interpretation
     What is it?
     Some key concepts

examined with some care. Interpretation touches most of our lives: we are at the receiving end of countless offers from people who want to explain to us our towns, our countryside, our institutions, our culture, our earth. Busily exerting all this effort to tell us 'how our world works' is a growing body of 'interpreters' – full-time, part-time, waged and voluntary.

Over the past two or three decades, we have come to swallow such terms as conservation, heritage, pollution, green tourism – do we need more jargon? So long as a new term is not too barbaric, and provided we can actually agree what we mean by it and can use it intelligently, it will do us little harm. The word 'interpretation' used in this context can be seen as a straightforward and appropriate metaphor, taken from language interpretation.

THE INTERPRETATION THREESOME

International affairs have moved on dramatically since the 1980s. Do you remember those exciting encounters between East and West – Margaret Thatcher of Britain and Mikhail Gorbachev of the USSR, for instance, amicably shaking hands at last, conferring and even exchanging laughter and smiles? The inevitable third party at all these tête-à-têtes was an unknown but instantly recognisable man – slim, balding, with a moustache – who stood discreetly behind Gorbachev, translating both for him and for Thatcher. Discreet, anonymous, and essential. Gorbachev spoke no English, Thatcher no Russian. It could be argued that the interpreter was, if not a Very Important Person in the accepted sense, just as important to the process of communication as the other two. Without such a skilled enabler there could have been no understanding between the two political leaders.

The 'environmental interpreter' is in exactly the same position. Visitors need to be introduced to places or features, to help their understanding of what these things have to communicate. The VIPs in this encounter are the feature itself (it could be a castle, a landscape, a silver candlestick, a pond, a coal-mine) and the visitor (tourist, student, citizen or casual passer-by).

The feature is a VIP because every building, every hill or valley, every living species of plant or animal, every craft, every artefact has not only an inherent value but also something relevant to say to each of us – if only we could understand its language! Its inherent value means that we must look after it properly (conservation), while we have a duty to try and understand its message.

The visitor is a VIP because he or she, as a human being, has power to help or harm the environment, to accept or reject it, to create, to conserve or to destroy. And this power can be applied not only to the wider environmental issues such as atmospheric pollution

Throughout the long years of the 'cold war', the people of the East and West misunderstood each other, starved of opportunities for communication and understanding. When at last President Reagan and Prime Minister Thatcher were able to meet President Gorbachev, and to chat and smile, *glasnost* encouraged the will to co-exist and to co-operate.

Language interpretation served as a 'mechanism' to enable communication to happen, a function that can serve as a metaphor for environmental interpretation. Many people today would welcome a similar reconciliation between humankind and our earth, between local communities and their own local environments.

Every generation needs opportunities to take an intelligent interest in its surroundings, and to develop an observant curiosity about the way people live and about the earth which is essentially our (and our descendants') sole resource for survival and civilisation. We need interpreters who will help us build an understanding of the world about us, giving us a better chance to relate happily to our world, and to manage it sensibly.

The two leaders with their interpreter at the Soviet Embassy, London, April 1989.

or land use in Antarctica, but also to immediate local and even personal matters such as whether to demolish the Victorian town hall, or whether to join a political party.

Understanding how our world works is a necessary element in the proper practice of such relatively humble activities as gardening, town planning, nature conservation, fitness and diet, family economy, even personal and community relationships. It can also contribute to the quality and enjoyment of every person's life.

The interpreter is not a VIP in the same sense as these two: he (or she) is there not for his own sake, but to serve both feature and visitor and the hoped-for relationship between the two. His attitude is essentially that of a discreet, loyal but anonymous servant, while his function is to be an intermediary, a broker of understanding and appreciation between the world and the individual. This function is extraordinarily important, and should be valued by society much more highly than it is – more highly, let us say, than entertainment, art or leadership, activities which in themselves depend on effective communication for their success.

So the process of interpretation requires a threesome. The diagrams overleaf express this triangular relationship, and try also to suggest the processes of giving and receiving that keep it alive. Later chapters will look more closely at each of these three parties to the interpretational process.

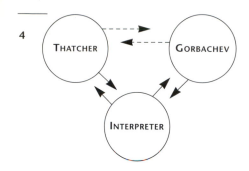

The language interpretation triangle

A WORD WITH MANY MEANINGS

It is difficult to be certain exactly what is meant in any given context by the words 'interpret', 'interpretation', 'interpreter' and 'interpretational'. This is mainly because the words are in fact used in several different ways. In this book, for example, the noun 'interpretation' will be used to describe the work, the profession of a full-time Interpreter; but it will also be used to describe the educational quality of his communication, and the process of enlightenment experienced by the visitor whenever this communication works. From time to time, we also cannot help using it in its earlier metaphorical sense: 'How should we interpret these bumps in the ground?' we might ask, or 'Have we interpreted the relationship between this landscape and its communities correctly?'

When we are talking, we have to rely on the context to make the precise meaning of our words clear. This works well enough if everyone involved makes the same distinctions, but causes confusion when they don't. No end of confusion – not just mutual misunderstanding but muddled thinking – arises from imprecise terms: to think clearly requires mental effort and a careful choice of words.

To try to make this clearer, I will illustrate it by typographic distinctions. Interpretation, printed like this in ordinary typography, could be used when the term means anything already listed in older dictionaries, whether literal or metaphorical. We would then know that the sentence 'I find it hard to interpret his strange behaviour' was not intended to have any new or special meaning. INTERPRETATION, printed in capitals, would describe the practical work or vocation of the Environmental Interpreter – probably researching, writing, designing or speaking to the public as part of the job. There is no knowing whether this kind of work will ever achieve its objective, namely *interpretation*. In italics, the term is reserved to describe the actual mental process whereby information, whether or not communicated through the agency of the Interpreter, is received as insight by the visitor. The correct use of the term *interpretation* must imply a successful transference or stimulation of ideas, evidenced by a consequent sense of enlightenment, of fresh insight, in the mind of the Visitor. This is the INTERPRETER's goal, and the sole validation of his or her work.

We need to distinguish these different meanings of the word, because by no means all INTERPRETATION results in *interpretation*. To put it another way, just because you have produced a leaflet or

> *It must have irritated some of his fellow panellists when the popular philosopher C. E. M. Joad, in the earlier years of the BBC's Brains Trust programme on the radio, came out with his oft-repeated catchphrase, 'It all depends what you mean by . . .' But he was certainly right.*

erected an information board, it does not mean that you will necessarily communicate any insights to your public. Even true facts and sound information may fail to generate insight.

INTERPRETATION seeks to encourage a special quality of understanding, not the superficial kind that knows the answers but not their significance.[1] The English author G. K. Chesterton wrote that what much modern science failed to realise was that there is little use in knowing without thinking. The criticism he levelled at modern science might today be better aimed at some examination techniques, but the conclusion of his remark is true enough. Perhaps the poet T. S. Eliot meant much the same when he wrote:

> Where is the life that we have lost in living?
> Where is the wisdom that we have lost in knowledge?
> Where is the knowledge that we have lost in information?[2]

INTERPRETATION is bound to include the provision of a fair amount of factual information; some will tend to generate understanding and insights (that is, to *interpret*), and some will not. Chapter 7 will consider this at greater length.

Now that the point has been made, the typography can revert to normal, and I trust that the reader will remember to think carefully which sense the word is meant to bear whenever it crops up. From now on, however, I will use the words Interpretation and Interpreter with a capital 'I' when the context is specifically Environmental Interpretation. This is certainly not intended to suggest that the only true Interpreters are professional or official ones. After all, most people find themselves explaining things from time to time (teaching a craft technique to a learner, communicating to a guest how the electronic fly-killer works, telling a child what a policeman is for), though to what extent these explanations qualify as Interpretation in the sense used in this book remains for the reader to decide.

Initial capitals will also be given to the terms Feature and Visitor when they are being used technically, and occasionally to other words when they are being used in some special sense. The list of terms on the following pages indicate the words for which readers should understand special meanings.

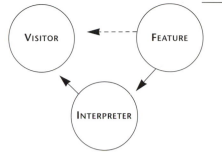

The Interpretation triangle phase 1
The message of the Feature, or the story it tells, is not clear to the Visitor directly, but the Interpreter is able to make sense of it, and communicates that sense to the Visitor.

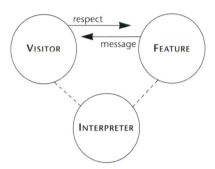

The Interpretation triangle phase 2
The Interpreter's aim is that in time the Visitor may be able to receive the message direct from the Feature, and respond to the Feature with appreciation and responsibility.

After the end of phase 2, we should ideally be left with a firm relationship between the Feature and the Visitor, while that between the Interpreter and the Visitor can fade away.

1. This is not to decry general knowledge quizzes such as Trivial Pursuit™, which can be great fun and can stimulate interest in all kinds of things. They do not, however, promote 'understanding' in our sense and would scarcely be claimed to do so.

2. Chorus from T. S. Eliot's pageant play *The Rock*, from *Collected Poems, 1909–1962*, Faber and Faber, London 1934.

There were perhaps a dozen of us, on the very rim of the Grand Canyon, Arizona. In front of us, her back to the spectacular scenery, stood a Ranger from the US National Parks Service; she was wearing a heavy jacket, which we thought strange on such a hot day. She proceeded to tell us about the Canyon – how all the variously coloured layers of rock were laid down, one by one on top of each other, in a period long before man existed. The rocks at the bottom are about one and a half billion years old. Above them is a layer of whitish limestone, deposited under shallow water many millions of years ago. Above that lies a layer of bright red rock, probably also laid down under water.

Here our guide dug in to one of her deep jacket pockets and brought out a couple of pieces of something that looked like Lego. The pieces were pale grey and red, and she stuck one on top of the other. She continued the story, and every time she mentioned a new layer of rock she drew from her pocket another appropriately coloured piece of Lego and added it on. By the end, her explanation had reached to the surface we were standing on, and her column of Lego was 15 inches high.

'Now,' she said, holding the column vertically, 'you don't see the layers like *that*, you see them like *this*.' And she detached the pieces one by one, reassembling them into a series of steps that simulated the stepped strata of the Canyon's sides. The reason, she explained, is that as the Colorado River has cut down ever deeper through the strata, so the weather has gained access to them, the upper layers being exposed for hundreds of thousands of years longer than the lower ones. Season by season, alternate heat and frost have crumbled the sides of the Canyon to form the stepped V-shape that we see today.

'People often ask me', she said, 'what is the best time to come and see the Canyon. I say, right now is the best time. If you had come sixty million years ago, it would still be a flat plain somewhere above the rock we are standing on. If you wait sixty million years more, you might find that it has all been washed away.'

This was Interpretation that left the audience with a sense of comprehension, tempered with awe. It was an experience we shall remember for a lifetime. And we never even thought to ask the Interpreter her name!

US Park Ranger acting as Interpreter at the Grand Canyon, Arizona. As a model practitioner, she is one of the dedicatees of this book.

Interpreting with discretion

To label the Grand Canyon with signs and noticeboards would be to provide an anticlimax for the visitor, and to insult one of the wonders of the world. There are some Visitor Centres there, but sited where they cannot offend. Few people would expect to stand at the edge of the Canyon with a guidebook in hand. A discreet, sympathetic and knowledgeable companion, who knows when to keep silent as well as when to speak, can enhance the experience. To be told about the place by a trained and understanding expert means that feelings as well as facts can be shared.

The north and south rims of the Canyon's winding, 250-mile course have so many bays, promontories and tributary canyons that there must be 1000 miles or so of Canyon 'edge', most of it far beyond the reach of visitors. The awe-inspiring scale of the landscape can absorb many thousands of visitors without diminishing its vast and beautiful loneliness.

LIST OF TERMS USED IN THIS BOOK

This list is offered not as a series of inviolable definitions, but as an attempt to explain the author's thinking. It is meant to be read, rather than used just for reference!

appreciate
More than just 'like' or 'be grateful for', this originally meant to 'value correctly' or 'know the real worth of' – and that is how it will be used throughout this book.

behaviour
Not a matter of being good or bad, or showing good or bad manners, but simply what people do, in terms of physical movement, demonstration of emotion, speech or other communication. This is the sense in which ethologists (students of animal behaviour) use the word; a novice ornithologist once wrote naively, but truthfully, "Birds are always behaving."

circumstances
This quite ordinary word, when applied to INTERPRETIVE PLANNING, will often denote the special set of factors that define a particular INTERPRETATION OPPORTUNITY or SITUATION.

code
The term is much used, with various meanings, in Communication Studies. In chapter 9 it denotes the system or pattern by which ideas or MESSAGES are reduced to SYMBOLS, which can be transmitted to the senses of another person ('audience' or Visitor). Speech sounds are Symbols used to encode Messages; so are various forms of writing; so, indeed, are gestures.

communication
Strictly speaking, this term should imply a two-way exchange, but we often use it to mean an attempt, successful or otherwise, to convey an idea or information (a message) to others, by some medium (speech, sign, graphics or whatever). The content of the message may or may not be interpretational. Most messages are not, so Communication is not the same as Interpretation – although it is part of the process. (The word 'message' here does not necessarily have the special sense given under the definition below.)

conservation
A more subtle concept than 'preservation'. Preservation implies trying to 'freeze' a thing or a place in the form that it currently bears, regardless of its past evolution or its changing relationship to the environment. It does not necessarily take into account how the thing or place may be used or kept in good order.

Conservation may be seen as the management of resources in a way that makes the most of them for all present and future uses – the basic principle of 'good husbandry'. Compromises are, of course, inevitable between one type of desirable use of a resource and another. In a given situation, nature conservation may have to be balanced against, say, architectural conservation or human welfare. The true conservationist has interests sufficiently broad to enable him or her to form reasoned opinions and propose imaginative solutions, based on the best available specialist information on all relevant matters. In some circumstances 'preservation' may provisionally be deemed an appropriate conservationist policy.

criticism
Used in this book to mean impartial assessment, not in its perhaps more familiar, everyday sense of unfavourable judgement. So when I write that I want people to be more 'critical', I mean that they should exercise their judgement more – to assess, rather than just to accept 'uncritically'.

culture

Used in this book without any value judgement, to mean the customs, manners and other manifestations of a social group, community or nation. This is not necessarily connected with notions of being either 'civilised' or 'barbaric'.

display

I have often used the term in this book to denote an exhibition whose main aim is to interpret some topic rather than to show a collection of artefacts. See also EXHIBITION.

education

It is often pointed out that this word means, literally, 'drawing out, forming'. The Romans coined the word *educatio* two thousand years ago, using it both to refer to the shaping of red-hot iron in the forge, and to describe the way they envisaged their children's upbringing. The word education should never be used to describe 'cramming' children for examinations. In any case, education in its real sense is not just for children but for all of us: it implies a life-long process.

environment

All that surrounds us. The physical environment includes the natural and the man-made, wilderness and countryside, villages and cities, the climate, the water we drink and the air we breathe, the universe beyond. The cultural environment includes social and political structures, the arts, language, human relationships. They all need to be understood if they are to be wisely managed, used and enjoyed.

environmental interpretation

This phrase is often used in Britain as a general term to denote what in this book is described as INTERPRETATION.

exhibition

I have tried to restrict the use of this term to mean a collection of objects displayed in their own right, as opposed to a display that is assembled to interpret some other feature or phenomenon (see DISPLAY). Thoughtful readers will realise that with this terminology we may speak of a display within an exhibition. This is very common in modern museums; it may include, for example, a display illustrating the food chain principle in the midst of a gallery exhibiting stuffed animals; or a display that interprets maritime oil rigs as part of a gallery exhibiting geological specimens. An art gallery usually houses exhibitions of works for view or for sale; but a retrospective exhibition that illustrates (i.e. seeks to interpret) the life and work of a particular artist would be, in this terminology, both an exhibition and a display.

feature

Generic term used in this book to mean the place (or site), object or phenomenon interpreted. It will be printed with a capital initial when it has this particular meaning.

form

Used in chapter 9 to denote the rhetorical mode in which an idea is communicated. See that chapter for further explanation.

green, greenness

A useful modern concept, which can be used of a process, a product or an activity. It is intended to imply that it is designed to do minimal short-term, and no long-term, harm to the environment.

green tourism
Tourism intended to cause minimal harm to the environment, including the local culture, and to provide fair rewards for local people.

guide
Commonly used to describe either a person who shows people round (a 'live guide'), or a guide-book or guide-leaflet. The context should usually make clear which is meant.

guided walk
The term is currently used in Britain to describe a semi-formal event at which a group of people are led on a walk, trail or ramble by a leader who punctuates the journey with expert comment on relevant aspects of what can be seen along the route.

heritage
All that we have inherited from previous generations, both material and non-material – not only regalia and stately homes, ceremonial and classical art, but also vernacular architecture, local tradition, landscapes, wildlife, ethnic culture, even beer mats. Perhaps we should include slums, rubbish tips and derelict sites, too, but most users of the term prefer to think chiefly of its worthier elements. Many use it to imply man-made features rather than natural ones.

heritage interpretation
A term that in some contexts is exactly equivalent to INTERPRETATION. Note the title of *Heritage Interpretation International* (see appendix D).

holistic
A term sometimes used to describe an all-inclusive, all-round, comprehensive view of a situation. Interpretation should aim to be holistic and attempt to consider Features in their total context, rather than narrowly. (This does not mean that Interpreters are meant to say everything there is to be known about every Feature!)

insight
A popular jargon word at present, it implies perceptive understanding – seeing to the heart of a matter. But what may be a novel revelation for one person may be old hat to another: one person's insight can be another's cliché.

interpret
See below, under interpretation.

interpretation
1. Explaining something observed or experienced to oneself or to another – e.g. literally, by translating something spoken in a foreign language, or metaphorically, by performing from a musical score; or by suggesting reasons for a phenomenon.
2. INTERPRETATION (in capitals). The tasks and activities carried out by a person in his or her capacity as an Interpreter; the profession, role or function of an Environmental Interpreter.
3. *Interpretation* (in italics). The internal process by which ideas communicated via an Interpreter actually create a sense of enlightenment in the receiver (or Visitor).

interpretation opportunity
A phrase occasionally used in this book to denote a situation in which a Feature of some kind can be seen as a potential subject for Interpretation.

interpretation point
The physical location where interpretation takes place, including perhaps in front of an interpretation panel, where the Visitor stands; in a lecture hall, where the Visitor sits, or at any point along a self-guided trail where the Visitor pauses to read a paragraph from a trail leaflet.

interpretational
Pertaining to the work, skills or profession of an Interpreter.

interpretative
This word has been used to mean both interpretational and interpretive, but it is ungainly and awkward to pronounce. In this book, interpretive is the preferred usage; see below for the meaning.

interpretive
Relating to interpretation, to do with the effective communication of ideas that lead to a sense of enlightenment or insight, or that are capable of, or conducive to, producing such an effect. By these definitions, one should usually speak not of interpretive literature, but of interpretational litera- ture (or just plain interpretation). Similarly, the title Interpretation Officer is preferable to Interpretive Officer.

interpretive plan
A carefully structured assessment of the factors that may influence Inter- pretation in a specific situation, on which reasoned proposals for a scheme of Interpretation can be based (see chapter 13). The term is occasionally ambiguous, as it can refer either to a notional plan (as in 'I have a cunning interpretational plan') or to the document embodying and expounding the notions (as in 'Do you want more copies of the plan?'). In chapter 13 I have often used the term 'plan document' when it is important to make clear that I am referring to the latter.

inter-relationships
The manner in which virtually everything is affected by, and explainable by, other things – e.g. geology influences geomorphology, which influences communications, which influences trade, which influences prosperity, which influences culture, and so on. A very important concept in interpre- tation, it is essential to an appreciation of 'how our world works'. (See also SIGNIFICANCE and HOLISTIC.)

introduction
This word will sometimes be used to refer to processes whereby the Inter- preter may introduce the Feature to the Visitor. The Interpreter often needs to take trouble to ensure that the Visitor's first meeting with the Feature (and possibly with the Interpreter also) will prepare him – sometimes emo- tionally, sometimes intellectually, sometimes physically – for the interpre- tive encounter. This is explained more fully in chapter 8.

landscape
Town or countryside as we see it, with all its geographical, natural and man- made elements. Some use the phrase 'cultural landscape' when they want to emphasise the man-derived qualities of those parts of the world's surface where most of us live. Others have coined the term 'townscape' for use where built structures predominate over farmland, woodland and wilderness.

medium
In general use the term can denote a go-between (as in the spiritualist con- text); a substance used to make or do something (such as artists' materials); or a channel of communication (whether referring to a technology or to an organised system of disseminating information such as the 'mass media').

L. T. C. Rolt remarks in his *Navigable Waterways* (1969): 'Everything that man has made has a voice. Every earth bank, every wall, baked brick or cut stone, every iron beam speaks of the men who made them . . .' Rolt wrote as an expert – a person steeped in industrial archaeology. Canals, bridges and locks mean something if, like him, you have learned their language.

This derelict lock on the Kennet and Avon Canal, near Devizes, has much to say through the materials of which is is built. The locks and bridges on this stretch of the canal were constructed, in about 1810, mainly of red brick from clay dug in a local pit. The brickwork was not strong enough to hold the hinges of the great oak lock gates so, as the canal was extended, stone was brought by boat from nearby quarries. The Great Western Railway, which bought up the canal in 1843, used blue industrial brick to patch up the locks and bridges that were beginning to crumble.

The word is too vague for use in precise analysis of the communication process, though it is often used loosely to describe the means by which we communicate – in general terms, the spoken or written word, diagrams, symbols, gestures, etc.; or, more specifically, leaflet, book, exhibition, film, slide/tape, live guiding, live demonstration, lecture, *son et lumière*, museum labels, interactive computer programme, etc.

Any proper analysis of the communication process will have to find a set of terms for more precise definition. So in most of this book the term will be used whenever a conveniently imprecise word is needed. Only in chapter 9 will it be given the specific meaning of a channel by which the senses of the recipient are stimulated – that is, sound or hearing, sight, touch, smell or taste.

message
Something significant that a Feature has to communicate to us, Interpreters and Visitors alike. The great pioneer of modern landscape interpretation, W. G. Hoskins, wrote: 'When I was young – and I have spent a lifetime of study since – I felt in my bones that the landscape itself was speaking to me, in a language that I did not understand, and I had to find out how to read it.'

nature trail
The term denotes a specified route along which travellers (usually on foot) may see and learn about wildlife. Interpretation may be provided by means of panels sited at appropriate stopping points along the route, or via a leaflet. See also TRAIL.

panel
In the small world of Interpretation, this term is often used to describe a surface dedicated to two-dimensional, interpretational graphics. This could be a unit in a larger, probably indoor, display, or an outdoor interpretation board. In this book I generally reserve the word to denote a surface that carries interpretational graphics; board or sign will be used for surfaces that carry non-interpretational material.

pattern of visiting
See VISITOR PATTERN.

presentation
In this book, the term will generally be reserved to denote the totality of an Interpretation exercise, as presented to and perceived by the Visitor; a PROGRAM is a presentation in this sense. Of course, the term has general uses as well; see INTRODUCTION for the circumstances in which, to avoid misunderstanding, that word will be chosen instead.

profile, visitor
See VISITOR PROFILE.

program
A familiar term among Interpreters in the USA denoting the carefully prepared PRESENTATION – words, visual aids and so on – with which an Interpreter addresses a group of Visitors. The talk at the Grand Canyon described on page 6 is an excellent example of a program. The term is little used in this sense in Britain.

promoter
The person or organisation that initiates a particular interpretation project. It is very often, but not always, the same as the PROPRIETOR.

proprietor
The ultimate head of an interpretation scheme: the person or corporate body that raises the money to start and to run it, and the person who, subject to any outside funding or other input, has the authority to stop it. Proprietors may be local authorities, businesses, or the owners of Features. They may have their own agenda of individual motivations, aims and objectives, but they should show respect and responsibility both for the Features they manage and for the public to whom they offer Interpretation. The proprietor is very often the same person/body as the PROMOTER.

script
The detailed plan, written or unwritten, of all that is to be said, done or offered to the Visitor in a PRESENTATION. A good PROGRAM will have a script, even if only a notional one. As with a film script, every angle, illustration, movement, word and pause needs to be included, because communication in most contexts involves much more than just words. To hope that if we look after the words the visuals, the movement and the ambience will somehow look after themselves shows an almost wilful lack of understanding. (Addresses to any or all of the five senses may be scripted into a presentation.)

signal
In defining the process of communication, this term refers to the stimulus that impinges on the senses of the receiver (the audience or Visitor). It might, for example, be a static pattern on a two-dimensional screen (graphics, drawing, photograph) received by the eye; or the sound of speech emanating from a loudspeaker, received by the ear; or raised bumps that can be sensed through touch by the fingertips (braille). The actual meaning of a signal consists in the CODE it carries.

significance
Another important concept: virtually every object or phenomenon, every Feature, is significant insofar as it points to or reinforces a general principle, or has something to say. The significance of a Feature may perhaps lie in its typicality, which exemplifies a principle; in its uniqueness or rarity, as

the exception that proves the rule; in the way it demonstrates INTER-RELATIONSHIPS, or in its influence. A single Feature may, of course, have many significances. Interpretation consists chiefly of perceiving and pointing out the significance of objects, actions or events. See also MESSAGE.

situation

Occasionally this word will be used here with an almost specialised meaning, namely the totality of all the factors that may affect an exercise in interpretation.

special event

In the general context of 'visitor attractions', a special event is a one-off public occasion devised to bring in a larger numbers of visitors than usual. This is in contrast to the regular or routine admission of visitors throughout a season. See the discussion of Special Events in Interpretation in chapter 10.

story

Used often in this book in the journalists' sense of a fact or sequence of facts seen from a human standpoint; the human element in the Interpretation of a Feature; the component parts of a THEME.

technique

The word is commonly used in a number of ways, referring to methods of doing things, or to skills in the doer. It can also be used to denote the various ways in which CODES and TECHNOLOGIES can be handled. See chapter 9 for further explanation.

technology

This term today normally denotes ingenious ways in which man has applied scientific knowledge to the solving of problems. Not all 'tech' has to be 'hi'. Chalk-on-blackboard is low-tech, for instance, but none the less useful, as is a guided walk. There are times when we want a word that can comprehend everything from virtual reality and holograms to visual aids and lecturing. In this book, the word technology is used as a generic term to cover them all – even the strictly non-tech ones such as direct speech.

theme

The notional thread that runs through, or conceptual framework that gives shape and individuality to, the presentation of an Interpretational message.

tourism

The term has two meanings, which need to be distinguished. The first is recreational travel, what many of us do on holiday; and the second is the whole business of managing and exploiting (not necessarily in a bad sense) places for tourists, and tourists at places. In the second sense, tourism perceives itself as an industry, and is prone to all the ethical problems that other industries face. The true Interpreter, as a person who seeks to cultivate insight and understanding, must assess the functions of tourism honestly, even if he or she makes a living from it.

tourist

Any of us once we have left our own front door, whether setting off to the opposite end of the world, or just taking the dog for a walk in the park. It is possible to wear the tourist's hat even when travelling to work, whenever we spare a moment to look around us.

trail

A special usage, borrowed from the USA, that denotes a specified route leading through scenery usually of wildlife or of historic interest (see NATURE TRAIL). By analogy, we now also have town trails, motor trails, cycle trails, heritage trails, mystery trails and sound trails (those guided by audio).

visitor

The audience or person to whom interpretation is addressed. It is a useful general term, even though people could be offered Interpretation in their own homes.

visitor centre

A term that implies facilities for visitors, under one roof. These often, but by no means always, include Interpretation.

visitor pattern

The complete set of parameters that describes the flow of visitors through an interpretation point or set of points. They include visitors' numbers, times of arrival, times of departure, activities and movement on site, etc., each according to times of year, week and day. A quantitive assessment (compare VISITOR PROFILE).

visitor profile

The parameters that describe and identify the kinds of visitors, in terms of age, groupings on arrival (i.e. singly, couples, families, etc.), social, economic and educational background, interests and expectations, etc. A qualitative assessment (compare VISITOR PATTERN).

Why Interpret?
Aims and motivations

2

The Grand Canyon (see page 6) is of course one of the world's most impressive sights. Most Interpretation is concerned with much humbler, sometimes even commonplace Features. But it is appropriate to start in the United States, for that is where Interpretation as we know it was first formulated.

Freeman Tilden's book *Interpreting Our Heritage*, written in 1957, crystallised and made widely public the notion of Environmental Interpretation, though the phrase itself was not one the author used; he called it simply 'interpretation'. He referred to it as 'a public service that has so recently come into our cultural world that a resort to the dictionary for a competent definition is fruitless.' This public service had evolved within the National Park Service of the USA.

North America is big, and the United States was fortunate that in the 1870s, not long after the end of the Civil War – at a crucial moment in its development as a nation – the idea arose of preserving some of the wilderness areas of the land as National Parks. This was a time of rapid development, ranches, mining, building, railroads; when Congress heard reports and saw photographs of the wonders of Yellowstone, on the borders of Wyoming, Montana and Idaho, it recognised that such an awe-inspiring landscape should be saved for the nation. Yellowstone was the first National Park, being declared in 1872 as 'a public park or pleasuring-ground for the benefit and enjoyment of the people' – the westward-pushing whites, that is, since the benefits the land had afforded to Native Americans for generations were at that time scarcely considered. By the end of the century Yosemite, Sequoia and General Grant (all in California) and Mount Rainier (in Washington) had been added. As the twentieth century progressed, more and more parks were created, some National Monuments, declared by Presidential decree, others National Parks, established by Congress.

By the year 1916, there were some twenty such Parks, and the National Park Service was established to administer and maintain them. By 1949 there were about 86 National Monuments (many primarily of historic rather than natural interest) and 28 National Parks. As the number of Parks was growing, so was the population of the USA; as people became better off and transport became easier, so the number of visitors increased. The time had come for new methods if the Park staff were to fulfil their formidable responsibilities for the safety and management of the visiting public, while at the same time help them to enjoy the 'wilderness'. The very size of some of these Parks is staggering to Europeans. Yellowstone Park comprises nearly two and a quarter million acres (3,471 square miles) – larger than the four English counties of Oxfordshire, Buckinghamshire, Warwickshire and Northamptonshire put together. But even such vast places can be damaged by accidental misuse, and greenhorn exploration of such areas can be dangerous. Visitors need guidance.

One necessary element in this provision was helping visitors to understand and appreciate what they had come to see. This was needed not only in the wilderness of the National Parks, but also in the historic contexts of the National Monuments. The style would need to be friendly and simple rather than pedantic and academic, so information and explanation had to be selective, concentrating on what was basic and significant. The National Park Service termed it 'interpretation'; they experimented with methods and techniques, and they trained their staff in communication skills.

INTERPRETATION COMES OFFICIALLY TO BRITAIN

The long and somewhat confused story of the many years of proposals, argument and wrangling that led to an Act of Parliament in Great Britain authorising the establishment of the National Parks Commission in 1949 is told with great clarity by John Sheail in *Nature in Trust* (1976). By the time of Tilden's book , authorities in Britain and Europe were facing their own problems. Britain's National Parks were (and are) young, and most of them are small compared with those in the USA, but then our country is only one fortieth the size. The first group of National Parks to be declared in Britain included the Peak District. This relatively open, hilly countryside is bordered by some of the most highly populated areas in the country – Huddersfield, Bradford and Leeds to the north; Barnsley and Sheffield to the east; Oldham, Manchester and Stockport to the west; Stoke-on-Trent, Derby and Nottingham to the south. All these conurbations are within twenty-five miles of the Park's borders.

Britain had to learn its own ways of welcoming but controlling visitors to its new National Parks, much of which are farmed, and all of which contain towns and villages. They may be comparatively remote, but they are by no means wilderness, and they remain private rather than national property. It is worth noting, however, that under the Environment Act of 1995 all Britain's National Parks were given direct responsibility for planning control within their borders.

The problems, wider than the boundaries of the Parks themselves, were expressed in an important book *Man and Environment* (1967) by Robert Arvill, who emphasised the need for educating the general public:

> [The citizen] must have much higher standards of education and information and a highly sophisticated level of awareness. It will take time to achieve this state, but a comparison of, say, the civilisation of 1914 with that of today suggests that it can be done.
>
> People need varying depths of knowledge to carry out their aims, but everyone needs some understanding of the 'natural' environment – even the people who see the country only at weekends. It is particularly important that the decision-makers in government and commerce, all the workers whose activities affect the countryside, scientists and teachers, and members of the professions who plan, manage and develop the land should appreciate the forces at work there. . . .
>
> The educational process must be continuously reinforced by a sustained campaign of information. . . . To achieve these aims will require new interpretative skills and measures to maintain better inter-communication. Television has a great capacity to stimulate, but the most vital need is for sustained 'follow-up' in all media of information.[1]

It was a small but highly significant personal decision made by one officer of the Peak District National Park which led to the importation from the USA to Britain of Park Interpretation, with a philosophy and a terminology to go with it. In 1966 Don Aldridge, the Peak Park's Information Officer (a post funded by Britain's National Parks Commission) was awarded one of the first Churchill Travelling Scholarships, to visit the USA to study interpretation as practised by the National Parks Service. A series of field trips was followed by two months at a National Park Service course on Interpretive Planning at Harper's Ferry, the Service's main training centre in West Virginia. On his return, Aldridge was invited to serve on the steering group for the Carnegie United Kingdom Trust's Leicester Museum Field Study Project. The activities of this group led to the launch in 1976 of the Trust's first five-year programme of promoting and aiding schemes of Interpretation in Britain.

No authoritative book expounding the principles of Interpretation was published in Britain in the 1960s, although articles and conference reports appeared in various professional journals, notably the *Museums Journal* towards the end of the decade. The newly established Countryside Commissions for Scotland and for England, Wales and Northern Ireland, which had absorbed the role of the National Parks Commission, and the Forestry Commission were developing their interest in Interpretation. Don Aldridge moved to the Countryside Commission for Scotland, and pioneered demonstrations and training in Interpretation at a new purpose-built centre at Redgorton, Perth.

1. Robert Arvill, *Man and Environment*, Penguin, Harmondsworth 1967. Arvill was the pen-name of a leading British environmentalist Bob Boote, Head of the Nature Conservancy Council.

2:1 Preserving heritage from oblivion

The Open Air Museum at Arnhem, The Netherlands, was founded in 1912 by citizens worried at the threat posed by rapid industrialisation to their country's 'wealth in traditions and regional diversity'. The lead had been given by Scandinavia; the museum at Skansen, near Stockholm, was set up in 1891, and the Friland Museum near Copenhagen ten years later. In some respects, the Open Air Museums of Scandinavia, the National Parks and Monuments of the USA and the National Trust in Britain can all be seen as national manifestations of the same awakening to the value of 'heritage'.

The Arnhem Museum suffered tragic damage during the Second World War, but the remains of the collection were skilfully restored and enlarged. The buildings – domestic, farm and industrial – are an eye-opener for visitors, showing how much our cultures have changed in the past century.

Britain now has many excellent open-air museums: St Fagan's, near Cardiff in Wales, and Beamish in County Durham, England, are examples (see also page 131).

A booklet, *Nature Trails*, was published by F. Warne for the Nature Conservancy Council in 1968,[2] and another, *Nature Trails in Britain*, listing 232 specific trails, was issued by the British Tourist Authority for European Conservation Year, 1970. Elizabeth Beazley, primarily an architect working in countryside recreation, was the first person in Britain to treat the nuts and bolts of Interpretation in book form, with *Design for Recreation* (1969) and *The Countryside on View* (1971).

In 1975 the two Countryside Commissions jointly published a two-volume *Guide to Countryside Interpretation*,[3] the first general introduction to Interpretation written for a British readership. In the same year (European Architectural Heritage Year), the British Tourist Authority published a booklet *Town Trails*, compiled by Brian Goodey and Michael Glen. Interpretation of the built environment was further boosted in 1979 by Arthur Percival's *Understanding our Surroundings*, published by the Civic Trust.

Also in 1975, after a series of conferences, the Carnegie United Kingdom Trust (CUKT) backed the formation of the Society for the Interpretation of Britain's Heritage (SIBH, now often operating under its briefer title Interpret Britain). SIBH has never been large, but it has provided a focus for those practising Interpretation professionally – whether full time or, more often, as just one aspect of their jobs. Here, people from national parks, country parks, museums, planning departments, stately homes, nature reserves, tourism and private practice discuss and promote Interpretation.

2. *Nature Trails* was written by Tom Pritchard and Philip Oswald of the Nature Conservancy Council, E. A. J. Buckhurst (Warden of a Field Studies Centre and a member of the Council for Nature's Youth Committee) and Peter Hope Jones. The first Nature Trail in Britain, according to this booklet, 'was opened in 1961, but there were very few until National Nature Week in May 1963, when over fifty were set up.'

3. By K. Pennyfather and D. Aldridge.

The CUKT's promotion of Interpretation was immensely influential. It did not merely hand out money, but scrutinised each application to ensure that projects were sound, and monitored them with care and good advice. A number of entirely new schemes arose all over the country during the 1970s and 1980s, some initiated by local trusts, others by local government. Voluntary bodies such as the National Trusts (for Scotland, and for England and Wales), Wildlife Conservation organisations and the Civic Trust and Museums took up Interpretation. Some were virtually starting from scratch; to others it was a matter of applying new philosophies and better techniques to what they were already doing. In some ways it was an untidy start, but it contained much good work. The problem has always been the difficulty of newcomers in agreeing what the real objectives of the exercise should be.

In 1980 the Centre for Environmental Interpretation was established at Manchester Polytechnic (now Manchester Metropolitan University), again with funds provided by CUKT. Sadly, after many years of invaluable work, the University closed it down in 1997. It is not yet clear which of its various functions may be taken over by other institutions.

UNDERSTANDING EDUCATION

'Interpretation', wrote Freeman Tilden, 'is an educational activity which aims to reveal meanings and relationships through the use of original objects . . .' He is describing, of course, INTERPRETATION (see pages 9–10), and telling us that its objective is to achieve *interpretation*. The term educational can also be separated out into two distinct usages: EDUCATION, the profession, the business of education; and *education*, the learning process that is achieved within a person.

Education is not a process reserved solely for formal situations in which you can identify the roles of teacher and taught. It describes the effect of influences from outside that make us what we are – intellectually, artistically, morally, socially. It includes what we learn in the family, what we experience in the community, and what we discover in our personal exploration of our environment, even the way we are affected by watching television or reading newspapers. Formal education is no doubt important but it has limitations, the greatest perhaps being that it tends to operate by injecting externally packaged knowledge regardless of whether a person is ready to receive it, rather than working from personal experience outwards (this will be considered further in chapter 5).

Another problem, especially today, is that education is often viewed too narrowly as a method of achieving what is, with unconscious irony, termed a vocation (a 'calling'). The word vocation was never meant to be a synonym for employment. Even in the world of adult education, which is only semi-formal, one office recently

The word 'education' can be seen as a metaphor from the forge. If your personality is to be made of iron, would you prefer it to be wrought in the forge or cast in the foundry? In a foundry, molten iron is poured into a pre-formed mould, and once cooled it must stay in that shape: any attempt to bend or re-shape it, any sharp knock, will shatter or fracture it. Iron wrought at the forge is tough but malleable. It can bend and withstand blows: it may show the dents, but it won't easily break. It can adapt to circumstances. The very word education, meaning 'drawing out' or 'shaping', implies the qualities of wrought iron rather than cast.

sent instructions to its tutors to *quantify* their learning objectives. No longer will phrases like 'to interest the class in . . .' or 'to help the students appreciate . . .' do. The *usefulness* of the course must be spelt out in practical terms – not always easy when the subject is German Romantic Composers or the Landscape of Loamshire.

Learning's usefulness does not consist merely in factual knowledge or technical skills. Wisdom is a higher quality, and so is imagination. Wisdom and imagination are both built on knowledge, of course, but great human achievements – whether in art, engineering or social provision – have not occurred through knowledge alone. Besides, knowledge itself is more than the memorising of facts. A full, rounded education must, if it is to lead to wisdom, train a person in clear thinking, sympathy, creativity, perception and many other qualities, which are not always recognised as important in formal education. Indeed, there may be educationists or politicians who are themselves short of these qualities, and even some – dare one say it? – who are insufficiently wise to be trusted to make sound decisions. By all means let us have educational objectives. How can an educator without a clear aim hope to know whether or not he or she is a success? But the objectives themselves must be identified and defined wisely and imaginatively.

SEEKING THE 'AAH!' RESPONSE

In our context, the aim in general terms will be to help the Visitor to appreciate better how the world works. This we hope to do by explaining or demonstrating the processes and principles that operate in a particular segment of our environment. We may be considering a natural feature, an artefact or an aspect of human behaviour – landscape, architecture or social history. We want visitors to feel that as a result of their encounter they are a little wiser, and understand better – that light has been shed, insights have been gained. This sense of enlightenment is crucial. Sometimes, especially in a face-to-face situation, a Visitor will show it by a delighted raising of the eyebrows and a rising and falling 'Aah!', as if to say, '*Now* I see!' This sense of enlightenment appears most readily when people receive answers to the questions 'How?' and 'Why?'

The important thing about the imaginary and rather stylised exchanges opposite is that they relate to the Visitor's experience on the site, and they deal with questions that may arise naturally. True interpretation is built on an experience, not an abstract concept. Information offered formally and off-site is unlikely to elicit the same interested reaction.

BENEFITS OF INTERPRETATION

The sceptic may grumble, 'Why take all this trouble? Does it really matter if Visitors are left puzzled or bored? Perhaps they came here just for the ride, and never meant to ask questions. Probably if we didn't keep on trying to interest them, they wouldn't even know what they were missing.' There are very good reasons why it *is* worth taking trouble. To start with, it benefits the Features, those places or objects that people go to see. If they are really attractive, interesting or important, they are worth conserving. If they are to be conserved, both political motivation and money will be required. If governments are to be persuaded to spend money on conservation and legislate for it, then strong and informed public opinion must do the persuading. And if strong and informed public opinion is to grow and be maintained, then the public must learn to understand and appreciate what we call our heritage.

Another good reason for Interpreting our heritage is just to give pleasure! Talk to any enthusiast and you will admit that the enjoyment to be gained from knowing all about something is immeasurable. Ask any person who has been on a well-conducted guided walk. I remember being one of a small party who were shown around the meagre remains of the ancient town and priory of Dunwich, Suffolk (a once-important medieval town now lost to the North Sea). The guide was a well-briefed 'ghostly friar' in appropriate costume. A fellow visitor turned to me at the end and said, 'I have walked here often before, but this is the first time the place has really come to life for me.'

Freeman Tilden knew how important this enjoyment was. People travel and visit for recreation (in its old sense of restoration of the spirits), some to get away from crowds, some to find company; some hoping for a sense of wilderness, others for a sense of history; others again to lose themselves in works of art, or – so

Information	Interpretation
'Totteringham Castle was built towards the end of the reign of Edward I, by Sir Miles Totteringham, Hereditary Groom of the King's Wardrobe. Originally it was surrounded by a 24-foot (7.32m) high curtain wall enclosing about 1.5 acres (0.61 hectares).'	'How did they find and fetch all the stone to build this castle? Why did they take so much trouble to build the castle, and why just here?' 'They wanted a castle here to guard this important river-crossing from attack, which they feared might come up-river or through that gap in the hills. The stone was all quarried from a hillside three miles away – you can still see the place if you walk up there – and was brought downriver by boats or rafts.' 'Aah!'
'Beech (*Fagus sylvatica*) is a native of Britain and Europe (except Spain), and may grow to a height of 142 feet. There are several varieties of beech, including the copper beech, weeping beech and fern-leaved beech. It is much used for furniture-making.'	'How did this clump of trees come to be on top of this hill? And why is there so little undergrowth beneath them?' 'It was planted by the local landowner to make an interesting feature on the horizon when he looked out of his drawing room windows. The trees are beeches, and their leaves make such a dense canopy that in summer there is little light to encourage plants to grow beneath. When the leaves fall they lie thick on the ground for months, as you can see, which is enough to suppress most plants except spring bulbs.' 'Aah!'

difficult to define – a sense of place. Why is it so pleasant occasionally to walk round a busy market, to stand on a clifftop, to lean on a farm gate and gaze, or to watch a craftsman at work? Few of us deliberately set out on such excursions intent on learning, although we must allow that to understand an experience is almost always to enhance it. What we see sometimes puzzles us. A discreet word of explanation can help a lot: that is why so many people travel with some sort of guidebook. Even the many of us who like to explore just by 'pottering about' actually find it satisfying because we feel it widens our understanding of our surroundings.

I have used the words understanding, appreciating and enjoying – you could say that these correspond roughly to our intellectual, aesthetic and emotional reactions to the world. The relationship of the three is fascinating: all can be good, all are valid. True understanding of anything – wildlife, art, landscape, buildings, motor cars – seems to affect people on all three levels. You can see this in the writings of the greatest scientists, the best landscape historians, the most perceptive critics of art and literature. Long experience in their subjects helps them see beauty and perceive 'rightness' – it also generates associations and memories that can be so strong that they bring tears to the eyes.

2:2 Getting to know a Suffolk crag pit

deliberately visited this quarry, or even come across it by chance, if they had not chosen to take part in an adult education local history excursion. The pit has been quarried for centuries as a source of lime for the land: this particular soft stratum of Suffolk rock is made up largely of corals and the shells of creatures that must once have lived in a shallow sea. Other pits dug in the same bed have produced a slightly harder-wearing (although all too easily erodable) stone; and the church that stands just above the pit (above) is built partly of it.

Why spend a weekend afternoon visiting a crag pit? Pleasure in education – for both giver and receivers. As for the pit, as it becomes more widely recognised to be locally significant, it is less likely to end up as a rubbish dump.

Chillesford Pit is an untidy hollow in a small hillside. It is doubtful if any of the people in this photograph (except local historian Bob Malster, on the right) would ever have

All these feelings can be beneficial to the Feature but, in the long run, intellectual understanding is what counts. Aesthetic pleasure and emotional associations do constitute a motivation for conservation, but intellectual understanding alone can provide a satisfactory conservation programme. Without true understanding, 'you always hurt the thing you love'.

INTERPRETATION STIMULATES ENQUIRY

Interpretation also encourages us to notice things that we would otherwise overlook. You can walk below the walls of the city of York without ever glancing up. But when you see a small sign, explaining that the gaps in the parapet once had wooden flaps to protect defenders from arrow fire, and then you lean back and see high above you just such a wooden flap that has been re-created to illustrate the point, you may well exclaim 'Aah!' and be grateful. Many a Town Trail guide leaflet will point the user to fascinating architectural detail which is probably never noticed by most of those who pass on the pavement below every day of the week.

My last justification for interpretation is perhaps the most important. We live in an age when individuals are so specialised in their trades and duties that, paradoxically, as our collective wisdom grows, so does our individual ignorance. In the developed world, one can live a lifetime without ever having to grow food, repair a house or dress a wound. Other people do these things for us; we leave it to the experts. But expertise in one skill often means ignorance and helplessness in others. An accountant can be ignorant about farming; a farmer may not feel the need to study a foreign language; a linguist may not be bothered with art; an artist can happily ignore microbiology; a microbiologist may have no interest in prisons; while a prison officer could be hopeless at keeping accounts.

And yet decisions about such matters as conservation, planning, manufacturing processes, medicine, raw materials, law and order, design and education have to be taken at national, county, district and parish level by representatives of the community. If there is not a general understanding of the basic principles on which the world works, we can only expect that our lives will be managed or mismanaged by others no wiser than we are. And we ourselves and our neighbours are quite likely, in our own ignorance, to spoil the environment for one another. Insights that can be gained from interpretation are essential to wise decision-making for the benefit not only of our own community or nation, but for mankind as a whole, and for the health of our globe. A new generation arises about every 25 years, so the processes of Education and Interpretation can never cease, and can never be complete.

At first sight, it may seem ridiculous to hope that explanatory panels, trail leaflets, guided walks and visitor centres could possibly help anyone to a real understanding of the way the world

A friend of mine, a keen and very experienced bug-hunter, is a fascinating person to go for a walk with. A Fellow of the Royal Entomological Society, he has spent his working life as a Post Office engineer and has discovered rare insects at the top of telegraph poles. You walk with him along a row of alders near a river bank, and suddenly he will say, 'Look! an upside-down fly!' You peer closely to find a brown fly resting head-down on the trunk – how he spotted it from eight feet away seems a miracle. He will tell you that this species always rests upside down, and almost anything else you may want to know about it. But even he cannot tell you why it rests upside down. Sometimes to discover that no one knows an answer is more fascinating than to be told it!

Basic but dull	Interpretation added	Principles revealed
This is a brick tower mill built in the early nineteenth century by James Anderson of Coplington.	This has always been a prime corn-growing region.	(a) The windmill is the product of commercial requirements
It was shown on an old map as Merryfield Mill.	Almost every village had its mill: grain and flour were too bulky to carry long distances by horse power.	(b) Old-fashioned transport systems had their limitations
Note the ogee-shaped cap.		(c) Building styles often reflect local tradition
The building is in the care of the Loamshire Windmills Trust. Key at Walbeck Farmhouse opposite.	The 'onion' shape of the cap at the top of the mill is very typical of Lincolnshire and neighbouring counties: you are unlikely to see this design in other parts of Britain.	

works. But there is more to this kind of site Interpretation than meets the eye. Good Interpretation does not just leave you with a fact or two; it reveals principles.

The interpretive comments in the box (above) may seem simple, but they are expounding principles. First, that our built environment has arisen through local needs, century by century; secondly, that the decline of this kind of building is due to social, technological or economic changes – in this case, the development in the twentieth century of bulk transport and centralised processing; thirdly, that fashion accounts for much architectural detail. Put these few principles together, and you get another important one: that buildings are what they are because of an interacting complex of factors – economic, social, geographical. The same principle is basic to the interpretation and understanding of landscapes, in which geology and soil, geography, communications, local economy and local tradition all interact to produce a characteristic local scenery.

Wildlife interpretation works the same way. Communities of plants and animals can only be understood, and therefore conserved, according to the principle that every species has its own preferences for soil chemistry, shelter, food, wetness or dryness, light or shade, and fellow wildlife (both plants and animals). The complexity of interactions between species is quite amazing. Good gardeners, good foresters and good naturalists appreciate this. But some others – the people who make decisions about drainage, or development, or farming, even some officials and councillors – may not.

Social explanations and historical backgrounds are implicit in interpreting buildings and land use. We cannot understand stately homes and parkland without appreciating the servant/master pattern of earlier centuries; the power of early kings and nobles to declare certain areas 'forest'; the dominance of the wealthy landowner who was able to eradicate whole villages in order to enlarge his park; the selfishness of some mill-owners, the philanthropy of others. All these things must be recognised if we are to understand our own past and cope with our own present.

Among the principles we find in such stories are the human tendency to scramble to the top at the expense of others; the part played by patience, wisdom and understanding in gradually modifying society for the better, and how lack of inter-communication can drive peoples or classes apart. Balancing these will be the truth that ambition has often led to innovation and technological improvement: research driven by the requirements of NASA may lead to better devices for the home and hospital.

Good on-site Interpretation does not have to be always preaching, but facts add up to form patterns, and the consistency of patterns can be read as principles. The human mind can process these without the moral always having to be pointed out. If we seek to understand the how and why of little things, the way the world works becomes clearer. But Interpreters must try to avoid being patronising and they must take care not to spoil the quality of other people's experiences in the clumsiness of their efforts to enhance them.

OTHER MOTIVES OF VARYING WORTHINESS

The conservation ethic. Where a species is rare, or a building fine, or a landscape beautiful, the chances of looking after it well are enhanced if the general public are in sympathy. Interpretation helps to open people's eyes, and to alert them to the need for conservation (see chapter 4).

To promote a worthy organisation. We are on slightly less secure ground here, because the worthiness of a particular cause will not appear the same to everyone. An example might be a children's charity wanting to create an exhibition to celebrate a major anniversary. It could tell a fascinating story, with a wealth of illustrative material displayed in one of its own buildings constructed many years ago to house orphans. The aims could be various: to celebrate; to reinforce the self-confidence of the organisation; to be a focal point for former inmates who wanted to visit their old home; to let the general public see what had been achieved; to encourage subscriptions. As long as the Interpretation is sincere, it would be hard to quarrel with this idea, even if a major object is to raise funds.

Similarly, a County Wildlife Trust may want to explain its achievements, justify its objectives and recruit supporters. If it attempts this merely by circulating appeal leaflets, then the

Interpretation content will probably be low. If it creates a display in a building near the entrance to one of its reserves, then good Interpretation will surely include explanations of the management of the site, and the role of the Trust will emerge quite naturally.

To make money. What of those professed Interpretation projects whose very existence is unashamedly to make a living for the proprietor, or which are funded by a local authority or Tourist Board because it is believed that they will help the local economy?

Now we must think clearly and honestly. First, there may be little difference between earning a salary as an Interpreter for a National Park, and setting up one's own Interpretation of one's own stately home, farm or watermill. Owners of stately homes can claim with some justice that fee-paying visitors are the only way they can afford to maintain their buildings. Earning a living, or a part-living, from Interpretation need not invalidate the Interpretation itself.

More importantly, is the scheme actually good conservation? Is the feature better looked after (in conservation terms) because of the Interpretation than it would be otherwise? Money has to be part of this equation – but so are questions of wear and tear. The conservation prospects for the wall paintings in the caves at Lascaux might well have been expected to be all the better for paying visitors, but their very presence brought humidity which did considerable damage to the paintings. For the sake of conserving the feature, visitors now have to be kept out.

Then there are places such as visitor centres built to Interpret a region – often new buildings, often well designed, such as Landmark in the Grampians of Scotland, and Living Legend in Jersey. The latter cost millions of pounds, and its avowed aim is to 'tell the Jersey story'. It offers an almost incredibly theatrical high-tech show, and one is left marvelling at the ingenuity with which modern science can be applied to entertainment. Good luck to it: it's fun. As Interpretation, it is rather like taking, not just a sledgehammer, but an automated pile-driver to crack a nut. But a hundred people will pay to watch a pile-driver crack a nut for every one willing to pay to watch the process done by a nut-cracker.

Other places have been built to tell stories, such as those of the Great Fire of London, famous battles and well-known legends. These are created not to conserve anything, but to make money from tourists. They should be judged as entertainment (see chapter 11), and their value, which may be real enough even if not interpretational, will be more fairly assessed.

Propaganda. Another loaded word, merely meaning 'promoting your own point of view'. Much interpretation is in fact undertaken for this reason. The environment lobby wants to explain why it believes a certain area of woodland should be preserved; the

In the diminutive Strike School at Burston, Norfolk, a tale is told of class arrogance in the earlier part of this century, when certain members of the gentry tried to crush the local Agricultural Labourers' Union. The village school-teacher and her husband, her assistant, were sacked for union activities; the children and their parents went on strike and refused to attend the school. Eventually they raised funds to build an independent school of their own in 1917. While the official school remained empty for two decades, the Strike School continued to function until the death in 1939 of Tom Higdon, one of the teachers involved in the original dispute (for the background, see B. Edwards, *The Burston School Strike*, Lawrence and Wishart, 1974).

Only a couple of generations ago, even to talk of the Burston School strike publicly and with pride would have been to risk social ostracism. It must be more than a coincidence that in the decades following the strike certain otherwise comprehensive guidebooks failed to mention the village at all. Yet I like to believe that today's land-owners, farmers, clergy and councillors are proud of this community's achievement.

Above: the schoolroom now houses a delightful display, produced by local amateur Interpreters, which tells the story well, movingly and, I think, fairly.

Right: stones on the exterior of the building are inscribed with the names of donors who gave money towards the new independent school. Most of the donations were from Trades Unions.

Just after the Second World War, two fascinating books were written describing the same place: Adventurers Fen in Cambridgeshire. Eric Ennion, a naturalist, had known and loved the fen for many years for its wildness, wildlife and beauty; he wrote about it just as it was being drained for agriculture. Alan Bloom was a farmer who had acquired it early in the war and turned it over to the production of food. Ennion was a passionate naturalist, and mourned what to him was a tragedy of destruction. Bloom was a passionate farmer, and was proud to have turned what he no doubt considered to be wasted acres into productive farmland. Ennion's book was an obituary for a wilderness, Bloom's a celebration of productivity. Both, in their way, are propaganda. One might be able now to look back with a dispassionate overview, and even apply Interpretation to the conflict of ideas that the draining of this fen exemplifies. It is hard not to reveal one's own sympathies, but the exigencies of wartime undoubtedly made it necessary to grow more food. One can only admire the energy and ingenuity of Bloom, and at the same time sympathise with Ennion's sense of bereavement.

Eric Ennion, Adventurers Fen *(1942; enlarged edn., Herbert Jenkins, 1949).*
Alan Bloom, The Farm in the Fen *(Faber and Faber, London 1944).*

Hundreds of thousands of pounds were spent preparing the former Central Electricity Generating Board's permanent exhibition (now under the joint management of Magnox and Nuclear Electric) at the nuclear power station at Sizewell, Suffolk. Its aim is unashamedly to portray the proprietors as benefactors to society, and nuclear electricity as an unqualified boon.

Department of Transport wants to explain why it is better to fell the woodland to make way for a bypass. An architectural historian would like to preserve a certain redundant building; a developer would like to demolish it and use the site for a new leisure centre. Each could mount an exhibition justifying his own view.

Truth is multi-faceted. Any simple assessment of a situation has to be partial, and audiences usually have neither the time nor the mental energy to sift through complex pros and cons, making it all too easy for the Interpreter to select the truths that reinforce his own point of view. The best advice one can give to those who wish to use Interpretation to promote their own beliefs is: be as fair as you can; let the evidence speak for itself; and be generous enough to accept that different points of view may be sincerely held.

Keeping up with the environmental Joneses. Perhaps the commonest mis-motivation for providing Interpretation is the kind of administrative correctness which thinks that because another council puts up interpretation boards, we had better do the same. This has caused many local authorities to propose and even carry out half-baked schemes without clearly considering their purpose. This is a great shame, since every unsatisfactory project detracts from the reputation and effectiveness of Interpretation as a whole.

Such misconceived projects can only be prevented by properly disciplined preliminary thinking: the importance of this, and ways to undertake it methodically, are considered in chapter 13.

Insights offered and sought
Interpretation's antecedents

3

Interpretation should have no mystique, and it is important to realise that it is not, in its essence, new. There are certain new factors, it is true. One is a general awareness that as we approach the twenty-first century the more highly civilised peoples of the globe are, as individuals, no wiser in their relationship to their world than earlier generations. This matters not just for people's personal pleasure and self-confidence (though this is not to be undervalued), but for the world itself. A second novelty is the self-consciousness with which the process of Interpretation is now being analysed, refined and practised. Just as the casual study of animal behaviour has become formalised into the science of ethology, and interest in human inter-relationships has evolved into the discipline of social psychology, so the urgency of the need to communicate our understanding of the world about us has resulted in the discipline of Interpretation.

There may be fresh motivations, unfamiliar jargon and new organisational structures, but the essential elements of Interpretation are old enough. Explaining the world has been a concern of man since he first started to communicate. Training children in prehistoric times must have had required insights and skills similar in kind, if less refined, to those required for good Interpretation: after all, upon each generation's understanding of its local world hung life and death. The inter-connections between weather, soils, plants and animal prey were probably appreciated by a larger proportion of a local population before cities were built and universities endowed. The aboriginal native of Australia knows the outback in a way that the professor from Sydney does not.

The sixteenth-century Native American, the seventeenth-century British sailor, the eighteenth-century German peasant and the nineteenth-century French farmer were all 'wiser in their generation' than we are. Today our collective wisdom may be greater, but it cannot all, by definition, be possessed by any single individual – and it is probably true that as we rely more upon others to advise us and to provide for us in everyday matters, the happier we are to abdicate our own share of responsibility for the world.

If we want to enquire into the ancestry of the Interpretation of

30   Insights offered and
sought. Interpretation's
antecedents

today, it may help to consider eight major traditions whose lineages have contributed to it. Four of these have been initiated mainly by experts eager to share their knowledge; and four by the natural inborn curiosity of people seeking experience and understanding, or 'wanting to find out'. In the first category I include the traditions of popular instruction; formal education; museums and collections, and conservation. In the second will be found educational self-help; hobbies; tourism and travel, and entertainment.

THE EXPERTS REACH OUT TO THE PEOPLE
Popular instruction

Publius Vergilius Maro, known familiarly as Virgil, lived near Rome in the 1st century BC. He is most famous for his epic poem *The Aeneid* about Aeneas of Troy. But he also wrote four books, *The Georgics*, about practical husbandry: on the cultivation of fields, the culture of vines and olives, animal rearing and bee-keeping. To Virgil, the poetry was certainly more important than the educational content but, in a sense, his books were a kind of how-to-do-it journalism. We have to remember, of course, that there were no mass media then: copies could only be circulated in manuscript, or read or recited to small audiences, most of whom were probably Roman country gentlemen and their families who no doubt employed farm managers anyway.

A revival of interest in all things Roman led a number of English writers in the eighteenth and nineteenth centuries to take Virgil for their model, and to try their hand at didactic verse – that is, verse that professes to teach. Very few people now read John Philips's *Cyder* (1708); John Dyer's *The Fleece* (1757), a poetical essay on sheep husbandry and the wool trade; or *The Loves of the Plants* (1789), a curious botanical treatise in blank verse by Erasmus Darwin, grandfather of the evolutionist Charles Darwin. In the same rather eccentric tradition is the *Ornithologia* (1827) of James Jennings, probably the only instructional bird book ever written in verse. Admittedly, some two-thirds of Jennings's instruction is crammed into his introduction and footnotes (which are in prose), but he clearly believed he was educating his public by mixing scientific data with poetry. He wrote in his preamble to the second edition (1829):

Since the appearance of ORNITHOLOGIA in 1827, the public attention has been more than ordinarily excited to Animal Natural History. The Zoological Society is mentioned in page 94. Its collection of living animals in the Regent's Park is now, under suitable regulation, open to the public at a very trifling expense, namely, one shilling each person. The crowds that daily visit the Gardens are almost innumerable. They are, at once, a fashionable, an agreeable, an amusing, and instructive lounge; and far exceed, in exciting interest, anything which could have been previously anticipated concerning such an establishment.

Insights offered and   31
sought. Interpretation's
antecedents

'An amusing and instructive lounge': that could serve as a modest statement of what the Interpreter tries to offer. Where Jennings writes 'lounge', we might use 'stroll'; and by 'amusing' he means not funny but entertaining. We shall pick up this two-hundred-year-old definition again in chapter 11.

A later British scientist of great personal repute who believed in writing for, and speaking to, the lay public was Thomas H. Huxley. In the second half of the nineteenth century he emerged as the most articulate supporter of Charles Darwin. As Professor of Natural History at the Royal School of Mines in London, and President of the Royal Society, his scientific credentials could scarcely have been greater. But a very important part of his achievement was his influence on English education through the advice he gave as a member of various royal commissions, and through his own direct activity as a popular lecturer. One of his most celebrated lectures was delivered to the working men of Norwich, when the British Association met there in 1868. It was entitled 'On a Piece of Chalk'. Aware that Norwich's own foundations are (literally) bedded in this rock, he started his lecture by holding up a piece of chalk. From this opening gesture, he enthralled his hearers with tales of geology and zoology – what could have been dry, dead facts were made to live by the way he related them to people's lives and experiences. It is significant that in his biography of Thomas Huxley, Edward Clodd headed a major section 'The Interpreter'.[1]

Science has had its popular literaure in the twentieth century, too. *Science for the Citizen* and *Mathematics for the Million* by Professor Lancelot Hogben of Birmingham University were published in the 1930s and sold tens of thousands of copies. Scientists have adapted well to modern media: the Royal Society's annual Christmas lectures for children have been relayed for many years on British television. They are models of good teaching and good presentation; tens of thousands of adult viewers watch them because they are so fascinating. The children who attend go not because they are told to, but because they want to – it is learning made entertainment.

The documentary film

For a while, the world's cinemas screened documentaries to support main feature films and to vary the entertainment of those who flocked regularly, often weekly, to the local picture palace. As well as newsreels, films expounded general topics to these mass audiences: cultural traditions, manufacturing processes, transport systems, railways, architecture and the arts. The voice-overs of these old films may sound patronising to us today, but they were products of their period: in their own social context they met a need, and they worked. Many specialist clubs and social organisations used to hire films from libraries that could not have prospered if

1. Edward Clodd, *Professor Huxley*, Modern English Writers series, Blackwood's, Edinburgh, 1902.

32   Insights offered and
sought. Interpretation's
antecedents

their stock had not been interesting, and their clients not eager to be interested. Even industry sponsored popular educational films. For their celebrated *Night Mail* (1936), the General Post Office commissioned a script from the poet W. H. Auden, and music from the composer Benjamin Britten – clearly, that film was intended to delight as well as to inform. The Great Western Railway Company produced excellent documentaries, one of which was *Between the Tides*, a classic exploration of intertidal wildlife on Britain's western coast. The ulterior motive may have been to stimulate travel, but some of the results were truly interpretational.

Radio and television started with cinema and the press as their standard. Interpretation was embedded in their entertainment, but they soon developed their own techniques of presentation. They discovered 'star' communicators – highly qualified specialists who, through their skills in exposition, became television personalities. Of these, older British viewers will recall Magnus Pyke on science, Jacob Bronowski on cultural history, Kenneth Clarke on the fine arts, and W. G. Hoskins on local history. Others of equal calibre have now taken their place.

Formal education

By the late eighteenth century, ideas about children's education were becoming more sympathetic and imaginative. Some advanced educationists were already advocating 'heuristic' education, or education through discovery, but they were well ahead of their time. 'The good Mrs Trimmer'[2] prefaced her *Easy Introduction to the Knowledge of Nature* (1782) with an explanation of her aims:

> The idea of the following little work was originally taken from Dr Watts's Treatise on education . . . his words are these:
>
> 'Almost every thing is new to children, and novelty will entice them onwards to new acquirements: shew them the birds, the beasts, the fishes, the insects, trees, fruit, herbs, and all the several parts and properties of the vegetable and animal world . . .'
>
> But delightful as these things are to children, if communicated in a way that is accommodated to their capacities, they can never be brought in their early years to attend to scientific accounts of causes and effects, or to enter far into each particular branch of knowledge.
>
> I therefore thought a book containing a kind of general survey of the works of Nature would be very useful, as a means to open the mind by gradual steps to the knowledge of the SUPREME BEING, preparatory to their reading the holy Scriptures . . .
>
> The good effects of this mode of instruction I have witnessed among the children of the poor, and happy should I be to see it universally adopted in our schools for the higher orders of children . . .

It is remarkable how perceptive some of the early Victorian educationists were. We can see this in some of the books addressed to

2. Mrs Sarah Trimmer (1741–1810) wrote material for charity schools, mostly on religion and natural history. She was perhaps the first person to denounce traditional children's stories for what we now might call their 'political incorrectness'. The phrase 'the good Mrs Trimmer' appears in a verse by C. S. Calverley of 1872, parodying the poet Jean Ingelow; it shows us how long the fame of a populariser of natural history could last in the nineteenth century.

children, especially those written by women, despite the stilted
language.

> EDWARD: What are you doing, Mama?
> MOTHER: I am examining the pretty little yellow flower, that we
>   found this morning in the hedge.
> EDWARD: How do you examine a flower?
> MOTHER: You cannot understand the method, my dear, until you
>   have learned something of Botany.
> EDWARD: What is Botany?
> MOTHER: It is the science that makes us acquainted with plants, and
>   teaches us how to distinguish them from one another. The term
>   Botany is derived from a Greek word signifying an herb or grass.
>   Do you not recollect what your aunt and I were talking of yes-
>   terday in the garden? I thought you seemed attentive to our
>   conversation.
> EDWARD: You said something about a very industrious man, who had
>   examined a great many plants.
> MOTHER: Yes, we were speaking of Linnaeus, a celebrated botanist,
>   who did so much to increase our knowledge of the works of
>   nature, that he was called the Father of Natural History. He was
>   born in Sweden, in the year 1707.
> EDWARD: Am I too young to learn Botany? I think I should like it
>   very much.
> MOTHER: By no means, my dear. It is so simple a study, that the
>   youngest persons can understand it, when the principles are
>   properly explained to them.[3]

I imagine that Edward would have been about eight. The language
has changed, but not children. The author, while writing a book
for children of Edward's age to read, incidentally describes very
well the kind of domestic scene that she imagines would be familiar to her young readers. Edward has overheard what his mother
and aunt were discussing in the garden, and his mother deliberately gets on with her hobby in front of him. Naturally his curiosity is aroused, and his mother just answers his questions. There is
something to look at, something to handle, and Edward is invited
to share the procedure.

   Such ideas eventually bore fruit, though learning about the
world through discovery has always had to tug against the more
mechanistic, 'no nonsense' view of education that prefers to base
teaching on the three Rs and the memorising of facts. Mrs Trimmer would, I am sure, have felt that those who are already motivated by a general spirit of enquiry will learn to read, write and
count all the more readily because they want to.

The museum tradition

The ancient Greeks invented the word *mouseion* to mean a temple
of the Muses – a school for, or collection of, the arts. The Renais-
sance revived the idea of art collections, and from the fifteenth

3. Anon., *Conversations on Botany*, 3rd
edn., 1820.

3:1 Commemorating a royal death

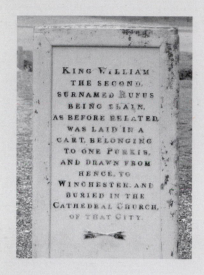

KING WILLIAM
THE SECOND,
SURNAMED RUFUS
BEING SLAIN,
AS BEFORE RELATED,
WAS LAID IN A
CART, BELONGING
TO ONE PURKIS,
AND DRAWN FROM
HENCE, TO
WINCHESTER, AND
BURIED IN THE
CATHEDRAL CHURCH,
OF THAT CITY.

Erecting a monument to record an event is an old tradition. At first, a chapel marked the presumed site of the death of William the Conqueror's son William Rufus, who was killed by an arrow in a hunting accident in the heart of England's New Forest, near Ringwood. In 1745, long after the medieval chapel had vanished, Lord John Delaware erected the Rufus Stone, so that 'the spot where an event so memorable had happened might not hereafter be unknown.' Nearly a hundred years later, a forest Warden named William Sturges Bourne, having found the stone 'much mutilated and defaced' (vandalism or weathering? we may wonder), had its remains covered in a cast iron structure – 'an iron case of supreme ugliness,' wrote a contemporary – with an inscription on each of its three sides (left). Just as with many battle sites, this place has no features surviving from William's day – even the oldest trees in the vicinity are younger than any William saw.

Note the sense of immediacy that a touch of circumstantial detail gives to the account: 'a cart belonging to one Purkis'. An interpretive monument as old as this is itself interpretable: the quaintness of its wording, the style of its lettering, the very fact that it exists, all speak of earlier ages than our own.

century personal collections by the educated rich began to appear across Europe. In the middle of the sixteenth century the English word 'cabinet' was coined – a diminutive of 'cabin', meaning a little hut or room, influenced by the Italian *gabinetto*, meaning a closet or chest of drawers. The new word soon came to mean a small room or a piece of furniture in which to store and display *objets d'art et de vertu*, interesting bits and pieces. The English statesman, scholar and writer Francis Bacon suggested that gentlemen with pretensions of scholarship and taste should own 'a goodly huge cabinet, wherein whatsoever the hand of man by exquisite art or engine has made rare in stuff, form or motion; whatsoever singularity, chance and the shuffle of things hath produced; whatsoever Nature has wrought in things that want life and may be kept, shall be sorted and included.'[4]

Such items were known as 'curiosities', a word implying 'things full of interest' or 'worth studying', without the dismissive overtones it has today. When the diarist John Evelyn, Secretary of the recently formed Royal Society, visited the physician and polymath Sir Thomas Browne in Norwich in 1671, he was enchanted: 'his whole house and garden being a paradise and cabinet of rarities, and that of the best collection, especially medals, books, plants and natural things.' Browne then conducted Evelyn on a tour of Norwich, and commented (very possibly as they passed the flint building that is now the Strangers' Hall Museum) that the builders of his day had lost the art of squaring flints. Eleven years later, Elias Ashmole bequeathed his large collection of curiosities and rarities to Oxford University, where it formed the basis of today's

4. Francis Bacon, quoted in O. R. Impey and A. G. MacGregor, eds., *The Origins of Museums*, Clarendon Press, Oxford, 1985.

Insights offered and   35
sought. Interpretation's
antecedents

3:2 The cabinet of the Pastons

The last of the famous Paston family of Oxnead, Norfolk, was the second Earl of Yarmouth, who died in 1732; his grandfather Sir William Paston had been a great collector. A contemporary painting (below) celebrating the collection now hangs in the Strangers' Hall Museum in Norwich. It depicts a photogenic jumble of items – musical instruments, shells, a clock, an hourglass, fruit (or wax models), a ewer, a tankard and a lobster. Among this clutter, almost buried in it, are a girl and a boy, themselves looking almost like exhibits.

By an interesting chance, an inventory survives of some of the contents of Oxnead. It includes 'Cheiny potts', 'Indian Kans', 'a shell, engraven with the story of Atalanta, standing upon an eagle's foot of silver', 'a paire of coaker-shell cups with covers' and 'a mother of pearle shell, the fashion of a boat, standing upon a silver and gilt foote upheld with two anchors, with two spoones in it, one christall and one amber' (quoted in R. W. Ketton-Cremer, *Norfolk Assembly*, Faber and Faber, 1957). The need to index and label collections, however crudely, comprised the very first attempts at museum interpretation.

The Yarmouth Collection *by an anonymous artist, c. 1665.*

36   Insights offered and
sought. Interpretation's
antecedents

Ashmolean Museum. Sir Hans Sloane started to collect plant specimens, minerals, antiquities and books; like Evelyn, he was Secretary of the Royal Society and later became its President. He
bequeathed his collections to be the founding nucleus of the British
Museum.

The relevance of these stories to Interpretation is to do with the
ways in which, in the eighteenth century, the educated members
of the public came into contact with such collections. First arose
the custom of gentlefolk visiting the great houses of the country,
to view not only the grounds and the architecture, but also the art
treasures they contained. If the owners were not free or inclined to
receive the visitors themselves, their higher-ranking servants would
undertake to show them round. When visitors asked questions, the
hosts or their servants had to be ready to answer and explain. The
second way in which the public encountered such collections was
if they were donated to an institution, and people were admitted
to see them. At the very least, objects had to be identifiable by the
visitor, and thus museum labelling was born. Older readers may
still remember museums in which labels gave only a brief identification of the object, the name of the donor, and the date of the
donation; some labels on stuffed birds would add their sex, the
date and place they were shot, and who shot them. As for interpretation – none! Museums have progressed since then.

Conservation

The conservation tradition is a more recent one, but its importance
to Interpretation is immense. A summary of major developments
in conservation in Britain is given in appendix A.

THE PUBLIC SEEK EXPLANATIONS

The process of sharing an understanding of the world requires, generation by generation, not just the initiative of those who care, but
the interest of people willing to be 'schooled'. Perhaps there will
never a general public enthusiasm for life-long learning, but there
has always been a proportion of people who positively seek knowledge and understanding, and plenty of others who are happy to
learn so long as it can be on their own terms.

Just as those who seek to communicate understanding today
have centuries of tradition behind them, whether they realise it or
not, so also there is a long tradition of individual searching for it. I
have suggested four key traditions – educational self-help; hobbies;
tourism and travel, and entertainment. All of these can be considered as mainly consumer-driven. Even though today much tourism
and entertainment is promoted commercially, it is people's appetite
for such things that characterises the market.

Educational self-help

Self-help has always been with us, but let us in this brief account highlight the sort of people of whom Samuel Smiles, Victorian author of *Self-help* (1859), particularly approved. That he was writing for an eager readership there can be little doubt: mid-Victorian England saw much conscious effort on the part of artisans to educate themselves, and a great readiness in many middle-class people with a social conscience to help.

Smiles was born in 1812, in the heyday of Mrs Trimmer, and was an exact contemporary of Charles Dickens. His father kept a shop in Haddington, Lothian; Samuel, after the manner of many of his biographical subjects, 'made good' by hard work, gaining entry to the University of Edinburgh where he qualified as a doctor. As Smiles was growing up in Haddington, David Livingstone, one year younger, was working in a cotton factory at Blantyre, Lanarkshire, 45 miles away. He too was to qualify as a doctor and later to achieve fame as an explorer and missionary to Africa. The Scots had a genius for self-help.

Most of Smiles's working life was spent in Leeds, Yorkshire, where he met another northerner of humble origin, nearly thirty years his senior. George Stephenson, son of a colliery engine-minder in the Newcastle area, worked as a boy as an engine fireman, earning enough to enable him to attend night school and gain a basic education. Smiles, with Stephenson's approval, wrote his biography, and then went on to treat of others who had made good, including two fellow Scots, the naturalist-cum-cobbler Thomas Edward of Banff, and Robert Dick, the botanist-cum-baker of Thurso.

It may have been partly the influence and popularity of Smiles's books that led to the establishment of many institutions for the further education of workers. Among the pioneers of this concept were the philanthropic mill-owners (father and son-in-law) David Dale and Robert Owen, who in the first half of the nineteenth century built splendid educational establishments for their workers and their workers' children at their mill settlement at New Lanark (Scotland again). Smiles is likely to have been aware of the developments at New Lanark, for they were taking place in his childhood.[5] The idea that working-class people with minimal schooling deserved opportunities to better themselves gradually became institutionalised. Mechanics' Institutes and other independent establishments were formed. The Working Men's College in Great Ormond Street, London, was founded in 1854 by F. D. Maurice (1805–72), a leader of the Christian Socialist movement and later Professor of Moral Philosophy at Cambridge. Early this century the young George Trevelyan found himself drawn there:

5. With great vision, the entire complex at New Lanark is currently being restored, apart from some of the factory buildings. The workers' housing is being converted into flats, and Owen's ambitious educational Institute now houses a Visitor Centre that tells the extraordinary story of this industrial settlement.

38   Insights offered and
sought. Interpretation's
antecedents

Evening classes were the staple of the Working Men's College, and I taught in some of them, at first going up once a week from Cambridge for the purpose. I don't think I taught well, but I made friends and liked the men, excellent samples of London folk . . . They were not in fact all 'working men', but the name of the College helped to keep away snobs . . . Men were not merely taught in the classes, but came to regard the College as a club and a home.[6]

All over the country popular lectures were organised. The Workers' Educational Association, brainchild of Albert Mansbridge, was founded in 1903 to provide Britain with a network of self-organising but centrally supported study groups.

The education system has always recognised the importance of youth groups (including youth centres, youth clubs, church clubs, scouts and guides, army cadets, young farmers' clubs and dozens more). It is a basic tenet of youth work that such groups do much more than keep young people off the streets: they can in some ways provide informal social and cultural education. Many run camping or touring holidays, and organise excursions to the countryside or to sites of interest. How effectively such experiences are interpreted depends on the understanding and training of the adult leaders.

Hobbies, clubs and societies
The origins and development of Britain's natural history societies have been chronicled in a delightful book by David Elliston Allen.[7] He traces them from the seventeenth-century 'herbarizings' or field excursions of the Society of Apothecaries, which apprentices were expected to attend in order to learn how to identify medicinal plants in the wild. The Society's physic garden at Chelsea, opened

6. G. M. Trevelyan, *Autobography of an Historian*, Longmans, Green and Co., London, 1949, pp. 23, 24.

7. David Elliston Allen, *The Naturalist in Britain – a Social History*, Allen Lane, London, 1976.

When I ran a boys' club in Kilburn, London, in the early 1960s, a neighbour of mine, a geologist, said he would be happy to take a small group of boys out on a fossil hunt. Bob did not know the local boys; I thought I did, and I doubted if his idea would work. I accepted his offer with some apprehension, and three fourteen-year-olds joined us one Saturday. It was never difficult to encourage the boys to come on an outing 'just for a laugh'.

After a hilarious and noisy journey we arrived at our destination, a chalk quarry. We pushed through some undergrowth and arrived at the chalk face. The boys had never seen such a place before. Bob started probing at the chalk with a geologist's hammer, and eventually turned round with a small piece of something white in his hand. He produced a lens, and handed it and the specimen round and asked if we could see the minute shell shape embedded in it. Yes, we said, we could. 'What you have there', he told us, 'is the remains of a creature that lived in the sea about a hundred million years ago, and you are the first people ever to see it.' When we got back home, one of the boys (who had no academic interests whatever) said, 'Could you leave us at the library? I'd like to see if they've got a book about fossils.'

I and my colleagues took boys from the club on many more outings, visiting the Sussex Downs, a Welsh hill farm, Hadrian's Wall. Always, these particular three boys would take their hammers. One winter, while camping on the South Downs in Sussex, we were walking over some rough ground when one of the lads spotted a shaped flint fossil, and called out, 'Look! An echinoid!' He picked it up, and an echinoid it was. And all this interest, knowledge and dawning understanding was started by a chance invitation that was nearly refused.

In the seventeenth century physicians and apothecaries used to explore suitable habitats for plants and herbs, and novices learned about the medicinal properties of plants from the senior members. Long before that, the idea of gathering specimen plants together into a special garden was already current. The earliest physic garden may have been the one founded by a member of the medical school at Salerno, Italy, in the fourteenth century. John Gerard, author of the famous *Herball*, who died in 1612, had his own garden near the Fleet river in London. The University of Oxford's Botanic Garden still occupies land given for the purpose in 1621.

The Society of Apothecaries set up its physic garden in Chelsea, then a village, in the 1670s. Amazingly, it has survived on the same site, its high walls insulating it from the built-up surroundings, and it is still used for research and study. To walk into it is to enter a calm, green world of trees, shrubs and other plants, accompanied by signs and labels that today are interpretational – providing not mere facts, but revelation.

The Chelsea Physic Garden has restricted opening hours, so enquire before you go.

in 1673, was used regularly for demonstrations led by expert botanists; approved non-members could also attend.

Field Clubs sprang up in the late 1770s, especially in the north midlands of England, which opened up natural history as an activity for ordinary people. Allen quotes J. C. Loudon: 'Wherever the silk, linen or cotton manufactures are carried on . . . the operatives are found to possess a taste for, and occupy part of their leisure time in, the culture of flowers.'[8] In Norwich, Thomas Browne's city and another centre of fabric manufacture, a favourite hobby was the breeding (or 'fancy') of canaries: 'It was common to find many a bedroom filled with nest-boxes.'[9] The hobbyists would meet regularly in informal clubs, often in public houses, to share their knowledge and discuss techniques.

The next century saw the fusion of these informal and formal traditions:

From these two quite separate stocks, the one rather avidly academic but with a well-proved role in promoting the advancement of knowledge, the other unambitious and convivial with its roots in the field, the equivalent of a natural hybrid, with all a half-breed's vigour, arose spontaneously in 1823. This was the Plinian Society of Edinburgh, a general scientific society which luckily happened to have its birth just as field classes had become all the rage at the two southern Scottish universities – and which, accordingly, made history, apparently almost without noticing, by including in its programme from 1825 at least occasional excursions into the surrounding countryside on foot.[10]

8. J. C. Loudon, *Encyclopaedia of Gardening*, 1822.

9. Revd Joseph Crompton, first President of the Norfolk and Norwich Naturalists' Society, in 1869; published in the Society's *Transactions*, vol. 1, 1870, pp. 13ff.

10. Allen, op. cit., 1976. The Society was named after the first century AD Roman scholar and naturalist Gaius Plinius Secundus (Pliny the Elder), whose monumental *Natural History* was first translated into English in 1601, and was long regarded as an important authority. He died of volcanic fumes while investigating the eruption of Mount Vesuvius that engulfed Pompeii in AD 70.

40   Insights offered and
      sought. Interpretation's
      antecedents

The earliest county Naturalists' Societies soon followed. The Natural History Society of Northumberland, Durham and Newcastle-upon-Tyne was the first in 1829, and was followed by many others over the next thirty years, including London in 1858. In 1841 Edward Lees, co-founder of the Worcestershire Society in 1833, published his book *The Botanical Looker-Out* – a significant title, which nicely reflects the informal enthusiasm of many of these Victorian amateur naturalists.

A major literary influence was the classic book by the Revd Gilbert White, *The Natural History and Antiquities of Selborne*, published in 1789. This was the first substantial book on the wildlife and history of a single parish, a kind of mini-survey in depth which caught the imagination of many country parsons and other would-be naturalists, many of whom began to keep records in imitation of those published in the *Naturalist's Calendar* of 1795, edited from White's papers after his death by John Aikin.[11] In almost every one of the local and county natural history books that followed *Selborne*, the authors declared their indebtedness to White. They include the Revd Leonard Jenyns, founder of the Bath Field Club, who edited *Selborne* in 1843. In 1846 he published his own *Observations in Natural History*, in which he recalled the 'ardour inspired by a first perusal of White's work', and claimed that the popularity of natural science in his own time was 'doubtless in a great measure owing to the influence which White's *Natural History of Selborne* has exercised on the present generation.'[12] These early Victorian societies were the forerunners of – even, in many instances, the very same as – today's county Natural History Societies. Although their first members tended to belong to the nobility, gentry, clergy and medical profession, they could make room for others of more lowly occupation: John Hancock of Northumberland (after whom the celebrated Hancock Museum is named) was the poorly educated son of a tradesman in Newcastle; Edward Lees was a printer, and T. E. Gunn, a founder member of the Norfolk and Norwich society, was a taxidermist.

An obvious spin-off from hobbies is the vast literature contained in specialist magazines: there are enough enthusiasts in Britain to make an amazing range of specialist journals viable. Most readers are hoping to learn, so each of these publications is potentially 'interpretive' – their editors and writers have the opportunity deliberately to publish material that, piecemeal and cumulatively, helps to explain our experiences of the world about us.

The Grand Tour

The first known printed guidebook in the world was allegedly *Mirabilia Romae* [Things to Admire in Rome], published in 1473.[13] In the eighteenth century, the concept of the Grand Tour reached

11. John Aikin had the distinction of being mentioned by name on the final page of White's *Selborne*. His daughter Lucy became a historian and biographer, and wrote of her childhood memories in Great Yarmouth, Norfolk: 'A flat, barren, sandy down, extending to the beach was our daily walk; but so much the keener was my delight when we accompanied my father on his professional drives through the shady lanes of rural villages on the Suffolk side. He was an admirable observer of nature – not a plant, not a bird, not a wild animal, escaped him; he knew them all, and taught his children to know and love them too.'

12. Revd Leonard Jenyns, *Observations in Natural History*, 1846.

13. According to Patrick Robertson, *The Shell Book of Firsts*, Ebury Press and Michael Joseph, 1974, repr. 1983. It was written by an author named Benedict and issued by the printer Adam von Rottweil in Rome.

Insights offered and 41
sought. Interpretation's
antecedents

its heyday: the sight-seeing journey through Europe was considered essential for every young man of Britain's upper classes who aspired to being cultured. Families made careful arrangements, negotiating introductions for their sons to celebrities and potential hosts abroad, and engaging older chaperones who were acquainted with the towns, cities, galleries and antiquities to be visited. After six months in Germany and Italy, you were meant to be able to make intelligent conversation. The popularity of the Grand Tour inspired guide literature, for example Thomas Martyn's *The Gentleman's Guide to His Tour Through Italy* of 1787.

Travel guides also began to be published in Britain at about this time, to popular spas such as Bath and Tunbridge Wells, places of interest such as the Universities of Oxford and Cambridge, and picturesque destinations such as the Lake District and Stonehenge. The range increased in the early nineteenth century, including guides to fashionable seaside resorts such as Brighton and Scarborough. These were mostly addressed to a genteel audience, and the text was largely devoted to description rather than interpretation. The arrival of cheap rail transport and the Bank Holidays Act of 1871 greatly increased travelling and brought it within reach of a new market. Thomas Cook's first packaged holiday tour was as early as 1845, when he took over 350 travellers by rail to Liverpool and North Wales for four days. To assist with the ascent of Snowdon he 'employed the only English-speaking Welshman he could find in Caernarvon'.[14]

Popularisers of guide literature for foreign travel included John Murray, whose series of *Hand-books for Travellers* appeared from 1836, and Karl Baedeker, whose celebrated series was published in Leipzig from 1872. Ward, Lock and Co. were publishing their Guides to Britain from 1896.[15] In France, the *Guides Michelin* have been popular since the early days of motoring, and have been available in English for over half a century.

After the Second World War, rail excursions in Britain never regained their old popularity. But there is a resurgence: *The Northumbrian*, *The Glasgow and Burns County Explorer* and *The Tattoo and Highland Weekend Break* are among the experiences on offer. You can make nostalgic journeys as well as dine in renovated Pullman carriages of the 1920s and 1930s along Railtrack routes; you can even travel from Paris to Venice in period carriages under the name of the *Oriental Express*. But the advertising for these always stresses luxury rather than opportunities to learn – 'Fondle the fabric of history as you traverse Europe.' Also popular are maritime cruises and terrestrial safaris, some with highly educational themes and expert leaders. At the more modest end of the scale, less demanding tours by coach or boat have the driver, skipper or a courier pointing out features of interest. Not surprisingly, the interpretational element is often inadequate in the humbler excursions;

14. Ibid.

15. In later editions, these became known as the 'Red Guides'; the earliest editions were bound in green.

42 Insights offered and
sought. Interpretation's
antecedents

the guides are sometimes ill-briefed, and may be unaware of what facts act to interpret, and what merely inform or entertain.

Entertainment

Some aspects of Interpretation undoubtedly derive from people's need for undemanding intellectual titillation. There have always been entrepreneurs who can make a living from laughter, games, relaxation and idle curiosity. For centuries, fairgrounds and circuses were venues for the presentation of 'marvels' or 'prodigies' – dwarves, bearded ladies, giants, two-headed lambs. Also displayed were fire-eaters, jugglers, trapeze artists and clowns on high stilts, parading elephants, lions and tigers, even camels and wolves – a mingling of strange accomplishments and strange beasts which made mind-blowing, merry entertainment. People willingly paid and were entertained, and probably did not much worry about whether everything they had seen was genuine.

In cities like London, showmen set up more permanent amusements. Madame Tussaud established her waxworks in London's Baker Street in 1835. The planetarium was not added until 1958, though an earlier one was on view in Munich as early as 1923. Thus entertainment and education were combined. The main showpiece of the nationwide 1951 Festival of Britain included themes as varied as wildlife and architecture, and was nothing if not educational – but it was popular, too.

The theme parks of today are in direct succession to these events. So are Robin Hood centres, hologram displays, Red Arrows aerobatics, shipwreck centres and even some aspects of county agricultural shows. To those who scan local newspapers for ideas for weekend family excursions, it may make no real difference whether to visit the village fête or a civil war battle re-enactment, a steam rally or wrestling in mud. Very few will pause to assess the likely interpretational content – what people are looking for is a good day out. But some members of the public, consciously or not, will choose experiences with a 'hint of culture'. They perhaps enjoy nostalgia, architectural magnificence, big gardens, animals or things mechanical to give flavour to their leisure.

This is a fascinating field for the Interpreter to consider. Where can he find an audience? Is it worthwhile trying to attract floating weekenders? Already press advertisements include open days at nature reserves, costumed events at castles or stately homes, *son et lumière* at the cathedral – entertainment with a message. Perhaps there may be wider scope for extending Interpretation into the world of entertainment, or into the leisure activities of the home.

The Very Important Feature
Conservation comes first

4

Because conservation is the prime, the underlying, the ulterior motive of Interpretation, it stands to reason that the Feature itself is the most important party to the Interpretation process. It is not there to be exploited; it must be handled with loving care. This is not just for the selfish and cynical reason that attractive and interesting features, if well looked after, can be made to generate money, but because they are parts of our world that matter – if they did not, then we would not consider them worth interpreting. We interpret in order to conserve.

There is a great deal worth conserving in this world. It ranges from natural wilderness – the deserts and the glaciers, the forests and the seas – to attractive man-made landscapes, such as the colour-rich woodlands of New England, the grassy Downs of southern England, the canal-crossed wetlands of The Netherlands and the vineyards of Tuscany. There are fine and interesting buildings – the châteaux of the Loire valley, the stave churches of Norway, the temples of Japan – indeed, whole towns and villages whose attraction lies in their form and variety as much as in individual buildings. But in stressing the famous and the spectacular we must not overlook the small and the local (village greens and commons, terraces of town houses, statues and street-names, hedgerows and gardens), which can be just as significant and valuable to the people who live nearby. There are animal and plant species, beautiful and useful, too numerous to name and too obvious to require illustrating by examples. There are archaeological and historic sites which are important monuments to the story of man; there are works of art and traditional cultures.

Each country has its own history of conservation. In Britain the story has two main strands, the conservation of artefacts, and the conservation of nature – and the two intertwine in the conservation of landscape.[1]

CAN WE INTERPRET THE SLUMS?

We interpret in order to conserve. Here, then, is a problem: is it somehow inappropriate to apply interpretation principles and techniques to unlovely features such as slums or refuse disposal,

1. The antecedents of what we may call the 'conservation movement' have been described in various books and journals relating to museums, architecture and wildlife (see appendix E). Some remarks on the evolution of conservation in Britain are given in appendix A.

an oil spill or a planning blunder? Aren't they part of our heritage, whether we like them or not, and don't they too need to be understood? Or is Interpretation to be limited by definition to the good and the beautiful? Surely we have all come across articles, exhibitions and film about the *Exxon Valdez* or *Torrey Canyon* oil spills. At Oświęcim, Poland, there is a museum that interprets the former Nazi concentration camp on the site we know as Auschwitz. The more this is considered, the more apparent it becomes that any Interpretation of slums, planning blunders or the horrors of Auschwitz is calculated to remind and to warn. The Interpretation *is* conservationally motivated: it is intended to promote respect and care, whether for places or for people, by exposing folly and evil.

The positive conservation principle is easily exemplified in nature conservation. Ben Lawers in the Grampian hills is a mountain famous for its sub-arctic flora; plants grow there that are unique in Britain. These species first colonised the slopes soon after the Ice Age glaciers retreated. As the lower slopes of the Scottish mountains gradually grew warmer, the arctic flora began to die out. But on the upper slopes of Ben Lawers and one or two other hills in the range, the climate is still 'alpine' enough for them to survive.

But a few decades ago Ben Lawers became too famous: visitors in search of interesting flowers used to range all over its slopes, not sure where to look, and sometimes collecting specimens of rare plants that should not have been touched. The National Trust for Scotland acquired the mountain, and now keeps it for the plants – and for people, too. A well-designed Visitor Centre at a convenient point of access minimises the overuse of narrow roads and helps visitors orientate themselves. Inside the Centre, the story of Ben Lawers and its plants is told and their vulnerability is explained; reference material is available for those who want it. Alongside the Centre is a short trail, which leads the visitor past living samples of many of the rare plants. Thus the main Feature is saved from damage, while the visitors get great satisfaction and leave with an enhanced understanding of 'the way Ben Lawers works'. Appreciation of the fact that some plants are specially adapted to survive in harsh conditions is a key to understanding basic principles of evolution and ecology – principles that, once grasped, can be recognised in operation in all sorts of other situations.

All over the world there are archaeological features of considerable fascination, which are vulnerable to erosion by the feet of visitors or other accidental damage. Books and television create publicity, which brings more visitors. The active interest of these people is valuable, for an interested public will be reluctant to see ancient monuments harmed; and yet persistent treading over the centuries can wear out even stone. The grand, evocative ruins of

Knossos in Crete, for example, are suffering from poorly controlled visitor access.

Weather, too, is an elemental agent of damage. Rain, frost and the heat of the sun, not to mention earthquakes and volcanic eruptions, can make catastrophic changes. The deterioration of archaeological sites once they are exposed means that in wetter climates, such as Britain, they either have to be filled in again to preserve what remains, or sheltered in a specially erected building, as at Caerleon in South Wales. The same principle can be seen at Dinosaur National Monument on the border between Utah and Colorado, where the exposed fossil remains of dinosaurs are protected *in situ* by a building on the hillside.

LESSONS FROM POMPEII

The eruption of Mount Vesuvius in AD 79 destroyed what may have been a beautiful and interesting city, but it also preserved the ruins for us, ready for the archaeologists of the nineteenth and twentieth centuries to uncover, for the fascination and education of hundreds of thousands of tourists every year. Pompeii can perhaps teach conservationists three things. First, that natural forces can destroy as well as create, while man can create as well as destroy. This apparently obvious fact can be overlooked by enthusiasts for 'nature'. How often do members of the public complain that trees or shrubs are being cut down in their favourite woodland? They seem not to be aware that the woodland they love best – with grand old trees and other younger ones among them, with bluebells, primroses or wood anemones colour-carpeting the ground – is the way it is because for centuries it has been sympathetically exploited by man. 'Exploit' is a word that has acquired a dirty colour, but its essential meaning is 'to achieve, to make something of'. Our bread is grown from seed descended from wild plants that our ancestors 'exploited', and sown in fields that have been won from the wilderness that our ancestors 'exploited.' All living creatures exploit their environments: it is the way they live.

The second issue raised by Pompeii is the other side of the same coin: should man just accept natural forces and processes, and never interfere or manipulate them (another emotive word)? For man's survival as a species, and for the survival of many individuals, such forces may sometimes have to be resisted or harnessed. Terrace cultivation in the Andes, irrigation systems in Egypt, sea embankments along low-lying coasts, the stone quarries of Barnack in Cambridgeshire, and the coal mines of the Ruhr – these are man's destructive/creative input into landscape, in much the same way as the dams of beavers or the mounds of termites. The motives are similar – domestic and economic.

Thirdly, nothing can remain the same for ever. There was a time when the city of Pompeii never existed; a time when it flourished;

At Knossos, Crete, is one of the most fascinating ancient sites of the Mediterranean, reputedly the palace of the legendary King Minos, dating from about the eighteenth century BC. Its hilly terrain is under constant erosion from the feet of the many thousands of tourists who visit it every year. Sudden, sharp showers send miniature streams gurgling down the steep paths, washing the sandy soil downhill. Yet who would wish such a fascinating place to be closed to tourists, or reburied to protect it from the weather?

Some structures on the site are reconstructions by archaeologists; others are modern, designed to shelter certain particularly vulnerable features, or to serve the convenience of visitors. It is not always immediately apparent what is truly ancient, what is reconstructed, and what is comparatively new.

Knossos is interpreted mainly by live guides and by guide books. But there must be many visitors for whom its significance in ancient history remains unclear, and others who find the place baffling, or even disappointing. Some may wonder whether conservation has been compromised by inadequate control of visitors.

The ancient sites of Greece, typifying Europe's cultural heritage, draw visitors from all over the world: tourism makes an important contribution to the country's national income. Perhaps more should be spent on conservation and interpretation, even if it is the visitors (local as well as foreign) who end up paying for it. Maybe some kind of two-tier system could be devised for such over-visited sites, offering a choice between limited viewing from a suitable viewpoint with appropriate interpretation, and more extensive but nevertheless controlled access for those willing to pay extra.

Top: visitors at the Minoan site of Knossos, Crete, on a rainy day.
Above: an eroding pathway at Knossos.

a time when it lay buried and virtually forgotten; and a time when its very skeleton became a popular tourist attraction. Each phase had, or has, its virtues: none could have been, nor will be, preserved for ever.

Conservation, as has often been said, is not just unintelligent, unscientific preservation. It is 'quality of exploitation'. Man is the only creature blessed with an overview of the world and the skills to look after it, as well as being cursed with a capacity to destroy it. Man alone is equipped to fulfil the responsibility of managing the world wisely and unselfishly on behalf of all living things. True conservation is wise and unselfish stewardship, intelligent and informed management. It has to balance the needs and opportunities of today, tomorrow and (as far as they can be anticipated) a million years ahead – just as long as natural forces permit. Pompeii is a unique site that needs its own conservation, management and interpretation. So is Knossos. So is the Grand Canyon. So is Stonehenge. So, potentially, would be any hill or river, any farm or vineyard, any town square, any village pond.

The Stonehenge problem

Stonehenge, in Wiltshire, is a good example of a world-famous site whose fame could be its destruction, whereas it was lack of fame that nearly permitted the destruction of the stone circle at nearby Avebury. In the seventeenth century local people, no doubt exploiting their world for the immediate benefit of their local economy, began to break up Avebury's sandstone monoliths to use for building. They devised their own way of going about it, heating the stones with big fires piled around them and then, when they were hot, drenching them with water. This cracked them into convenient pieces. Now Avebury's remaining standing stones have achieved celebrity, and are protected by English Heritage.

Stonehenge, on the other hand, a much smaller monument, is visited by hundreds of thousands of people every year. The problem is how to save it from its admirers. Gone are the days when you could walk among the stones, scramble over some of them, even carve your initials on them; today, you are not allowed anywhere within the enclosure that surrounds them. There is a visitor centre explaining their history, but it is off-site – this is no doubt partly intended to cut short the time you spend at the site itself ('Interpretation as a management tool', some would say). Meanwhile, as the existing system gets more and more clogged up, ambitious and imaginative plans have been proposed for re-routing local roads, creating hidden car parking space, controlling access. The next phase of Interpretation, it might be argued, could be to construct a replica, or to consider whether a virtual reality experience might occupy and entertain visitors even more effectively than the reality itself.

Here is a real dilemma: interpretation is ideally based on first-hand experience, and yet its main loyalty is to the Feature. Visitors are not so important that the Feature can be sacrificed to them.

GREEN TOURISM

The same problem is endemic in tourism. How does our 'right' to visit the Galapagos Islands balance the right of the Islands to their own survival – or is it only man that has rights? When one nation exercises its 'freedom' to test atomic weapons on coral islands, who has the authority to insist that similar habitats must be protected from the comparatively harmless curiosity of scuba divers?

Green Tourism is the concept that has been devised to address these problems. The idea is that the only permissible tourism should be of a kind that does not interfere with the qualities of the place itself (including its wildlife) or with the way of life and culture of the local inhabitants. Theoretically this ought to mean that an undeveloped resort would not construct casinos, marinas, golf courses, fish and chip shops or burger bars – nor, if the principle were to be applied strictly, hotels. Visitors would be expected to stay in local homes, eat local food, travel by traditional forms of transport and amuse themselves by simple sight-seeing.

But advocates of Green Tourism are not so naïve as that. The 'benefits' of tourism (they mean money) must, they say, be shared by the local community, not hogged by outside entrepreneurs. Here the thin end of the wedge of realism is being gently inserted. People in developing communities will naturally want extra facilities for their own convenience and enjoyment. A more prosperous community will probably number among its members some who see advantage in making money for themselves, not just for the general good. Who are visitors to say that they should not? The idealism of Green Tourism is sound enough: the problem is human nature. In reality, the application of these principles can do little except perhaps slow down the processes that are gradually making the world the same all over, and educate us all in the need for moderation and self-restraint.

Green Tourism does not apply only to developing parts of the world: there are also Green Tourism initiatives in the wealthy West. But if these are to have a positive and lasting effect, both the visitors and the locals must be 'educated' in specific 'environmental conservation'. Interpretation must be a major element in this process, both directly and indirectly applied. Directly applied Interpretation would have to include comment on the tourism itself, interpreting it to both tourists and locals. Such focusing on specific problems involving visitors' own activity is not entirely unknown (see page 84 for consideration of the Yorkshire Dales 'Landscapes for Tomorrow' project). The Norfolk Wildlife Trust's Broadland Visitor Centre at Ranworth used to greet visitors at the entrance to its interpretational exhibition with a pile of garbage (old bicycle wheels, plastic bottles and other junk dredged from the waterways), placed in front of a floor-to-ceiling photograph of the beautiful Broadland that they had come to see. Possibly some visitors were shocked or offended, but the chances are that this unspoken message got across.

Conscientious tour promoters make sure that their couriers explain to visitors how important to the local community certain aspects of their behaviour can be. It may concern dress requirements, the removal of shoes before entering a mosque, or local customs regarding price haggling, tipping, gifts and hospitality. To explain these matters effectively to first-time visitors requires some 'interpretation' of the local scene. Done well at a critical moment in the visitors' experience, it can be highly effective.

Less directly, Interpretation can dwell on the values, virtues and vulnerabilities of a site in the hope of revealing truths to the Visitors which will enhance their enjoyment. A plan for Interpretation undoubtedly helped Ben Lawers (see page 44). If they are impressed, however, they are likely to go home and spread the fame of this 'unspoilt gem' to their friends. A fresh batch of visitors will arrive there the next year, to be treated to the same Interpretation. Even if the convinced and converted come home satisfied, and never return to that spot again, they may well have had their appetites whetted, and begin to look for other unspoilt paradises to explore.

Perhaps the best that Interpretation can hope to do in the short term is to modify Visitors' behaviour to the site's advantage, by engaging their understanding and sympathy. In landscapes like those of Britain's Peak District, Yorkshire Dales or Lake District, where the fields are bounded by dry-stone walls (undressed stone without cement or mortar), visitors may not realise that to clamber over them is not only dangerous, but damages the walls. This could enable farm animals to escape and might require hours of work to repair. The Lake District National Park's Centre at Brockhole, Cumbria, has a special section of wall with a pile of stones beside it, with an invitation to visitors to try their hand at wall-repairing. Some have a go, others watch – but all should leave with a greater respect for Cumbrian dry-stone walls and those who have to maintain them.

The mid-term value of Interpretation may be mainly political. That is to say, the mere fact that a site is interpreted demonstrates that someone is trying to manage it for the use, enjoyment and education of the public, and encourages a constant, even if modest, flow of people to visit it. Statistically, a visited, managed site is less liable to vandalism, and any attempt to change its use, or to hamper such provision for public enjoyment, will be seen as a retrograde step. On the other hand, a site that local people are

One site that has had to wait many years for interpretive treatment is the spectacular (though comparatively little known) Roman shore fort in East Anglia, known as Burgh Castle. About two miles inland from Gorleston-on-Sea, near Great Yarmouth, Norfolk, this impressive Roman monument is tucked away on the edge of a promontory of land surrounded by the sea on the east and the wide marshes of the Broadland rivers to the west. A flint wall (above), much of it still standing fifteen feet high, extends for about 425 yards around three sides of the site of a fourth-century military fort: it is one of the most extensive Roman structures in Britain.

Until recently, the only information greeting the visitor who (perhaps on the strength of a puzzling feature on the Ordnance Survey map) tentatively explored this remote corner was a notice alongside a public footpath a few hundred yards away saying 'Burgh Castle Roman site', and, at the site itself, three signs announcing: 'It is an offence to climb on the walls.'

Visitors could have been equally well deterred by some simple, friendly explanation of what the structure was, its age, why it was built, and a reminder that Roman concrete, even after surviving for fifteen centuries, is vulnerable to wear and tear. Norfolk Landscape Archaeology and the Norfolk Archaeological Trust, in association with various other organisations, are currently working on a welcoming scheme of interpretation for Burgh Castle.

Another Roman site in Norfolk is Venta Icenorum, location of the civitas capital provided by the Romans for the remnant of the Iceni tribe after the defeat of their queen and leader Boudicca. Here again, there has not until recently been any on-site explanation: the land was in private hands and fenced off against trespassers.

A few years ago it was acquired by the Norfolk Archaeological Trust and the whole site laid out in a pattern that welcomes visitors. Fencing, stiles and wooden steps are placed in such a way that one can walk round the outside of the former walls, or along the top of the bank on which they stood. Helpful interpretive panels by Norfolk Landscape Archaeology bring to life what otherwise is little more than a large, rectangular grassy field surrounded by an earthwork.

There is a small, landscaped car park, and it is possible to walk right down to the little river Tas, which no doubt in the town's heyday served as a waterway, for one edge of the Roman town wall ran along the river bank. The site is not supervised: to make it so accessible is an act of faith in the public on the part of the Trust and of English Heritage.

Looking at an interpretive panel at the site of the Roman town of Venta Icenorum, Caistor St Edmund.

hardly aware of, though currently safe because no one except botanical or archaeological specialists ever go there, is more at risk from sudden unwelcome mismanagement or 'development'.

There are two sides to the question of access. Specialist conservationists may see Interpretation as a means of easing the stress on vulnerable sites, of moderating visitor behaviour rather than attracting visitors. But this is not what the regional Tourist Boards normally believe to be the role of any Interpretation they may be willing to subsidise. Tourist authorities see Interpretation as being itself a 'tourist attraction' – a visitor-friendly service that makes people want to recommend the place to their friends and come back another time, and thus to increase 'visitor input'. A recent proposal for a programme of tourism development from a District Council states its aims as being 'to improve the visitor experience and increase tourism spending in the town. A key priority is to enhance the public's enjoyment and understanding of the parish church through interpretation. . .' and 'to encourage visitors to explore the church, influencing their length of stay.'

THE TOURIST INDUSTRY

The unattractive phrase 'tourist attraction' is much used in the tourist industry. The term 'tourist industry' is itself slightly revolting to an outsider: which of us likes to think we are raw material to be processed, like so much oil or sisal or timber, by people who want to manipulate us, exploit us and take as much of our money as they can? However, tourist attractions there are, whether we like it or not; and probably we all seek them out from time to time, however selectively. We need somewhere to park the car, to fill up with petrol, to find refreshments, and to meet other physical needs in reasonable comfort. Managing all this are the thousands upon thousands of workers in the tourist industry.

Interpretation's best gift to Tourism is its long-term tendency to promote the protection of whatever qualities give a region its character and interest. In this function of protection, Interpretation is just an agent, helping the Visitor to understand the Place. The more that visitors appreciate the Place, the more anxious they will be to see that it is not spoilt. If it remains unspoilt, then visitors will come. If meretricious attractions are invented just in order to entice yet more visitors, the chance is that these newcomers will not be interested in the Place so much as in the Attraction. Then potential enthusiasts for the Place may begin to desert it, its character will change, property values may drop, and the local inhabitants, in the long term, could lose out. Understandably, in an era or location in which work is in short supply and earnings are not high, they may opt for cash now and never mind the environment. That is exploitation in the popular sense, if you like. If the residents spoil their own district in the process of making money, at least (they may argue in justification) they will have earned enough to be able to go somewhere nice for their holidays. However, educated societies as they progress do tend to become more concerned with quality and more discerning. Even if we have not reached it yet, there will come a time when the majority of people will be grateful that earlier generations struggled to protect the best in their heritage for their descendants.

Tourism occasionally exploits

In western Ireland, in County Clare, lies one of the most distinctive and interesting landscapes in the British Isles – the Burren. It consists largely of exposed surfaces of limestone rock, in the crevices of which grow a variety of lime-loving plants. At its most attractive, it is something like a giant rock garden, and geologists and botanists love it. Up to now, it has been moderately accessible at its edges, less so in its central parts. This is just what conservationists would wish, since there is enough for casual visitors to admire from the roadside, while anyone with specialist interests can find ways of penetrating further to the heart of it.

In the early 1990s the Irish national Office of Public Works announced plans to 'open up' the Burren as a tourist attraction. This would mean new roads, new facilities for parking, refreshments, toilets and all the tourist infrastructure, and a grand new Visitor Centre at Mullaghmore to 'interpret' the Burren to the hoped-for influx of sightseers. This would be rather like erecting a new visitor centre, with full supporting facilities, in an ancient forest, and then creating a new road network to enable visitors to get there. Of course, once such a facility is in place it is important that managers publicise it for all they are worth, so that the promoters can maximise the returns on their investment, and the politicians can justify their planning decision on economic grounds. This Burren project became something of a *cause célèbre*. As soon as it was announced, Irish conservationists expressed their indignation, while the press and Burren-lovers from other countries started to campaign to prevent it. It became an occasion for attacks on the very concept of Interpretation. The scheme is now shelved.

Not so the proposals of the Cairngorm Chairlift Company to develop 'attractions' on the northern slopes of Cairn Gorm, Scotland (at 4,084 feet above sea level, the fourth highest mountain in Britain). The Company hopes to construct a funicular railway to carry 250,000 visitors each summer to an 'interpretation centre' and a 250-seat restaurant at a height of 3,600 feet, less than 500 feet from the summit. The promise of an influx of paying tourists and the provision of an educational facility are seen by opponents of the scheme as bribes to sway planning authorities to override local conservation considerations.

To those who do not know the Cairngorms, the plan is likely to sound outrageous. Yet some who do know the place point out that the sheer size and extent of the mountain range would dwarf any such development into insignificance, and that the scheme will merely enable a few more people to enjoy the region's splendour and to support its conservation. Whatever the rights and wrongs are, the cases of the Burren and the Cairngorms at least remind us that there may always be a risk of enfeebling a golden goose by forcing it to lay too many eggs.

It is unfortunate, but almost inevitable, that Interpretation gets dragged into the argument. However good the Interpretation that any proposed Centre may offer, planners and planning enquiries will have to consider whether it can compensate for any consequent damage to the Feature. One might also ask whether such Centres would ever be impartial in their accounts of the development itself, the controversy it aroused and its impact on the environment. Dare Interpretation, in other words, turn the spotlight upon itself?

'Interpretation as a management tool'

This phrase (which fortunately seems to be going out of fashion) has often been used by cynics to describe the ploy of building a Visitor Centre at some already over-visited location in order to divert the highest possible number of cars. There, they will cause the least possible traffic disruption to the area as a whole, and their occupants be detained for as long as possible by harmless occupations – Interpretation being as harmless as any. It is known as the 'honeypot' principle: the Centre is the pot, Interpretation is a suitable brand of honey. If you can't actually squash the wasps, at least you keep them under control.

There are more benign ways of employing this principle, however. If a woodland nature reserve has sensitive areas which you would rather, for the sake of the wildlife, keep undisturbed, you can create a footpath network that allows visitors easier access to certain parts of the wood, but does not lead them to the vulnerable parts. This is not actually Interpretation, of course, though it can be an essential element in Introduction (see chapter 8). By the same token, providing a car park, toilets, visitor centre and shop at the entrance to an ancient monument may be a valuable means of controlling the movement of the public, but is not Interpretation: that will depend on what you put in the Visitor Centre. But visitor control may be vital to the wellbeing of the Feature. A good example is the Visitor Centre run by Cadw at Tintern Abbey, Gwent, in Wales, through which you have to pass before you have access to the abbey ruins. Most visitors, finding themselves confronted by an interesting display, look round it first before exploring the abbey site. This is sensible and logical; at the same time, Cadw staff can monitor their visitors.[2]

In certain circumstances, the management of the Feature can be modified to suit the requirements of Interpretation without harming the Feature itself. If you want to show visitors how coppice woodland is managed, you could create a path to give access to an already coppiced area, or you could develop a demonstration coppice alongside a path that already exists. If you have an industrial archaeological site which, for safety reasons, has to be mostly back-filled or fenced off, it may be possible to leave one feature open, safely railed, and interpreted. A good example of the transformation of a difficult and rather inaccessible area into an interesting site is the Llyn Llech Owain Country Park, in Carmarthenshire (see page 107).

In many cases, the provision of interpretation and accompanying facilities for visitors generates an income which can at least in part be spent on the conservation of the Feature. The hundreds of thousands of pounds spent on raising Henry VIII's warship *Mary Rose* from the sea bed off Southampton in 1970 could partly be justified on the grounds that once the ship was restored it would

2. Cadw is the Welsh equivalent of English Heritage; the word means to guard or protect.

generate enough income from visitors to house, staff and maintain it. If it were not for its potential attraction to the public, even its archaeological and historical importance might have been insufficient to save it.

LONG-TERM BENEFIT

The public's support for conservation is not enlisted only at visitor centres and tourist attractions. Well-led guided walks may reach fewer people, but impress them more deeply. Public demonstrations and explanations of skills as varied as bird-ringing, sheep-dog handling, bricklaying and picture-restoring inevitably earn respect for specialist experts – whether in the countryside, the building industry or the museum – and they stimulate appreciation of the features they are trying to protect. Opportunities to participate directly in conservation projects may be among the most effective means of all. The true value of Interpretation must be seen as long-term and cumulative – the gradual education of the community and informing of public opinion until parish, district and county councillors, and even Members of Parliament, are sufficiently informed and sufficiently wise to make sound decisions.

5 Red carpet treatment
Understanding the visitor

When a language interpreter builds the bridge of communication between two people with different languages, he or she has to understand not just the language of each, but their capacity to understand the interpreter. It is possible to translate a speech in Russian into a style of English that is technically correct, but still not easy to follow. The interpreter must be able to turn a message into a form that the listener can quickly grasp. In terms of Environmental Interpretation, this means that the Interpreter must not only know what the Feature has to say, but be able to communicate it in a manner appropriate for, and intelligible to, the Visitor. To do this successfully means knowing what sort of person the Visitor is.

This may sound easy, but to understand people is not that simple. It is the complexity of man, as an individual as well as a member of society, that has given rise to such specialities as psychology, social studies, behavioural studies, group dynamics and educational psychology.

THE GENERAL PUBLIC – WHO THEY ARE

Individual people have certain things in common. The lucky ones have two legs and are mobile. They have five senses all busy receiving impressions from their environment. They use language, and have a capacity to recall, to think ahead, and to make comparisons. They tend to be frisky and small in childhood, they grow physically and mentally at a certain more-or-less predictable rate, they have the potential to become wiser as they accumulate experience, they slow down in old age. They are, to a certain extent, gregarious; certainly, they are socially interdependent.

Secondly, individuals are genetically the product of their parents and, through them, their remoter forebears. Height, colouring, build and other features are indicators of their ethnic and family origins. They may inherit varying capacities for different kinds of physical and intellectual activity. Even variations in temperament (optimistic, shy, resilient, ambitious, contemplative) or talent (musical, athletic, intellectual, caring) may have a genetic component.

5:1 English as a foreign language?

THE ANIMAL KINGDOM
'Looking at animals another way'

ARACHNIDA
Almost all terrestrial with a few in fresh water. The prosoma carries a pair of chelicerae, a pair of pedipalps which may be sensory, grasping or otherwise modified, and four pairs of walking legs. The opisthosoma generally lacks appendages except for the spinnerets of spiders and the pectines of scorpions.

The introductory panel shows certain phyla linked together. This is not meant to imply a greater significance than to provide a more convenient layout to Animal Kingdom.

Hypsibius evelinae
A tardigrade found in moss

Here are four label texts carefully copied from a 'new' display mounted in a national museum in the UK a few years ago. The museum clearly thinks that the display is innovatory, up-to-date. But in reality it is addressed to the sort of visitor that scientific museums used to expect in the past: students, of whatever age, who are already biologically literate.

We should think carefully before we complain about this. Such museums were established to amass and look after collections of specimens for research; the curators are scientists whose main work will be scientific. It is only since the survival of most museums has been seen as dependent, both politically and financially, on public support that skills in Interpretation have been widely deployed in their galleries. Interpreters, whether in museums or elsewhere, must beware of using technical terms that most Visitors will not know – whether such terms are genuinely familiar to the Interpreter, or just copied from a textbook.

Thirdly, individuals have all had different experiences in life. Some are brought up in loving families, others are not so fortunate. Some have always had enough money, some have not. Some are lucky in the amount of mental stimulation they received as children, others less so. These experiences work on our genetic basis to produce mixes of character, social skills, intellectual activity and ability which vary almost infinitely from person to person.

On top of this is a fourth layer: our actual accomplishments and skills, what we have been able to make of ourselves. If we have inherited potential, we may or may not achieve it. Differences in genes and environment are always helping or hindering us along the way.

So people do vary enormously from one to another, in fitness, in experience, in mental agility and stamina. They vary in height, weight and age. They vary in their interests, and in the way their minds work. Other people are not exactly like you; and there is no reason why they should be. And yet, like you, they have feelings, emotions, hopes, interests, embarrassments, fears. A good interpreter needs to work hard to understand what makes people behave as they do – it is not a subject taught at school. Of the various ways of studying people, I would like to refer to three.[1]

TRANSACTIONAL ANALYSIS

The phrase may be jargon and for that reason off-putting, but in fact it means what it says: a system for analysing the bases on which we transact our dealings with one another. The underlying principle is that our 'ego state' – the mode in which we conduct any encounter or 'transaction' with another – can be one of only three kinds, Adult, Parental or Childish.

The Adult is unbiased, unemotional and logical: it is exercised whenever we try to be rational, fair and honest. **The Parent** is exercised whenever we express our instincts to control, advise or correct others; sometimes it is authoritarian, and may manifest itself in dogmatism. **The Child** is the part of us that wants to be loved, corrected or relieved of responsibility; it plays and laughs, but may respond to difficulties with sulks or petulance. We can regard adult behaviour as a balanced, central position between the other two – equivalent to coping rationally, wisely and sensibly.[2]

A transaction is a single element in an exchange of communication between two or more people. The role of the analysis is to help us read between the lines of what people say (some examples are shown on the facing page). The importance of this to Interpretation is real, but subtle. In the conversational exchanges that may take place between a guide and his party, the guide has the option of treating them to a dose of his Parent, in which case he will sound bossy or patronising; or to his Adult, to which they will react with more enthusiasm, and will more willingly engage their intellects.

A nervous, insecure guide may seek security by trying to adopt a Parental pose, subconsciously hoping that the Visitors will play Child. It is quite possible that they will; but if they see through him and realise that he is trying to assume a role, they may subconsciously recognise his Child, sympathise, and respond with Parent-inspired support. This may, uneasily, help both parties through the encounter, but the learning opportunity will have been very much impaired.

1. Each is a speciality in its own right; for further study, some relevant books are listed in appendix E.

2. This way of looking at our transactions has been expounded in two popular books by Eric Berne: *Games People Play*, and *What Do You Say After You Say Hello?* Both are available as Penguin paperbacks.

HUSBAND: Darling, I wish you wouldn't always interrupt me when I'm talking.

WIFE: Sorry, love. I got carried away.

Here, the husband is in Parent mode, trying to address the Child in his wife. However, she responds in Adult mode, hoping to engage the Adult in him.

*

WIFE (rather desperately): Where on earth did I put my glasses?

HUSBAND: I think I saw them on the kitchen table.

Here, the wife is probably in Child mode, appealing to the Parent in her husband. He responds as Adult to Adult.

WOMAN: Sylvia always looks much more attractive than I do.

MAN (impatiently): Can't you ever stop fussing about your looks?

Here, the woman's Child is uppermost: she would like Parental reassurance. But the man unkindly responds in Child mode. An Adult response might have been something like 'That isn't so, actually. Your personality makes you much more attractive.' Whereas if he said, 'Now, now, dear, of course that's not true,' we might suspect that he was not really being objective, but rather ineffectually playing the Parent.

Just as an adult can communicate in Child mode, so a child can be Adult:

FATHER: Sam! How the hell do you think I can concentrate with all that bloody noise?

SAM: Would it be better if I took my radio upstairs?

Here, the father is in Child mode, for he has lost his control. Sam, however, has responded with a sensible suggestion in Adult mode.

If Visitors feel insecure, they may play Child. The proper role of the Interpreter is not then to play Parent, but to bring the relationship back to Adult–Adult. People can be stimulated to exercise their intellects better by an Adult–Adult invitation to consider or debate a point, than by a patronising Parental, 'Now, what have I got in my hand? A tape-measure? Well done.' Rather than words, a group's interest may often be better engaged by a little of what drama producers call 'business' – that, is suitable action on the part of the Interpreter. Explanation can follow.

Telling a story may seem a good way to engage an audience, though it may disguise an Interpreter's contempt for his listeners: 'These people don't know the first thing about history, so I'll tell them a ghost story.' The audience may sense this, and respond with their Child ('We are grateful to you for telling us such a lovely story') rather than their Adult ('Are you able to tell us anything more significant about this place?').

There is not necessarily anything wrong or shameful about the Child ego-state. It can be positive and useful, and we cannot sustain Adult mode for ever. Laughter is associated with the Child in us, and occasionally the Guide can endear himself to an audience by revealing that he is Child as well as Parent and Adult. Visitors may presuppose that an expert guide must be jealous of his dignity, while they themselves should be submissive and respectful. But if the guide quite spontaneously climbs a tree to collect a sample of lichen, or spits on his finger and rubs it on a piece of stonework to highlight faint scratched initials, or trips over a bramble and roars with laughter, his uninhibited behaviour signals that he is not afraid to be laughed at or to shock. Visitors may be driven by this to the verge of assuming the offended mode of Parent, but are more likely to smile and settle down to Adult – by far the most constructive mode for both parties to operate in.

A guide can establish a constructive Adult–Adult relationship partly by avoiding a tendency to dogmatise or patronise (both manifestations of the Parent), and partly by choosing methods of expression or illustration that will stimulate the Adult in the listeners. This means 'provoking' them (Freeman Tilden's expression, though not exclusively his idea) to intellectual reaction – that is, constructive thinking. This is more likely to happen when the Interpreter adopts the mutual exploration of a topic, rather than the Parental mode of lecturing ('Don't you lecture me!' is the cry of those who resent a patronising tone). To lecture is fairly easy – you keep the audience in their place and avoid interruption. To engage an audience as fellow-adults is harder.

INTERPRETATION FOR CHILDREN

Children, especially younger ones, may accept the friendly Parent approach. But there comes a time in all children's lives when they are grateful to encounter an adult who addresses their own Adult – that is, one who seems to listen, to invite help and to respect young opinions. Youngsters may not quite understand everything adults say to them, but their self-esteem is enhanced and their self-confidence boosted.

It is often said by the highest authorities (including Freeman Tilden) that Interpretation for children is quite different from Interpretation for adults. I spent many years as a professional youth worker, and I believe this is only partly true: while the practice may be different, the principles are the same. The important thing is to accept that the differences between adults and children are less to do with intelligence and the essential capacity to understand, than with the extra years in which adults have accumulated experience. And, sometimes, adults' accumulated experiences make it *harder* for them to understand a new idea: experience can make one cynical, inflexible, insecure, opinionated.

If the Interpreter, teacher or youth worker understands people and the characteristics of the different phases of their lives, he or she will come to realise that they are essentially the same at all ages – it is just that the range of a person's experiences, together with his or her repertoire of responses to problems, grows year by year, just as the body passes through a natural progression of growth, maturity and decline. These patterns of development are common to all of us. Adults have learned a few tricks to cope with defeat, disappointment, embarrassment and stressful relationships, whereas children are less sophisticated.

Children may be quite eager to answer questions put to them by a stranger; adults are more wary. If a Park Ranger asks, 'Why do you think these trees have patches of white paint on them?' children won't mind having a go – the satisfaction of getting the answer right may outweigh the humiliation of getting it wrong. Adults, feeling that they are expected to know even if they don't, often think it safer to conceal ignorance and not answer at all. A knowing smile can even imply, 'I know really, but I'm not saying.' And if you do know, you may keep quiet because you are afraid of being seen as conceited. If embarrassed by questioning, adults can always look at their watches, exclaim about the time, and hurry off towards the car park; children are somewhat less subtle.

Children like climbing trees, we think, and adults don't. But many adults would love to climb trees. In societies where people use coconut palms, adults climb them readily enough. However, we can be inhibited by fear of being laughed at; furthermore, most of us are probably not fit enough, and we wear unsuitable clothes. Children like games, adults don't. Nonsense! Children don't like boring games, any more than adults do. And adults play their own games readily enough. Once again, a sense of propriety tends to overwhelm us regarding what activities are normal and what may make us look silly. The sense of what may be socially proper is not particularly logical, but is something we gain as we grow up, as we learn not to behave in unconventional ways.

This is particularly true of adolescence, when not to behave in conformity with one's peers seems almost unthinkable. Teenagers combine elements of immaturity and adulthood in a confused and confusing mixture. One of the biggest hindrances that adults encounter with teenagers is the latter's assumption that adults will always try to patronise, manipulate or control them. They become suspicious. They are also particularly vulnerable to embarrassment.

Two contrary strategies have been tried by those who work with young people. The first is to minimise the embarrassment factor by isolating them from their peers, fear of whose opinion is the biggest inhibition. This sometimes works as a ploy within a family, but is rarely feasible for an outsider. The other approach may be easier for an outsider than for parents: it is to trust teenagers and to relate to them as Adult-to-Adult. Invite their opinions, and respect them; show no surprise at the gaps in their knowledge; discuss with them as equals; do not show resentment of bad manners; relate to them as fellow human beings, not from a position of superiority.

In Europe and Scandinavia, many young people's natural history organisations are run by the members themselves.[3] These thrive on the principle of delegating responsibility to autonomous local groups. The intensity of activity, study and experience of the countryside that members of such groups plan and achieve puts many adult organisations to shame. The young people learn from

3. The age range is usually from about 14 to 22, so that there are young adults taking the lead, especially at national level. But their authority is still subject to the votes of the members as a whole.

5:2 Interaction and first-hand experience

What young lad could ignore the opportunity to pull a big lever and watch and hear the signal clank into position? The former railway station at Tintern, Gwent, has been made into a Country Park. Lawn is now where the track was, but the platform, waiting rooms, signal box and part of the signalling system are still there – a sort of not-so-ancient transport monument, accessible for exploration.

Children will insist on trying the lever, while parents look on with a smile and perhaps a touch of jealousy – they would like to have a go, too, but are afraid of looking silly or childish. On the other hand, if a live guide were to invite them personally to operate the signal system, they would be delighted – that would provide them with the pretext they were hoping for!

For a generation that knows neither steam engines nor manual signalling systems, the experience would be meaningless without some explanation. Interaction with the environment, especially the feature being interpreted, is an experience from which we learn directly. A second kind of interaction occurs with teaching media, such as operating touch screens, talking to a live guide, playing an educational card game. Interaction is valuable at both levels – but the first is fundamental, while the second is just a good teaching ploy.

experience and hard work, and from one another. They learn, too, from any adults who earn their respect by joining in on their terms. Some members become professional biologists and conservationists; those who do not will remain informed amateur naturalists and supporters of conservation throughout their lives. This pattern of organisation has had some successful imitations in Britain.

Adults and adolescents are not essentially different from one another or from younger children, and there is no proof that we need separate sets of educational or Interpretational principles for different age groups. Any differences between the messages and means of communication that an Interpreter addresses to adults, and to children and adolescents, should be the result of intelligent and sympathetic adaptation of the same basic principles.

It has often been said that scripted interpretation should be pitched at 'the intelligent fourteen-year-old'. The truth is that the better you write or speak – which, for Interpretation purposes, means the more simply and clearly (see chapter 14) – the wider the age range that will be able to understand you. 'Children must not be talked down to,' wrote Enos Mills, an American precursor of Freeman Tilden, in 1920.[4] Many children are quicker on the uptake than adults, some of whom have limited experience and knowledge anyway. But children may not have developed the self-discipline or mental stamina to go on trying to understand something that is not clearly put. If it is hard work being at the receiving end of Interpretation, it will nearly always be the Interpreter's fault.

THE EMBARRASSMENT FACTOR

One of the strongest inhibitors for all of us is embarrassment. We are all susceptible to it, and we all develop different ways of dodging or hiding it. Self-isolation is one. Another is to adopt the behavioural norms of a social group to which we would like entry. The underlying worry is social insecurity, the fear of not being accepted. Some people will pepper their language with four-letter words, because not to do so might appear weak or fastidious. Others will express their keenness to conform by careful choice of dress, or by their activities – tennis or cricket may be unacceptable because too posh, snooker or football may be okay. Fly-fishing for one group, coarse fishing for another.

Once your chosen norms are established, and the longer and firmer you hold to them, the more you find yourself locked into a certain lifestyle or behavioural pattern, and the harder it becomes to break out of it. Anxiety about potential embarrassment is much more real and widespread than we may imagine. Even those who know what to do and how to behave at, say, a formal dinner, might feel out of their depth at a Roman Catholic mass. Those who are self-confident in a discussion group might feel awkward walking into a pub full of strangers.

4. Enos A Mills, *The Adventures of a Nature Guide*, 1920.

Interpreters should remember that the situation in which they encounter Visitors may be unfamiliar and potentially daunting to those Visitors. Many people will be ill at ease in an art gallery, cathedral or stately home, or on a guided walk in the countryside. How, they wonder, do we find our way about? Should we speak in whispers? May we ask questions? Will my ignorance be exposed? Will I be unwelcome or a nuisance if I bring a child in a push-chair? Imagine someone who does not often enter museums, but nervously decides to try one. Is there any entry fee? Should I go up to the reception desk on arrival? Can anyone walk about anywhere they like? May I touch the exhibits? If I don't understand something, is there anyone I can ask? If so, what sort of person will they be? Will I make myself conspicuous? What will the regular museum visitors think of me?

The best steps to reassure the apprehensive visitor are, firstly, to recognise the reality of other people's sense of insecurity in novel situations, and then to take positive steps to reduce insecurity by making everything clear. If there is a necessary sequence for viewing displays, then the very layout should make this clear. If, on the other hand, there are several rooms and it does not matter what you look at first, then the entrance to each must be equally welcoming, and perhaps labelled to entice the Visitor in. Doors should either be open, or else clearly marked (e.g. 'Collection of Clocks: Please come in and have a look'). A closed or unmarked door can be very worrying – is it the way out, another gallery, or the curator's office?

Some well-intentioned methods of trying to help can actually create embarrassment. It is irritating if an over-helpful staff member at a Visitor Centre leans over your shoulder as you are studying something, interrupts your reading and begins to expound the matter in his own words. A well-trained member of staff will have learned when it may be helpful to chat to visitors, and what is the body language of a person who would like to ask a question but is too nervous to do so. Where face-to-face interpretation is the preferred formula, there is even more that the provider must learn.

Contexts

Perhaps the biggest lesson is the positive one of creating contexts: what people may be afraid to do or say in one context, they will be happy about in another. A guide introducing himself to a party of people must smile and say who he is – this, and the way it is done, will affect the Visitors' behaviour. More than once I have been shown round premises only to discover at the end that the 'guide' to whom I have been talking so familiarly was in fact the owner. Think how it would then feel to have made some disparaging remark about the choice of décor!

> *Notices are a practical way to make things clear for Visitors. For instance, even a sign saying 'Welcome to Digglesworth Town Museum. Please come in and look round' instantly removes two uncertainties: yes, the public are welcome; and yes, we are free to wander round.*

A friendly introduction can go a long way to disinhibit Visitors: 'My name is Helen, and I am one of a team of volunteers who help show people round. I may not be able to answer all of your questions, but I'll be happy to try. Have any of you been here before?' – right away the visitors know where they are. It may help to go further: 'I am sorry we have roped off certain areas of the house. It is just that we have so many visitors that walking everywhere would soon wear out the carpets. You see, the owners still use all the rooms when they are at home': this both explains things and puts us at ease, and the guide seems to be someone we could talk to.

Furthermore, Interpreters often have some control of the physical contexts in which they will be helping Visitors. The ambience of a building can be welcoming, confusing or daunting. A large, grand foyer may be suitable for a business that is out to impress or to humble its visitors; but it can also spell 'Unwelcome'. A reception desk isolated in a large entrance hall is positively frightening. The receptionist may be so smart as to make the rest of us feel shabby, or so preoccupied with internal telephones or paperwork that we feel intrusive, or so unwilling to catch our eye that we feel unwanted. In Visitor Centre contexts, chairs or other seating will indicate that we are welcome to sit down. If staff members carry some simple identification (a lapel badge, perhaps, which can be read from at least six feet away!) we will not be worried that we might be addressing a fellow-Visitor, the chairman of the county council, or the window-cleaner. On the other hand, some uniforms indicating official status can be ambiguous and/or daunting, with overtones of traffic wardens or customs officers – people whose job it is to catch you out.

Where the Interpreter has a static indoor group to address (as in a seminar, lecture or public meeting), the very layout of chairs and tables can inhibit. When the speaker or officials are seated on special-status chairs at special-status tables on a raised (and therefore, by implication, special-status) dais, you cannot help feeling that these people are claiming some special status. And that implies that *you* don't really count for much. If a meeting is not too big, and chairs can be set in a circle or part-circle, there is an immediate implication that every one present is entitled to join in. Speaking from the back of a meeting where all the chairs are in straight rows facing the front can be daunting: half the audience ahead of you turns round to discover who you are. This is unnerving for most of us, but perhaps it is fun for extroverts.

If you are working with a group of people for longer than an hour or so and you would like them to take some active part in discussion or in a simulation exercise, you can structure a situation conducive to participation. Visitors may at first be nervous about speaking to one another, but familiarity with television interviews and game shows may give us ideas for how to get people mixing, talking and working in teams. Game show and other formats are now familiar and acceptable: they are recognisable norms of society, have no class bias, and so can be entered into with comparatively little trepidation. We have all seen losers who smile and shake hands and winners who grin, and there is no humiliation.

Pretexts

Finally in this section, a word about pretexts. Many of us would privately like to do certain things (talk to strangers, perhaps, or try out new situations), but are inhibited from attempting it in case we may be thought forward, childish or selfish. We may have sat in a railway train opposite an interesting-looking person, and not dared to speak. But if the attendant brings round tea or the train rocks violently or the window needs opening or closing, we have a pretext for speaking. Special events can also provide pretexts, opportunities for members of the public to try something new which they would not otherwise have known how to begin. Bird-watching, country dancing, painting – all sorts of activites can contribute to our better understanding of the world.

Not long ago a colleague of mine devised a painting day on a National Trust heathland property. It was advertised locally, beginners were welcomed, an experienced artist was on hand to introduce the day and to advise, and an exhibition at two local venues

5:3 Motivated to use the eye

All concentration, the artist studies the countryside he is painting. He is enjoying a week's leisure course at Losehill Hall, the Peak National Park Centre at Castleton, Derbyshire, which includes exploring and learning about the special qualities of the Peak District landscape. Even if he has some initial qualms, anyone who chooses such an experience is likely to become an enthusiast. The duration and intensity of holiday courses like this are likely to increase understanding and appreciation of the environment much more effectively than a casual interpretational encounter.

Wayside interpretation and some visitor centres are deliberately intended to attract the attention of casual passers-by, or those vaguely looking for something to do. Both of these categories are very important in the effort to spread greater understanding of the world we live in, but the very best interpretation situations occur when individuals consciously commit themselves to an educational experience – an afternoon guided walk, a series of adult education classes or a week's holiday course. Tutors of such courses should think, plan and teach 'interpretationally'. Otherwise many a lecture, anecdote or statistic will miss its mark. Even to some experienced teachers, interpretation may be a new concept.

was promised. Also in the programme was a short introduction by the site Warden, who explained the characteristics of lowland heath. The structure of the day offered both a context and a pretext, and it worked. The thinking was that if people are encouraged to hear about a certain type of landscape and its features, and then to look at it and record it on paper or canvas, then their understanding and appreciation will be enhanced. Interpreters can be creators of contexts and providers of pretexts – the two can dissolve inhibition and promote interaction and involvement.

GROUP DYNAMICS

Group Dynamics is an analysis of the way that people interact with one another within groups. It is relevant because very often the Interpreter's Visitors come in groups – whether the twos, threes or fours of family parties, friends or organised groups, or just a number of strangers assembling for some event. Each individual, their behaviour and the way they react to any interpretational exercise will, to some extent, be affected by the others in the group.

To every gathering of people, individuals come with personal reservations or preoccupations, prejudices or worries. You may have seen that wonderful sketch by Joyce Grenfell in which, while singing a hymn in church, she suddenly remembers that she has left the cooker on at home; while she continues singing in apparent conformity with every one else, her actual words change into an expression of her own growing anxiety. Some members of a visiting group to a Countryside Heritage Open Air Museum may be having misgivings about having come at all. Others may have personal problems on their mind, or be wondering whether they have won the lottery. Children, especially teenagers, may be hoping that none of their friends will be there – how terrible to be seen walking around with one's parents! One person may have toothache, another feels cold, a third wants to get home to watch a favourite programme, and a fourth doesn't like the shape of the guide's beard. Someone may see something that reminds him of something else, and embark on a train of thought that is miles away. Such miscellaneous preoccupation is often referred to as the person's, or the group's, 'baggage'. It is invisible, but real enough, and may account for occasional strange behaviour or abruptness. A newcomer to this kind of situation may remain rather stiff and polite, until he or she has had time to observe what the norms of such a group might be. All this preoccupation will affect the interactions and relationships between the group's members.

In any group, it can be seen how individuals tend to seek and fulfil suitable roles within it. One may want to ensure that the party doesn't get dispersed; there may be a group joker, or a self-appointed explainer, or one who tries to bring the loner fully into the group. There may be one who habitually disagrees, a constant

The guide Waga, reeve of Carlisle, must have been disconcerted on the occasion of Britain's first recorded guided walk, at 3 p.m on Saturday 20 May in the year 685 (the account is recorded in an anonymous Latin Life of St Cuthbert*). Waga was showing a party of clergy the city wall and a marvellously constructed fountain in it which, he explained, had been built long ago by the Romans. Bishop Cuthbert of Lindisfarne was paying no attention, but stood, leaning on his staff, with his head bent towards the ground. Suddenly he raised his eyes to heaven, sighed, and exclaimed: 'Oh, I think that the war is over and that the result has gone against our army.' The rest of the party immediately forgot their guide and turned to Cuthbert, anxiously asking what had happened . . . So much for Waga's carefully prepared 'program'!*

nonconformist. An awareness of these processes may help the Interpreter, as an outsider/insider, to regard the group's behaviour sympathetically, and to feel more confident in his or her own role. The Interpreter cannot remain a complete outsider: by definition, if you are present in the group, you are a member of it (complete with your own set of baggage), and immediately new sets of relationships and interactions come into play. If you are leading a guided walk, the others in the group will have certain expectations ('Here's an expert, he or she will be confident') and probably certain apprehensions ('Will we be asked questions that show us up? Will this person be approachable?'). The group may contain someone who makes straight for the leader (the Interpreter, in this context) and tries to impress, which may cause another member of the group to become irritable or suddenly go quiet. The dynamics of the group are continually evolving – and the behaviour of individuals evolves with them.

THE CONCEPT OF COGNITIVE *SCHEMATA*

As well as the hundreds of books and articles on Transactional Analysis and Group Dynamics, even more has been written on aspects of educational psychology and learning processes. Since Interpretation is an educational activity, what experts have discovered must be of relevance to us. One example is the way a person builds up an understanding of the world about him, from childhood onwards. Every child, from birth if not before, is accumulating experiences. To start with, these will be miscellaneous and somewhat unrelated. He will experience mother and father, bed and food, light and darkness, sounds and smells and tastes. From these elementary beginnings he builds up a personal understanding of these and other phenomena, with every fresh experience adding to and modifying that understanding, while the mind accumulates the information and gradually makes sense or patterns from it. In this way people come to develop what psychologists call *schemata* of related experiences. We build up a *schema* or notion of what 'mother' means – the reality, rather than the word – or 'food', or 'pain'. Every added experience clarifies and adds detail, and we begin to discern patterns, to explain to ourselves 'the way the world works'.

Every new experience, every new bit of information, has to be subconsciously attached to the existing *schemata* already in our minds. If this works well, we get more accurate and more serviceable concepts as we grow up. The wider our experience, the more balanced our understanding. But new experiences or new information are not always easy to fit in to an existing *schema*, which can leave us puzzled or confused. It is a bit like dominoes: a new domino can only be added to the existing pattern on the table if there is a valid point of connection. Otherwise, one just has to hold on to it until a connection becomes possible. The game may end without a particular domino ever being used.

This way of looking at learning can help Interpreters. First, it may explain how some people can find it very easy to accept a particular new piece of information: they can relate it to previous knowledge or experience. Others may not cotton on to it so quickly. In face-to-face situations, the Interpreter may notice that some of the audience are nodding, while others frown slightly. The frowners may be having difficulty fitting the new information into their existing schemata: there may be a mismatch. The 'Aah!' response (see chapter 2) is a signal that a new piece of information has provided a domino that links two otherwise loose ends – or a missing piece of jigsaw that makes sense of a previously incoherent pattern.

The *schemata* principle helps to explain how, at different ages, we all have progressively clearer and more complete concepts. A one-year-old is only just beginning to appreciate that things fall to the ground – and enjoys proving it; a toddler's concept of distance may be limited by the push-chair journey from home to the shops; a small boy or girl sees a family pet as something to cuddle, not yet as something that requires conscientious care and money to maintain. Notions such as responsibility develop throughout childhood, while the significance of a multicultural society may dawn in adolescence. Young adults may have already begun to find that what they once considered certain has become doubtful, that few things are as simple as they first seem. All the time, people are accumulating experiences or receiving information, sound or otherwise, which either reinforce or modify the *schemata* that make up their personal interpretation of the world. Our *schemata* do not consist of watertight compartments of understanding: they overlap and interact, so that a new 'perception' may modify several *schemata*, and create a knock-on effect. The point in life when one's *schemata* harden and become inflexible may be different for each person according to their habits of thinking, but there can be little doubt that, for many, to adjust thought patterns in middle or later life is not easy.

Another practical lesson to learn is the importance, when offering people a new idea, of attaching it to their existing understanding. If you are explaining something to advanced students, you will find that, for their specialist topic, they have highly developed *schemata* to which new pieces of relevant information can be fitted. Where Visitors are virtual novices in an area, then the Interpreter must use some ingenuity to find a connection. People welcome stories that appeal to their humanity – we are all human and share basic human feelings. Jesus spoke in parables because his audience knew, from their own experience, about vines and sheep and weddings and water: they could appreciate the significance of his metaphors. This may be a good reason for an Interpreter some-times to make a point in two or more different ways – if you deal out two or three dominoes instead of one, there is more chance of a player making a connection.

The *schemata* concept has one more great relevance to Interpre-tation. It recognises the 'grains of sand' principle. The big ants' nest is constructed by thousands of ants, each making hundreds of journeys: each time they bring one grain of sand or fragment of leaf to add to the pile. Such is the gradual process by which *schemata* are built. But the simile is helpful in understanding the way people learn only if we think of the grains of sand as each hav-ing to fit into place. This is the difference between learning parrot-fashion (which requires quite a lot of effort, for which motivation may be lacking), and insight. Not every fact that a person is offered – or even learns by heart – will 'fit' any of that person's existing *schemata*; and if it doesn't fit, then it can have no useful function, and will be ineffective: 'Effective knowledge is a matter of neat architecture, not of random piles of building bricks, however high they may be heaped.'[5]

Interpreters may worry sometimes that their contributions to people's understanding are too small, too trivial, to be of much effect. But these little experiences and insights are just what *schemata* are made of. This is the way the historian's knowledge, the politician's wisdom, the psychologist's skill are built up. What is more, the quality and relevance of each experience and each piece of information are vitally important: it is possible for us to build up lopsided, distorted, misleading *schemata* if we constantly see only one side of every matter, or take on board false informa-tion that seems to fit. One genuine new insight is worth a hundred irrelevant facts. The Interpreter might do well to adopt the motto: 'Not quantity, but quality'. So the fifteen minutes that an Inter-preter spends showing children a butterfly's wing through a lens, or explaining to adults how thread was spun in the days before factories, may not be so trivial after all.

The aim of this chapter is not to give a sufficient exposition of psychological, behavioural and educational theory, but merely to demonstrate that Interpretation cannot afford to be ignorant of them. Certainly, they should feature in the training of all Inter-preters, part-time and amateur as well as full-time and professional. The more widely such instruction becomes available to everyone, the better for us all.

5. Prof. Terence Lee, 'Some thoughts on informing, revealing and persuading', *Interpretation Journal*, 47, 1991.

Seeking the message
The conscientious researcher

6

WHERE THE FACTS ARE TO BE FOUND

Good Interpretation can only be based on the Interpreter's under-standing, and understanding must be based on knowledge. But our world – even our own little local world – is so full of interest and variety that no one person is knowledgeable enough to know every-thing about it.

If you believe in Interpretation as an important educational activity, then you must agree that even the simplest Interpretation project deserves scrupulous research. You cannot help people to an understanding of how the world works by offering them inaccu-rate or misleading information. If the initiative for an Interpreta-tion project comes from someone whose motivation is not primarily educational, but more to do with money-making or pres-tige, it is easy for them to be cynical about academic integrity – 'Heavens, man! It's only to keep a handful of ignorant grockles happy, after all!'[1]

It is not only out of respect for the Visitor that the Interpreter should strive for a proper understanding of the Feature, but out of respect for the Feature itself. Everything worth interpreting is wor-thy also of affection and understanding; it is difficult to speak with enthusiasm and authority about something one only partly knows and understands. Getting to know the Feature may mean spending a great deal of time and trouble. On countless occasions a local government planning department assigns its most junior, least-trained member of staff to prepare a leaflet for a new walk route or town trail. In the days of the Manpower Service Commission there were many teams of young persons occupied in scripting Interpre-tation boards or leaflets. The amazing thing is how well they coped, but some appalling misinformation found its way into print.

Most interpretation is concerned with places. It is because a cer-tain place may best be understood in terms of, say, landscape or ecology, architecture or industry, that we tend to see 'countryside' (wildlife) and 'heritage' (buildings) as being the main divisions. But this is quite an artificial and false distinction, often indicating more about the background and interests of the Interpreters or pro-moters than it tells us about Interpretation itself. Nevertheless,

1. This inventive but patronising term, used by local residents in popular tourist areas to denote their visitors, seems to have originated in south-west England.

whether you are working in countryside or heritage, most of the features interpreted will be localised.

A local historian may be well informed about the growth and development of his or her town, village or district, but not have the holistic outlook or breadth of knowledge that we have already suggested is essential in Interpretation. Local history needs, for instance, an appreciation of building materials and building styles, land use, communications, industry and trade, and the relation of these local matters to those of the rest of the region and the country. Ideally, the local historian should be an expert in transport history; geology; industrial processes; family, church and social history; local government, farming – and no end of other matters besides.

Consult the experts

One secret of successful research for Interpretation – since the time-scale is often uncomfortably short – is to identify and consult experts. Most are generous with their knowledge if they know that the questioner is genuinely interested, and why.

• Do not try to get the experts to do all your work for you! Restrict yourself to specific enquiries, and perhaps ask for advice on where to find an answer, rather than demand the answer itself.

• As a courtesy, send a stamped addressed envelope for their reply.

• Be considerate if you are asking them to meet you: offer to go to them, or to meet them at a place convenient to them. Avoid asking people to meet you at mealtimes, as it may be embarrassing for them; but if they suggest it, then agree.

• Go prepared with questions, paper and pencil, and do not waste their time.

In one interesting interpretation project concerning a watermill in Derbyshire, the site was ancient but the main buildings were only about a hundred years old; all the machinery was still in place because the mill had ceased production only a few years earlier. A committee was formed to prepare the mill for opening to the public. It comprised a member of the family who had owned the mill; an industrial archaeologist; a historian; an engineer; an adult education organiser; and the curator of another mill, already opened to the public, who was an expert on the history of milling. Between them they produced sheaves of excellently researched papers, with far more material than could ever be offered to casually visiting members of the public. To each person on the committee, every detail of his or her contribution seemed essential. They then called in a firm of professional Interpreters to

help translate all this knowledge and understanding into Interpretation for the visiting public.

The Interpreters were definitely not experts on mills; indeed, they were probably as ignorant of milling as most of the expected visitors would be. Their first task therefore was to study the material, absorb it, and seek to reshape it as its sense dawned on their ignorance. Because they were not experts, it was probably easier for them to pick out the ideas and themes that struck them as helpful, and to put aside certain other information, however authentic, as being more likely to muddle lay people than enlighten them. But without the expertise of the committee, their task would have taken four or five times as long, and they would no doubt have missed some important truths altogether.

• Be sensitive about the use of tape recorders, which can be very offputting; always ask first. Recording may be appropriate for oral history (see appendix E), but is not always comfortable for an expert answering specific questions.

When a project of any size is intended, it is helpful if experts can be persuaded at an early stage to make themselves available to give advice as and when it is needed. The very least that should be done is to find experts who will agree to check text in draft for factual errors.

To be an expert, incidentally, may carry one or two handicaps as well as advantages. To start with, you may be so specialised that you do not know much about the way your own speciality relates to other disciplines. Some architectural historians will know more about materials and how buildings were assembled than how the buildings were used. There is a whole discipline of study, for example, about the way the timbers of medieval buildings were jointed and put together. It is a very specialised field, and it would be unreasonable to demand that an expert in it should also know how butter was made in the buttery, or how land tenancies worked in the middle ages, or details of the families who lived in a particular house in the sixteenth century. And yet the story of the house cannot be satisfactorily communicated to the Visitor unless the researcher/Interpreter is informed on these matters, too.

The same principles apply in quite different disciplines. Some ornithologists know more about the identification of birds, and their breeding habits and migration, than they do of their economic value to man down the ages. Not all geologists are interested in the industrial processes by which we make use of minerals. It is common practice among archaeologists today to draw on the expertise of art historians, forensic scientists or botanists to supplement their own knowledge. One of Britain's leading landscape historians, Dr Oliver Rackham, started as a botanist: his studies of woodland ecology led him eventually into land use and landscape history.[2]

Learning from local people

Expertise does not have to be academic. We are all experts on certain limited subjects – our own lives and memories, for instance. We are also experts on what it is like living in our own home, town or village. Older people are experts on the changes they have seen, the work they have done, the people they have met. Many of us have hobbies on which we can speak with authority. Good academics in subjects such as landscape or social history will always seek out ordinary people with long memories to help them.

Interpretation researchers may find some of their most illuminating material in conversation with people who can recall, say, trams, farm horses or steam-rollers, or those who were employed

George Ewart Evans gathered material from ordinary country-dwellers for his fascinating and much acclaimed books on changes in rural industry and farm life in Britain, including The Horse in the Furrow *(1960) and* Ask the Fellows who Cut the Hay *(1956). His own essential expertise was in researching and writing oral history. It was the people he talked to – such as Allen Cobbold the blacksmith of Battisford and Joe Row the farm-worker of Blaxhall – who were, almost literally, experts in their own fields.*

2. He is also a first-rate expositor. See, for example, *The History of the Countryside*, enlarged and further illustrated in 1994 to become *The Illustrated History of the Countryside*, a classic example of an interpretive book (see appendix E).

When I was preparing material for a booklet on Norfolk's Waterways, I met an elderly gentleman who was the last of a family that ran a yard where wherries were built and repaired. He obviously enjoyed explaining how the boats were serviced – they were hauled up on the river bank, the old tar burnt off them with flaming oily rags on the ends of sticks, then re-tarred. The very last of Norfolk's trading wherries had been built at his family's yard. He recalled that the names of all the craft built there were crudely listed on a beam in the workshop – but the site was later occupied by riverside houses and apartments, and he had no idea what had happened to the beam.

in long-closed factories, mines or workshops. You need to go out and seek this kind of material – getting into conversation with strangers can be surprisingly rewarding once you have overcome any initial shyness. Accept first-hand reminiscences (though never forget how easy it is to misdate even one's own memories), but be wary of hearsay or 'local tradition' ('They do say that bank was built by the Romans').

Libraries, museums and record offices
Most Interpretation research will probably be carried out with the help of libraries or archives – though research may seem too grand a term to describe the simpler kinds of investigation. If your interpretation is site-based, you may well start by a visit to the local history library. Many branch libraries have local history sections, and it will be worth looking through as many books on your parish, town or county as possible, using the books' indexes to find mentions of the feature you are interested in. Take notes on all relevant points, and also note where each author got his information. See if there is a bibliography – a list of other relevant books and articles – at the back of the book.

Some books are unreliable, especially if they have been poorly researched: never believe that because you find something in print it must be true. Even excellent books such as Nikolaus Pevsner's *Buildings of England* series have occasional major errors. You may find that information in a standard work like Eilert Ekwall's *Concise Oxford Dictionary of English Place-Names* has been superseded by more recent research. Articles in magazines and newspapers, and many locally produced guide booklets, are among the least reliable sources, but they can often give you a 'lead' on a story.

If in doubt about the authenticity of a story, try to get back to the author's original sources. Good books usually identify these, either in footnotes or in a bibliography. Check everything that you can. You may need to search half a dozen books before you can be sure that you have a date or a name right. If you still suspect your source, make a note of the fact: it may be better to write in your

Interpretation script 'It has been suggested that . . .', or 'According to one observer . . .', or 'Local tradition has it that . . .', than to risk being caught out by the next researcher who follows the same path as you, but with greater skill or luck. Your pride should imbue you with a horror of offering false information.

Always seek authenticity, keeping an eye open for period accounts. If a Victorian book offers a contemporary description of the building of Tower Bridge in London, it may have more circumstantial detail, and a greater ring of truth, than the same story rewritten by a journalist today. If a Directory of 1853 lists three saddlemakers and a coachbuilder working in your town, it is probably correct. Beware, however, of trying to date things too precisely by this method – some entries may have been out of date by the time they were printed, while it is not unknown for a new building or railway to be described as 'open' prematurely. Even maps and plans have occasionally been published that show railways, roads or canals that were never constructed.

If you are looking for a historical slant on your subject, certain easily obtainable classics of topography and biography have indexes which are always worth skimming. These include the notes of John Leland, Henry VIII's official antiquarian (sixteenth century), and the diaries of Samuel Pepys, John Evelyn and Celia Fiennes (seventeenth century), Daniel Defoe (eighteenth century) and William Cobbett (nineteenth century). I looked up my local market town (Harleston, Norfolk) in Mowbray's *England Illustrated* of 1714, and was amused to see it described as 'a little dirty town situated on the river Waveney' – recently it won a Best-Kept Town award.

Many local history libraries have good runs of nineteenth- and even eighteenth-century newspapers. Here you may find material that may not be recorded anywhere else – biographical information from local obituaries, for example; reports that demonstrate the events for which a Corn Hall was used on days other than market day; advertisements for local products or services, or announcements of forthcoming events.

Local museums may hold artefacts, photographs, early advertisements, sale catalogues, old books or other items that can sometimes provide unique pieces of information. Museum curators are often able to suggest other sources that may be helpful to you, or introduce you to enthusiasts who have studied the place or the topic before. Long-established local solicitors' practices have been known to come up with fascinating documentary material from the eighteenth century.

Record offices are major sources of information. Regionally they are administered by County Councils, and nationally by specialist branches of the Public Record Office. In general terms, record offices are chiefly concerned with looking after original and manuscript documents, while local history libraries hold published material. But systems are not identical everywhere: in some counties, archive photographs may be held in the local history collection; in others, in the record office. Some counties merge their record office and local history collections into a single unit, while others keep them in separate buildings; some larger counties divide such reference material between two centres. In London, each borough has its own collection. Scotland, Wales and Northern Ireland have their own particular institutions concerned with the preservation of archives and source materials.

All these collections exist to serve the public – no one need be shy of walking in and asking how to get a reader's ticket (free), or how to use the facilities. It may seem a little daunting at first, but before long the set-up becomes familiar. Anyone who has used several libraries and record offices becomes aware how very different they can be in comfort, accessibility and service. The more you explore, and the more help you seek, the more fascinating and useful sources of information you will find.

Finding illustrations

While you are researching for facts, remember to make a note of any potential illustrative material – photographs, engravings, old newspapers or other documents. Note down clearly what the items are, what points they illustrate, their clarity and suitability for reproduction, their dimensions, and exactly where they are to be found. Illustrations can be as eloquent as the spoken or written word in an interpretive message – they are not just a form of decoration to make a publication or display more attractive. The choice of illustrations is as serious as the choice of words.

You never know what suitable material may turn up. In one search for material on a country park, it was found that an early nineteenth-century artist had made a series of neat little watercolours of buildings in the parish. Even unlikely buildings or scenery may have been the subject of local photographers, or have featured on early picture postcards.

I found by chance an 1857 engraving (originally published in the Illustrated London News) of the then newly built Corn Hall of a certain town; more recently, the building has served as a cinema and dance hall. At a local history talk, I mentioned that lightning had destroyed a statue, clearly shown in the engraving, which used to crown the entrance of the building.

A woman then told me that she was in the market place during the thunderstorm when this happened, and remembered part of the statue crashing to the ground.

A mid-nineteenth-century rector of the parish, who kept a very full diary, commented on an extraordinary lawsuit that followed the erection of the hall, in which it was claimed that part of it was built over a public right of way. 'It was said', he wrote, 'that an attack would be made on the Corn Hall, indeed ten extra police were sent from Norwich.'

Not all buildings and places have such variety of picture and anecdote to illustrate their story – but if you don't enquire such gems could lie hidden for years.

Old photographs are sometimes the only record of a scene now vanished, like this one (right) of a former wharf and warehouses at Hardley Staithe at the end of a dyke or short canal connected to the river Yare in the Norfolk Broads. The old view can be of great interest to visitors – but a poor, faded photograph, perhaps never very clearly focused, tends to lose clarity when copied for reproduction in a display or publication.

When the Broads Authority wanted to erect a panel at Hardley Staithe to explain its former commercial activity, this picture, showing the staithe in its decline probably early in the twentieth century, was all there was to help today's holiday-makers visualise its past.

Artist Martin Warren, using a magnifying lens, made a drawing from the photograph (below), enhancing the contrasts and highlighting features that were almost lost in the general blur. What is more, by giving a little extra height to the trees, and extending the area of water at the bottom, he was able to change the proportions so that the final illustration fitted the space allotted to it.

Museums also hold much good illustrative material – not just pictures, but old posters and notices, commemorative pottery, trade tokens and tools – which can be photographed or drawn. Old photographs and engravings can reveal important facts about the past use and appearance of buildings, or the existence of features now long vanished. Even faded photographs can be used for illustration. If they are severely damaged, it can be a good idea to have them copied by a competent artist in the form of line drawings, with necessary tonal enhancement. These can be better than the photographs themselves, since the artist can enhance significant features without distorting the truth.

Some local newspapers keep a selection of the photographs they have printed; otherwise, the photographers themselves may still have the negatives. It may also be worth writing to the local paper to enquire if any reader has photographic or other relevant material which can be copied for the purpose of a publication or display. Individual members of the public must hold a vast amount of interesting material.

If local sources fail, there are picture collections and photographic agencies which may be able to help; many are listed in publications such as *The Writers' and Artists' Yearbook* in the section on picture research. Try also the National Portrait Gallery, and other art galleries and museums for photographs of paintings and engravings that may illustrate your subject. Remember that charges will usually be made for the reproduction of material from commercial agencies and institutions.

If you happen to be offered original material (paintings, engravings, old photographs, old documents) for use in display contexts, please *never* display the originals unless you run a properly equipped museum. It is heart-breaking to see local displays in which documents or old photographs are fixed to boards by sticky tape or drawing pins, or displayed in full sunlight, or immediately over radiators, or in an atmosphere that is too damp or too warm. The first thing to do if you are offered any such material is to get good-quality photocopies or photographs made, preferably by a professional photographer, and use a copy in the display. Make sure that a second 'master copy' is kept safely for posterity – perhaps deposited with the local record office, subject to the permission of the copyright-holder or the owner of the original. Due acknowledgement should be made in the display of those who have helped to provide material, and the rules of copyright must be followed scrupulously (there is more about this in chapter 12).

Maps as sources of information

Among the most valuable sources for historical and topographical detail will be maps.

Ordnance Survey maps should be the first enquiry, including the earliest one-inch series of the 1830s and the six-inch maps of the 1880s. There are few more enjoyable ways of getting to understand twentieth-century Britain than to explore it with the aid of an 1880s six-inch map! Ask your county local history library how to obtain photocopies.

Tithe Maps are another extremely important resource for English and Welsh parishes: the series dates from the 1830s when the tithes of farm and other produce due by law to the local Rector were 'commuted' (changed into cash payments). These large-scale manuscript maps, usually beautifully drawn, indicate every field and plot, house and stable. They are generally accompanied by a schedule, which is keyed numerically with the plots on the map and reveals the owner, the tenant and the use of every inch of ground – and often the name of every field.

Enclosure maps were made over a long period (most of them between about 1750 and 1850); they were prepared by order of Parliament to show how the former open fields or commons of a parish were to be shared out proportionately between the existing landowners. Here is documentary evidence of the landscape before local enclosure, and of land ownership at the time. Try also to find a copy of the relevant Act of Parliament.

Estate maps are another source of information, and so are the maps and particulars prepared for the sale of estates, mills or other properties.

There is an enormous quantity of other material available, among which are often the former contents of 'parish chests',[3] and records from local manors and estates.

Archives and collections

Many national archives are accessible, some more so than others. Most of the national Public Record Office material is kept at Kew. Many learned societies and other institutions have their own collections or databases. The larger and older established national learned Societies – such as the Royal Geographical, the Linnean and the Society of Antiquaries – have valuable collections of documentary and other items. Even local societies may have collections.

There is no space here to list even a small part of the categories of information to be found; I have mentioned just some of the most helpful sources. Potential researchers should feel reassured that information is accessible, and that advice and help are available. There are many good books on how and where to research local history (see appendix E).

THE IMPORTANCE OF BEING METHODICAL

The most important thing is to be be methodical, and never to rely on memory alone. Memory is quite capable of confusing and

3. Until a few years ago parish documents, some of them many centuries old, were often kept in old chests in the parish church. I remember one such collection in which the documents at the bottom of the pile had rotted with damp and were all stuck together. Now such material will usually be found in the more reliable care of the appropriate county Record Office.

transposing facts, and even of losing information altogether.[4] Perhaps the most important thing to record is where you actually found the information. There is nothing more maddening than needing to check a fact, or wanting to look back at some account that you remember reading, and being unable to recall where it was. Users of computers may like to store their records in databases. All researchers will evolve their own methods: the important thing is to have one.

ARCHIVING YOUR INFORMATION

Interpretation projects are often undertaken in rapid bursts. A job has to be done within three months – the end product is an interpretation scheme, perhaps an exhibition or a publication. The task is then completed. What is to happen to all your research material? The interpretation itself may incorporate as little as a tenth of it. Who should keep all these hard-won data?

When the work has been undertaken for an organisation, the organisation itself should keep it. In a few years' time, another member of staff might need it, and it would be a pity to have to start the whole process again from the beginning.

In some cases, material may be deposited with the county library's local history collection, provided it is ordered and intelligible. Where such work is an element in a project commissioned from a professional researcher or Interpretation consultant, I suggest that it should be a requirement that a copy of the information

4. 'I can never remember whether it snowed for six days and six nights when I was twelve or whether it snowed for twelve nights and twelve days when I was six,' Dylan Thomas, *A Child's Christmas in Wales*, radio broadcast, 1952.

Keeping research notes

One sound method is to rule and photocopy blank sheets in three columns. In the first, narrow, column, state your source (you can invent a code for it as long as you also remember to keep a separate list of sources and codes!), with page number (if appropriate) and where you found the source itself. It is all too easy to forget where you came across a particular document or book, and posterity, too, may be grateful.

The second (widest) column is for brief notes or quotations from the source. Write neatly: what is adequate just to prompt your memory tomorrow may prove incomprehensible in six months' time.

The third column is for you to enter, perhaps in capital letters, key words to act as a sort of non-alphabetical index, so that when later you skim over your notes looking for references to specific places or topics, they will catch your eye, and the process will be speeded up.

Eventually you may need to transcribe selected information into a separate file for each heading. If you are researching, say, a former gentleman's estate which is now a Country Park, you may need files headed 'Family'; 'House'; 'Staff'; 'Gardens'; 'Woodland'; 'Events', and so on.

Aylsham Mill, Norfolk (right), was built in the late 1700s by one Robert Parmeter, in anticipation of the canalising of the River Bure which would enable wherries to reach the mill on the outskirts of Aylsham. Norfolk Heritage discovered, in a book of 1804 by the agricultural writer Arthur Young, a description of Parmeter as 'a considerable farmer, and a very intelligent, sensible man.' Next it was learnt that a local firm of solicitors possessed an eighteenth-century plan of the proposed canal – which turned out to be signed by Parmeter as one of the proprietors of the new Canal Company.

Modern flour mills, successors of Parmeter's on a nearby site, had inherited an archive of documents from earlier years. These included old papers and photographs and a brochure prepared for the sale of the watermill in 1914, with full particulars of the machinery and a plan of the whole mill complex.

The county Record Office had an earlier plan of the same site, dated 1855, showing the property of a Samuel Parmeter. Nineteenth-century trade directories, of which the local history collection of the Norfolk County Library had a full series, demonstrated that the Parmeter family had also traded in coal and other goods from the canal wharf; and that, after a couple of generations, they had gone into partnership. After the 1850s, the name Parmeter ceases to appear in the 'trades' section of the directories; instead, among the 'gentlemen', is listed a Robert William Parmeter, solicitor and Clerk of the Peace.

goes to the commissioning body, even if additional fees have to be paid for the time it takes to assemble the material in a form that will be accessible to future users. I have seen an excellently prepared and illustrated report of this kind, made in connection with a management plan for a Country Park. It was produced by the consultant on his own initiative, and became invaluable for an Interpretation team called in to work at the same Country Park a few years later. I am also aware of research work that was undertaken in connection with a major Interpretive plan, the results of which were never used – nor, apparently, even wanted by the client who paid for them.

WALKING IN THE VISITOR'S SHOES

Last in this review of the research process, but perhaps first in terms of importance, is on-the-ground exploration. Here we are researching not just the background, not just the story, of the feature; but the context in which the Interpretation is to be delivered. Whether it is a guide leaflet, a display on the walls of a visitor centre, oral

*A good reason for researching
your route on foot is that you
may get talking to people along
the way. Sometimes you may
actually go and knock on someone's door: 'Excuse me, but my
map shows a channel connecting
your farmhouse to the waterway.
Can you tell me what happened
to it?' 'Yes, it was filled in only
ten years ago. Those iron rails
and a dip in the ground are
all that remain to show where
it went.'*

*Or you see an elderly gentleman
sitting on a seat overlooking the
river. 'Have you known this river
long?' 'I've lived here nearly all
my life. My father used to work
on the barges. He'd be away
from home for four or five days
on end, going in to the market
town with loads of malt from the
old malthouse over there.
They've turned it into holiday
flats now.'*

communication ('live guiding') or something else, your Interpretation will be addressed to live people in a given spatial context.
Until you have put yourself literally in the position they will
occupy, in the very circumstances in which they will receive
the Interpretation, you cannot satisfactorily plan what to say and
how to say it. In other words, you are not in a position to begin
scripting.

There are positive and negative reasons for this. You may be
Interpreting, let us say, a length of river waterway. You have discovered in your documentary research that there used to be a wharf
and a range of warehouses at a certain place: is it worth mention-
ing, and are there still any traces? Yes, there are the remains of low
walls and a brick foundation at the water's edge. You can point out
the site, explaining to visitors just what to look for and what story
these features have to tell.

Your walk along the waterway may reveal all sorts of little features that intrigue or puzzle you: a bridge that seems to lead
nowhere; slots in the stonework of a lock; a building that looks as
if it might have been a boathouse. If these puzzle you, then they
are quite likely to puzzle some other visitor. You should try to find
the answers.

Negatively, you run the risk of offering information that does
not really relate to the visitor's on-site experience. You may have
read that further along there were once iron ore diggings on a hillside near the waterway, and that for a short period the ore was
carried downriver by barge. Can the site be seen from the towpath?
You go to check, and find that it is now obscured by a belt of woodland. You may still want to mention the story, but you won't be
able to say, 'On the far side of the river you can see the scars in the
hillside . . .'

If you have prepared a script for a guide leaflet, you will make
one last visit to the site before taking it to the printer. You will walk
precisely the same route that you recommend your visitors to walk,
stopping at the same points that you suggest they stop, and reading your guide text as conscientiously as you hope they will. You
may find even at this last minute that there are improvements you
can make in the wording, especially in directions how to proceed
or where to look.

Frog into prince
Turning information into Interpretation

To be a good servant of the conservation principle, Interpretation must be based on fact rather than opinion or fancy. This is easier said than done, especially for any Interpreter with an axe to grind. Ideally, of course, Interpretation should try to be objective, but a person with strong convictions cannot easily keep them to one side. It is possible to read all sorts of messages as we study the world about us: we could interpret the rainforests of South America as a wonderland of wildlife, an important genetic resource, the home of peoples who live in symbiosis with the forest, or a tale of man's greed and wickedness. Perhaps all are valid messages from the forests. But there are also those who see the message 'a wonderful opportunity to raise the standard of living of a poverty-stricken people'. It is a fact that the forests are being destroyed at an alarming rate; it is also a fact that many of the people of South America are starving. Any Interpretation of that region that wilfully conceals either of these major truths is doing Conservation a disservice – for Conservation consists in making the wisest decisions in the light of all known factors. Its effectiveness will depend to a large extent on conservationists' reputation for frankness and integrity.

THE MORALITY OF INTERPRETATION

In an ideal world, perhaps, the role of Interpretation would be to expound facts, truths and problems, but not to press for specific solutions. The exhibition at the Visitor Centre at Bradwell-on-Sea Nuclear Power Station, Essex, would demonstrate not only that nuclear energy is clean and economic to produce, but also that it can be dangerous, and is expensive to decommission. Nature conservationists could tell us how they cull deer and kill squirrels; farmers might show us videos of the way that intensively reared animals are kept, and animal rights activists might explain how research on living creatures has led to the mitigation of the suffering of millions of men and women. If politicians were honest and logical, they would acknowledge the valuable ideas of their opponents. They would dispense with dogma. And there would be apologies instead of cover-ups. But we do not live in an ideal world.

Where does the Interpreter stand among all this? I believe that Interpreters should seek to be honest. They should be concerned to offer truths, and should as far as possible help visitors come to independent conclusions. Education, especially training people to think clearly, is more useful than brainwashing. The difficulty is that Interpretation as we know it, the presentation of little bites of fact in informal contexts, can never claim to offer the 'whole truth'. It should, however, try to offer 'nothing but the truth', with as few predetermined conclusions as possible, and should be fair in its politics. That it has to be 'political' is obvious: understanding how the world works must lead to decisions about how to manage it.[1]

INTERPRETATION AND POLITICS

There have been honest attempts to integrate Interpretation into political processes. An interesting one was the Landscapes for Tomorrow scheme, in the Yorkshire Dales National Park.[2] The Yorkshire Dales form an attractive landscape of hills and deep valleys, remote villages and farmsteads. It is a green countryside devoted mainly to the rearing of sheep and cattle, and its fields are characteristically divided by rough walls of pale limestone. The future of such beautiful scenery, ever popular with visitors because it seems to be a survival from a quieter, less mechanised past, is a matter of constant debate. Planning control is in the hands of the National Park Committee.

The scheme was an experimental project which ingeniously blended Interpretation and planning consultation. A carefully devised travelling exhibition portrayed typical landscapes of the region, illustrating the ways that different management policies might affect their appearance. Media included audio-visuals, specially prepared paintings depicting possible landscape outcomes, conventional two-dimensional screen displays, and a floor game – a sort of giant snakes-and-ladders. The exhibition, which was well staffed, toured to a number of accessible sites in the region, and the public were invited to take part and comment. The scheme was monitored by a university professor and his team, and modified as it proceeded to take into account what the organisers were learning from the exercise. The public's reactions and suggestions were recorded, and their opinions fed back to the planners.

The authors of the report suggested that what the scheme was doing was merely extending Freeman Tilden's vision of interpretation by adding an extra stage in which the Visitor, having passed through the passive, subjective phases of awareness, understanding and concern, became involved in an active simulated planning exercise which introduced the objective realities of economics, national policy and conflicts of interest. Taking part was a genuinely interpretive experience for members of the public, which was intensified by the political extension.

1. 'Politics', as used here, means the principles and practice of managing society. It does not necessarily imply any particular political system, let alone one that depends on confrontation. It is not intended to bear overtones of deviousness and self-interest.

2. Reported in 1992 in a publication of the National Park Committee; see appendix E.

Frog into prince **85**
Turning information into
Interpretation

Interestingly, this exercise was promoted not in the context of the usual party-based district or county council, but in that of a National Park, which exercises planning powers through a committee of representatives of county, district and local councils, with nominees from the Secretary of State for the Environment. It would be good to think that such consultation exercises might be undertaken in other contexts, but vested interests do not trust public opinion, and they and professional planners may feel a little insecure in allowing public consultation so high a profile.

If the outcome of an interpretation project is genuinely open-ended, then the facts to be offered will be chosen even-handedly, and the basis of their selection will be as much to do with what the visiting public can assimilate as what the promoters want them to hear. This question of assimilation – the Visitor's capacity for taking things in – is important. It is not just a matter of quantity of information (though too much will surely be a turn-off), but of its apparent relevance to the visitor in that place at that moment. Little, clear and relevant will be more helpful than comprehensive, complex and wide-ranging – though we all know that this is what real situations are like. One clear sentence from Margaret Thatcher may have helped Mikhail Gorbachev understand what she stood for more effectively than a forty-minute speech – especially if his mind was already preoccupied with problems of economics or his own political future. The visitors that Interpreters are going to meet will not have prepared themselves beforehand by putting their affairs in order, or doing an hour of relaxation exercises. We dare not assume that they come ready to receive a lecture. We shall be grateful if they go away remembering a single thing – so that thing had better be something genuinely significant.

INFORMATION THAT INTERPRETS

Here are some groups of informative statements, which we shall assume to be true in a hypothetical context.

Group A
1. The toilets are situated in the stable block.
2. It is an offence to climb on the walls.
3. This notice is sponsored by Hardkick Holdings Ltd.

I defy anyone to claim that any of these statements could conceivably be called interpretation. They may be necessary, but they are not significant or enlightening. A thoughtful person might wish to enquire what it is that Hardkick Holdings hope to gain from their act of sponsorship, and the discovery might contribute to an understanding of how the world works – it might even inspire. These are not bad statements – they are perfectly good, but they are just not interpretive.

Group B
1. This house was built by the third Baron de Grouchy.
2. This weed is known to botanists as *Senecio vulgaris*.
3. A bomb was dropped on this hill during the Second World War.

What marks should these statements be awarded for their capacity to enlighten? None. One cannot imagine what the house in the first statement looks like, but there are probably twenty more interesting and revealing things to be said about it. If not, why point out the house at all? Who was de Grouchy, and when did he build it? The second statement is about as unhelpful as they come. The third statement sounds promising at first, but then disappoints. Was anybody killed? No? Big deal.

These statements look like attempts to Interpret, but they fail. Interpreters should beware of offering information that invites the response 'So what?' – unless they can confound a sceptical audience with a riveting story to follow it up.[3]

Group C
1. We are standing in an oak wood.
2. This is a dove-cot.
3. The fortifications at the top of this hill are about two and a half thousand years old.

These statements are 'information', and are probably a necessary element in Interpretation because they could (though scarcely on their own) lead to a sense of enlightenment in the hearer. Statement 1 might enlighten people who had heard of oak trees but never before realised what one looked like; or people who knew about oaks but had never thought of them actually forming a wood. But the chances are slim. Statement 2 similarly might provide limited enlightenment to someone who had heard of dove-cots but never actually seen one, but the Interpreter listening out for a responsive chorus of 'Aah!' is likely to be disappointed. Statement 3 might get a reaction from those to whom two and a half thousand years seems an impressively long time, but it leaves unanswered some far bigger questions: who lived here that long ago, and why did they fortify the top of a hill anyway?

Group D
1. All the brick needed to build the walls of this factory were made from local clay and brought upriver from the brickyard by barge.
2. The apertures in the wall of this and other barns are for ventilation: without them the hay or the grain stored here might rot.
3. Any creature that lives here at the edge of the sea has to develop some system to survive being submerged by salt water twice a day.

3. I am told that other interpreters in the USA have also advocated the 'So what?' test. I would guess that the idea originated (as it did in my own experience) in interactive teaching.

Now we are getting somewhere! Each statement contains five essential elements.

- They relate directly to what the visitor can see or experience; note the words 'this' and 'here'.
- They deal with the 'how' or 'why' of the situation.
- They express a fact or 'story' which can be further built on.
- They have some underlying appeal to visitors' humanity – the hard work and planning involved in building a factory; the processes of gathering food manually; the animal struggle for survival.
- They hint at general principles that visitors will see exemplified elsewhere if they keep their eyes open.

All right, you could respond with 'So what?' if you were in a bad mood or otherwise preoccupied. But people with open minds may see in this kind of information the promise of a fascinating initiation into a new range of knowledge, though they might not put it that way.

Mere knowledge does not guarantee enlightenment, but it is usually much more satisfying to know how and why than merely what and when. Someone facing a tumbledown structure half-enveloped in brambles might ask, 'What is that heap of old bricks?' Better than to reply 'It's a ruined building,' or even the equally accurate answer 'A lime-kiln,' would be to say, 'It was a sort of oven where people used to burn chalk to make lime for mortar.' The fuller answer assumes that the enquirer wants to know how and why the structure was used, rather than just its technical name. After a couple of further questions the term 'lime-kiln' will enter the conversation, and the enquirer will end up thinking, 'So that's what a lime-kiln looks like!'

Turning information into Interpretation is at least partly a matter of deciding which information is going to be helpful to the audience – the Interpreter has to select. This selecting process can transform a bundle of bare facts into Interpretation. What are the principles on which to select and reject? The aim, remember, is to introduce the Feature to the Visitor, and to promote understanding, even rapport. It is best to start not by selecting random pieces of information, but to consider what is the main and most pertinent message that the feature proclaims.

THE NEED FOR A THEME

The most effective interpretation always has a clear theme, a simple message. Very often it can be summarised in a single sentence. I well remember a visit to a newly built visitor centre at Risley Moss, near Warrington, Lancashire. There the chosen theme was explicitly proclaimed at the very entrance to the display, once in words, and once in a visual image. The words were 'What is a mossland? – a shallow saucer of clay holding a wet sponge of peat.' It was such an extraordinarily unexpected statement that it was arresting. Beneath this was a little bracket on which stood – a clay saucer containing a handful of wet peat. I have forgotten virtually everything else in what was quite a big exhibition, which explained the varied uses of this area of waterlogged land over the centuries, and the lives of the people who lived and worked here. But I shall never forget that one truth – a definition that was not just a dictionary meaning, but a fundamental explanation of a landscape and its story. Like many good interpretive statements, it had both an immediate and a global significance: it explained the story of Risley Moss; and it proved how man's activities are constantly prescribed by nature.

A further virtue of the 'theme' principle is that it helps ensure that not every site of a given kind offers an identical message. True, 'Man's Impact on the Environment' seems to crop up rather often as a theme – but it is a title, a chapter heading, rather than a statement. It is more helpful when preparing Interpretation to formulate the theme not in the form of a noun-phrase, but as a sentence or 'message statement'. 'Man made this landscape' is better than 'Man's Impact on the Environment' because it is a statement, and is specific. 'Fashion in Architecture' is a title which might be applied almost anywhere; but 'The builder of this grand house wanted to show that he knew the latest Italian fashions' is a specific statement relating to a particular Feature. I am not suggesting that such statements should be blazoned above the entrance to a display, or printed as a title to a guide leaflet; rather, it should be constantly in the mind of the script-writer as he prepares the text, with the intention that a Visitor who studies the whole display or reads the whole leaflet, and is then asked what it all amounts to, might spontaneously summarise it in the very same words as the unwritten message statement.

You may have come across summaries of plays or opera plots in programmes or encyclopedias: Mozart's *Don Giovanni* in fifteen lines; Gilbert's *Gondoliers* in a paragraph; Shakespeare's *King Lear* condensed into three sentences. One could go further and sum up the plots in single newspaper headlines: 'Statue Horror Ends Roué's Seduction Bid'; 'Boatmen Chuck Throne after Paternity Muddle'; 'Mad Monarch Undervalues Loyal Daughter'. It makes a good Interpretation training exercise: the results are not likely to be suitable for incorporation into interpretational texts, but they are often very witty, and the game concentrates the mind wonderfully.

The choice of one theme implies a rejection of others. If you have done your research well, you will have a wealth of fascinating fact and usable illustration to hand; without it, you would never have known what your options were. Now a choice must be made, and three-quarters of this hard-won material, possibly even more, will have to be put aside.[4]

4. Information well researched should never be thrown away: it will be useful to someone somewhere. Perhaps the range of your Interpretation material might include a more detailed follow-up booklet, or a series of specialised leaflets for interested enthusiasts.

Frog into prince   **89**
Turning information into
Interpretation

The question of relevance in what you choose consists of two separate elements – the significance of the Feature, and the Visitor's capacity for relating to it. The two must somehow be brought together. It would be possible to assume, for example, that a specially significant story of a certain European Protestant cathedral is its early association with a famous saint. But the topic of medieval saints may not ring a bell with a high proportion of twentieth-century visitors; a more relevant kind of message might be the extraordinary expenditure of labour, skills and money required to create a building of such size and grandeur many centuries ago. Can the two stories be made to merge? The answer is probably yes. The theme that merges the two stories may be something like 'Medieval devotion to a miracle-working saint enabled this church to be built in thanksgiving to God.' It does not have to be told from a religious point of view, but it should be based on an appreciation of religious feeling at that time, which is not so very different from religious feeling today. In its exposition, the theme would have to exploit our human capacity to sympathise with people of other times and places.

Among recent subjects of Interpretation are two country parks, very different in size, but similar in certain respects. Both were formerly estates surrounding a gentleman's country manor; both are interesting for their woodland. In the larger of the two, Norbury Park, near Leatherhead, Surrey, one could almost lose oneself in the woods. One sees plantations, new or mature; former coppice and new coppice; ancient yews on a parish boundary; neglected areas; occasional signs of damage by storms, deer or squirrels, and frequent signs of felling, trimming and planting. There is a sawmill operating in the heart of the park, and a workshop where timber is made into posts, gates, benches and signs. One theme will have to be: 'Even attractive woodland like this is a working, productive environment requiring efficient but sympathetic forestry.'

The other (see overleaf), Nowton Park near Bury St Edmunds, Suffolk, still has something of the quality of a landscaped garden. Much of the woodland lies in a great belt screening the perimeter of the park. Its other trees are grouped decoratively – a fine avenue of lime trees, clumps at focal points in the parkland. Here the Interpretation statement is 'This landscape is the legacy of a wealthy middle-class Victorian family: designed for leisure then, still used for leisure today.'

Even if only an implied theme statement were received, even if Visitors forgot all the information offered in support of it, the Interpreter should be satisfied. Interpretation exists to communicate concepts that matter, not incidental facts that do not. At Nowton the Victorian owners, the Oakes family, are mentioned by name; at Norbury the visitor is told how many acres of woodland there are. But names and figures often have a valuable function as

7:1 A pleasure-ground for gentlefolk

The great avenue of lime trees (left) at Nowton Park, on the outskirts of Bury St Edmunds in Suffolk, was one of the final touches in the development of a country estate by four generations of the local Oakes family of bankers. Like so many other successful Victorian dynasties, they strove to fulfil the traditional English image of landed gentry. Gentry needed a fine house and a landscaped park to surround it, a belt of woodland to mark the perimeter, clumps of trees to vary the scenery, and an ornamental pond or lake, a folly, and an impressive approach to the big house through an avenue of trees. This meant a great deal of planting; here it included tree species from all over the British Empire.

In 1985 the house and park were acquired by St Edmundsbury Borough Council. The house was leased to a school, and the estate became a Country Park. Visitors can only properly appreciate what the park has to offer if its earlier story is told. Interpretation at Nowton is therefore based on two complementary and interwoven themes: the pleasure-ground for the gentry (now become a pleasure-ground for the general public), and trees (planted as a private amenity, an arboretum, for sport and for prestige, and today used for nature conservation and timber products).

A great entrance to the park, from which a driveway was to have led along the avenue to the mansion, was never built: these rows of trees testify to an ambition unfulfilled.

props and aids: they give circumstantial immediacy to a story, without being themselves necessary to understanding.

HOOKS AND HANDLES

The Interpreter's themes are sometimes said to be made up of 'topics', but I prefer the journalist's term 'stories'. 'Topic' sounds a little too static, too academic; 'story' suggests movement and life. Journalists will sometimes say to one another about some potential news item, 'Can we make a story out of it?' What this usually means is 'Can we find a human angle that our readers can identify with?'

Stories that are going to be of any use to an Interpreter have qualities of both relevance and interest. Relevance is more than an objective matter of fact: to the Visitor it is a subjective matter of personal feeling. To engage the Visitor's real attention and involvement, a story will need one or more qualities that we may call 'hooks' – grabbing qualities. This is not a new concept; three hundred years ago, the satirist Jonathan Swift wrote:

Frog into prince 91
Turning information into
Interpretation

From this brief survey of the falling state of *ears* in the last age . . . it is manifest how little reason we can have to rely upon a hold so short, so weak and so slippery, and that whoever desires to catch mankind fast must have recourse to some other methods. Now, he that will examine human nature with circumspection enough may discover several handles, whereof the six senses afford one a-piece, beside a great number that are screwed to the passions, and some few riveted to the intellect. Among these last, curiosity is one, and, of all others, affords the firmest grasp: *curiosity*, that spur in the side, that bridle in the mouth, that ring in the nose, of a lazy and impatient and a grunting reader. By this *handle* it is, that an author should seize upon his readers; which as soon as he has once compassed, all resistance and struggling are in vain; and they become his prisoners as close as he pleases, till weariness or dullness force him to let go his gripe.[5]

Swift's 'handles' are the same as our hooks, except that his metaphor reminds us that the writer is trying to grab the reader, while ours implies that the story itself may, like the seed capsules of the wildflower burdock, have its own built-in ability to grab.[6] Let us consider some of these hooks or handles. They do not, as Swift points out, engage only the mind, but may be connected to any of the senses.

Curiosity, in particular, requires a teasing element in a story or situation, something that demands to be explained. It could be a riddle or puzzle to which the listener feels he must find the answer; an occurrence so strange that the reader can't wait to hear the explanation; or a sequence of events where he just has to discover how it all ends. In Environmental Interpretation, the Visitor's curiosity is involved whenever a process is demonstrated, or a human dilemma posed. It could be an explanation of how canal boats can climb hills by means of locks, or how a camera obscura works. In the world of wildlife, the story might be the curious behaviour of the baby cuckoo in its foster-parent's nest; or how alder trees spread their seeds. The alder, which loves to grow where its roots will be wet, often drops dried 'cones' into a river or ditch; they then drift for yards or even miles downstream until they get tangled in vegetation on the river bank, and there germinate. Alders often line river banks continuously for hundreds of yards. If it were possible to show a person this process, either in real life or by film, it would have something of the miniature drama of a game of Poohsticks.[7]

Movement is another hook. People love something that moves, or machinery that works – a live lizard, a model steam engine, those marvellously intricate moving sculptures of the sort first produced by Roland Emmett. If, at a show, you want to get people walking up to your display rather than anyone else's, you will need something conspicuous that is either spectacular or that moves. Flat, vertical surfaces covered with dozens of little photographs are

The title of a popular television comedy based on the characters in a television news studio is Drop the Dead Donkey. *The dead donkey must have been some story that never reached the screen; stories that are worth broadcasting have both relevance and interest. The story of the Queen Mother choking on a fishbone did reach the nation's screens, but was of more interest than relevance. Other items, such as news of yet another scientific breakthrough, may seem rather boring, though their relevance may be grudgingly acknowledged.*

5. Jonathan Swift, *A Tale of a Tub*, 1704, section XI; my italics.

6. Burdock (species of *Arctium*) has large brown burs with little hooks that can get caught on clothes.

7. See A. A. Milne, *The House at Pooh Corner*, 1928, chapter 6. It is not only children who have the capacity to concentrate for a while on the trivial: the essays of Jean Henri Fabre, whose studies of insect behaviour helped to pioneer the study of animal behaviour, make delightful reading. Even the trivial can be both fascinating and immensely significant.

In one of the great museums of
Paris, several series of old-
fashioned farming tools are
displayed in glass cases. Two
things prevent them being boring
– the sheer artistry with which
they are placed within the cases,
with dramatic lighting; and the
coin-operated equipment that
activates archive film showing
exactly how they were handled
and used.

8. See also the references to participation
in chapter 11.

9. A Victorian title.

tiring to look at, the captions are often dull and the layout amateur. But tether a camel in front, install a large fountain or hire a
falconer to fly an eagle about, and the crowds will gather. I am not
recommending irrelevant attractions, but the hook of movement,
of something happening, is a real one.

Humanity is an important hook, perhaps the most important
of all: some element in a story with which any Visitor can identify,
whether or not he is predisposed to be interested. It means making
it easy for a Visitor to put himself, in imagination, into another
person's shoes. So a story of how, less than a hundred years ago, a
coalminer would walk home at the end of a day, in full view of the
community, covered in black dust, then strip off and sit in an iron
tub in front of the fire while his wife poured warm water from the
copper over his shoulders, will enable most of us to sense what it
felt like in the days before baths and running hot water.

The humanity element can transform a lifeless topic into a
lively one. While it may be difficult to engage the interest of visitors in the geology of a quarry, it is much easier to interest them in
the risky skills of the quarry men. When we watch a basketmaker
deftly weaving a lobster pot, we are marvelling at his craftsman-
ship rather than wondering what species of tree the cane is from.
We do not mind being told it is willow, so long as we can watch.
And curiosity insists that we are told just how the pot catches the
lobster, and how the fisherman extracts it without being nipped by
those enormous claws. We go away understanding a little more
about the qualities of common trees, the lifestyle of marine crus-
tacea, and the ingenuity of man. Trivial, but significant. Interpreters should always strive to tell the story, even of inanimate
objects, in human terms.

In some situations humanity and movement coincide to make
a double hook. People with no real appreciation of archaeology
will stand for hours to watch a dig. Archaeologists at many urban
excavations insert special viewing platforms into the temporary
fencing, so that passers-by with time to spare can watch; sometimes, on-site exhibitions explain what they are up to.

Involvement is another hook, reinforcing those of humanity
and movement.[8] True interaction with Visitors is not easy to
improvise, but it can be incorporated into pre-planned events like
guided walks. In autumn, a Fungus Foray[9] is always popular – a
search for mushrooms and other fungi with the guidance of an
expert, sometimes followed by preparing, cooking and eating them.
Occasionally the public are invited to spend an afternoon planting
trees, or learning how to coppice. So long as activities like these
offer explanations as well as practical experience, they are an excellent vehicle for Interpretation.

Shock is a hook with several forms, the basic thesis being that
our interest is easily engaged by horror, scandal, fear, surprise,

7:2 What on earth is going on?

Most of us are easily fascinated by the sight of people engaged in work that is unfamiliar to us, and if there is an air of mystery or anticipation, so much the better. These young people have a stand at a county agricultural show to publicise their youth group SPLASH (Society for the Pursuit of Local and Social History).

Some months before the show, they buried a wall of bricks and some bits of old iron, then replaced the turf and watered it so that the scars became invisible. Then, on the two days of the show, they painstakingly staged an 'archaeological dig'. They were never without an audience.

It was only a fake, of course, so its interpretational value was slim. But the exaggerated care with which the investigators unearthed their find was a fair representation of how tedious archaeological excavation can be. Visitors came, stopped and watched – and read the display material that explained the group's interest in local history.

amazement, gore or disgust. In the Moyses Hall Museum, Bury St Edmunds, are displayed the skull and scalp of William Corder of Polstead, convicted for the murder of Maria Marten in the Red Barn in 1828. I cannot imagine what exactly this display interprets, but the showcase is obviously a great success.[10] Many an English house or abbey ruin has its tale of ghosts or underground passages, or both. Most visitors love to listen to such stories, even though they usually provide more misinformation than truth.

There are positive ways to use such fascination, and some horror stories can be told in all honesty. Teenagers can be grabbed by the macabre, especially if it is made to seem respectable: a group of volunteers I spent a day with, who had volunteered to wash bones and skulls at a cemetery site, positively enjoyed scrubbing the clay

10. There is a melodrama based on the event, *The Murder in the Red Barn*, so that the display could be said to interpret the reputation of the play. And it may be unexpectedly enlightening to discover that the only inhabitant of this Suffolk village to achieve lasting fame was a murderer whose bodily remains are today treasured and displayed to the public. Just as relics of saints used to fetch exorbitant prices among the faithful, so the rope with which Corder was hanged was allegedly sold at a guinea an inch.

off the leg bones of Anglo-Saxons and cleaning their eye sockets with a toothbrush.

Superlatives can easily be captivating: the deepest lake, the largest parish church, the rarest plant, the oldest town. *The Guinness Book of Records* is perennially popular. Comparisons can also be effective: the guide at the Grand Canyon (see page 6) used them to convey a sense of its depth. She had established in advance that several of our party came from Manchester, and she had done her research. If we could pile three (or was it four?) Manchester Town Halls on top of one another on the bed of the Colorado river, she told us, even the top one would still be invisible from the Canyon's rim.

Gadgetry often exerts great fascination, and so can be another hook. Who would not like to get their hands on the resistance-measurers that archaeologists use when they survey an open site before a dig? They walk along with a sort of frame, prodding the ground ahead with probes, while at each prod the electrical resistance is memorised by computer. When they get back to base, the results are printed out in the form of a crude plan on which the significant patterns of buried evidence can be traced.

To watch mammal traps being set in a hedgerow for live surveys – or to learn how to set them yourself – and then next morning go to see if you have caught anything can provide harmless excitement, an insight into the lives of the mammals and scientific data as well.

Novelty could perhaps be our last hook: wear a hard hat and descend a coalmine; set out on a walk at dusk to listen for nightingales, or at dawn to hear the dawn chorus; try your skill with a bow and arrow; climb the steps to the top of a tower. A new experience enjoyed, together with something of its significance, may be remembered for a lifetime. High-tech gimmicks retain amusement value for remarkably short periods, and are not necessarily any better at conveying truths than more old-fashioned methods: interactive videos have not half the pull that they did five years ago. Virtual reality is likely to wear thin soon – but climb a tower, let a falcon perch on your arm, or stook sheaves of corn, and you will experience reality itself.

> It is true, and an indication of the barbarity of the times, that in 1306 King Edward I of England, having captured the relatives of Robert Bruce through the treachery of the Earl of Ross, hanged and disembowelled Robert's brother Nigel, placed Robert's child Marjory in a cage at the Tower of London, and imprisoned his sister Mary in a cage hung from the wall of Roxburgh Castle. These rather horrible facts may engage a visitor's interest enough to enable the Interpreter to build on them something more significant. The story, for example, suggests one reason why the medieval barons of the Scottish borders were so anxious to maintain castles of their own, whether grand or modest.

Left: working in an allotment garden.
Below: learning to fish.

Certain hobbies and sports interact so closely with the natural elements in our world that those who pursue them can hardly fail to learn interpretively. Gardening is one. Once you get past the beginner's stage, you quickly recognise that different species of plant prefer different soil types and soil chemistry, and different degrees of moisture and shade. They have to be sown or planted at times of year that suit them. You learn about biennials and perennials, genera, species and varieties. Organic gardening, where you accommodate the natural habits of plants and animals rather than dominate them with technology, takes you further – until, almost without realising it, you are recognising principles of botany and ecology.

Fishing is another such hobby – even the differences between coarse, game and sea fishing are a lesson in ecology. Fishermen will often sit for hours on a river bank, or wade through the shallows of a trout river, noticing the behaviour not only of their quarry, but of kingfishers, dippers, terns, dragonflies or mayflies – and how rain and wind, sunshine or tide, affect them and their habitats.

Ramblers, climbers, naturalists, birdwatchers, steam buffs, industrial archaeologists, local historians, photographers, visitors to historic sites, suppporters of Amnesty International . . . Through their different pursuits and experiences, and the encouragement and advice of fellow-enthusiasts, all can become wiser about the world.

8 Introducing the Feature
First impressions and ambience

In diplomatic circles, the language interpreter probably does not have to be concerned with the stage management of a summit meeting. Others decide how the visiting Prime Minister or Head of State will be conveyed from the airport, and by what route; by what entrance and through which state rooms he or she will pass; whether or not there are to be fanfares or guards of honour; and whether the interview itself will take place in an atmosphere of relaxed and informal comfort, or in dignified and formal pomp. The interpreter just has to be there at the meeting, and get on with his job when told to.

In Environmental Interpretation, the Interpreter is often in a position to control these matters to a certain extent, and very important they are. If the Feature's message is to be heard, understood and respected, the Visitor needs to be made suitably welcome and comfortable. Distractions should be minimised, and the actual introduction to the Feature must be properly planned.

A checklist of procedures for the diplomatic visit would probably run something like this:

1. Choose a time
2. Invite the visitor
3. Brief the visitor
4. Choose the route
5. Create the ambience
6. Dress the potentate
7. Dress the interpreter
8. Welcome the visitor
9. Stage manage the encounter
10. Point out the potentate.

Every one of these elements, I suggest, has a direct equivalent in Environmental Interpretation, and is worth examining carefully. They do overlap somewhat, and the sequence is more a matter of logic than of timing; but the virtue of this kind of analysis is that it may help to identify small but important processes that somehow need to be woven into the experience that Interpretation offers the Visitor.

1 CHOOSE A TIME

The potentate's aides no doubt keep a fixture diary, and know his or her schedule months in advance. They will also know the best times of year, week or day to receive important visitors. This may depend partly on the convenience of the potentate, partly on the convenience of the visitor, and partly on the nature of the visit and its likely programme.

This kind of consideration is very clearly demonstrated in some wildlife Interpretation. A certain wildflower meadow, which has survived in an area of intense arable farming, is opened by the county wildlife trust to the public for just one weekend a year. Visitors can see orchids and a host of other attractive flowers in bloom, photograph them, examine them closely and smell them. The timing is crucial, because the flowers will only be at their best for a few days, and would risk damage if visitors were free to come any time they liked. Botanists from the trust go out the day before the public come, and mark a circuit through the meadow that passes suitable clumps of plants, and stick explanatory labels beside them. No one would want meadows normally to have their plants labelled – but for a special open day it is an entirely acceptable exercise in simple interpretation. Gardens, too, have to be open to the public at the appropriate intersection of two time scales – time of year to suit the garden, and time of week and day to suit the visitors.

Guided walks tend, naturally, to be concentrated in the months of most daylight and warmth, but many programmes of walks continue on a lesser scale throughout the year, with themes or routes appropriate to the season (see page 163). Some excursions will be determined by the tides. Though it may be possible to rustle up enough walkers for a two-hour winter exploration of, say, a bird-haunted estuary to justify arranging for a guide, it is unrealistic to keep all Interpretation schemes going all year. To try to keep a small visitor centre, popular in high season, open throughout the winter is likely to prove a waste of staff time.

Promotional material for staffed visitor centres and other attractions may fulfil certain specific functions in addition to the general one of making the place known. One is to make clear exactly when a place is open – in the northern hemisphere, seasonal opening often begins with Easter weekend, then ceases again until the main summer run from, say, the beginning of May until the end of September. But for indoor, well-heated and permanently staffed attractions (larger museums and hands-on science centres are good examples), promotion may be intensified to encourage out-of-season visitors with a different programme of activity.

The direction of the sunlight may be a consideration in some walks. Photographers know how much it matters to get the sun in the right position, but even without a camera, trying to study a feature with bright sun behind it is most uncomfortable. A good guide will remember this – at what point in a circular tour will the Visitors be facing the sun? A certain route may be best walked clockwise in the morning, anti-clockwise in the afternoon. Which combination of direction and time of day is best for that particular circuit?

Similar principles operate when planning urban, as well as country, walks. On a town trail, one tends to walk less briskly and with shorter distances between stops; in chilly weather, this can be an uncomfortable experience. Buildings, too, look more attractive in bright weather; and town walks are likely to be less fraught with risk in the reduced traffic of a Sunday morning.

2 INVITE THE VISITOR

Here we are concerned with the actual method and style of invitation (in many sites, additional visitors are deliberately not sought). An effective invitation must be comprehensive, giving essential information such as place, date, time and subject. It is all too easy to leave out something of basic importance when drafting a poster or a press advertisement. But other factual information should possibly be included in the promotional literature, to reassure potential Visitors and make them less apprehensive. Advice about free parking, the availability of refreshments or special activities for children, whether beginners are welcomed, when an event is planned to end – all these may make the difference that encourages a family to come.

'Something for all the Family!!'
'Loamshire's Most Amazing Collection!!!'
'Try Your Hand at Milking a Yak!!!!'
These promotions are intended to imply 'Wow! Are you going to enjoy yourselves!'

'Your Ancestors' Bones'
'Buried Treasure'
'Piecing Together the Past'
These are slogans that will appeal to someone already half-hooked on the idea of archaeology.

Then there is the matter of the 'tone of voice'. An Interpretational invitation must combine the almost contradictory qualities of advertising and integrity. Promotional advertising has a language and typography of its own. Do you, as a provider of Interpretation, wish to copy it? It depends, perhaps, on the audience you want to attract. Sometimes you will be preparing an event or an experience with a particular market in mind. Clearly the promotional style must match the intended market.

While some enthusiasts search for a specific form of entertainment and experience that they know they like – backpackers, wildlifers, church-crawlers, steam buffs or ghostbusters, for instance – many people set out in search not of a specific topic so much as a general 'buzz': something new, something pretty, something to watch, something to keep the children occupied, something to buy. Promotion of interpretational attractions has to bear this in mind. The concept of Interpretation may not be a draw in itself!

3 BRIEF THE VISITOR

The invitation must leave no doubt in the mind of the intended visitor just what sort of experience is prepared for him. People may be nervous about committing themselves to an unknown experience. As well as the elements already covered, there may be further matters to clarify.

• How to find the Feature will be one. Just naming the village or the street may not be enough: it is frustrating to drive round a strange place searching for a sign that one is not even sure will be there. Perhaps a diagram or map should be provided, with clear indications of the position of the incoming roads.

• Is the facility accessible to wheelchairs, or are there steep slopes or stairs to be climbed?

• Will there be a lot of walking to do? A large zoological garden such as Whipsnade in Bedfordshire may dismay visitors who arrive without realising its sheer extent.

• Is any particular clothing or equipment essential or useful? Wellington boots? Binoculars?

• What are the admission fees, if any? Are there price concessions for the elderly, the young or the unwaged?

Ensure that any fears or doubts on the part of the Visitor, or embarrassments on the occasion itself, are avoided. Doubts may cause a potential visitor to decide not to come, just in case there *are* any problems. Embarrassment on just one occasion may mean that a return visit is never made.

4 CHOOSE THE ROUTE

The approach to a new place, a new experience, can be almost as exciting as the place or experience itself. Certainly, it can enhance it. To approach the city of Lincoln from the south provides a long-distance view that can be breathtaking. If it is a summer's morning and the mist is just being dispersed by the sun, you may see the great cathedral towering above the haze across the valley of the river Witham. If only such conditions could be guaranteed every time a coach carried sightseers to the city!

The cathedral city of Ely, rising out of the fens like an old-fashioned ship in full sail, could perhaps be approached by river. To arrive by boat at a riverside settlement may provide a better

8:1 Internal combustion engines not welcome

These forms of transport are neither too fast nor too comfortable. They slow you down to a pace that matches the scenery and prepares you to appreciate the traditional, basic but specialised farming practices that such a landscape requires. Tracks criss-cross this wide, rough, gently rolling land, and the signs are painted not on upstanding posts, but on great boulders.

Part of the heathland was purchased in 1905 to protect it from development. Since then the Verein Naturschützpark (VNP) has acquired further land, much of it designated as nature reserve. Sheep-farming continues, but visitors are welcome. The characteristic old farmhouses have mostly been made over to other uses, but are well looked after. One is a museum of the Lüneberger Heide; others are hostels where visitors may stay if they want to do more than a day's walking. But no cars are allowed.

If you visit the protected parts of the Lüneberger Heide in north Germany – a wonderful heathland landscape of heather and juniper, sheep and bees – you will not have access to the heart of it by car, bus or rail. You will have to enter it on foot, on horseback or by horse-drawn waggon.

understanding of its former commercial dependence on water transport than a pedestrian tour of the wharf could ever do. It is not merely a matter of viewpoint, though this may be important; there is also the theatrical relevance of the gesture.

Some farms that are open to the public carry their visitors around their extensive acres by tractor and trailer. Towns or cities may offer circular tours in open-topped buses or horse-drawn carriages. You can fly in a helicopter or small plane deep into the Grand Canyon. More exotically, you may visit the temples of the Maya by mule or the Sahara by camel, or approach even remoter sites by swaying rope bridges over deep ravines.

Interpreters have not always got the resources of boat, plane or saddle but, if they have, they should use them. Commentaries offered on *bâteaux-mouches* in Paris, or barges on the canals of Amsterdam, or boats along the river Thames might relate the waterborne experiences of their passengers to stories of the waterways themselves. Not just stories of smuggling (the popular coastal and riverine equivalent of ghosts and underground passages), but explanations of what waterway traffic was really like, and where and how water transport interconnected with the roads. This is very well done on certain boat tours of the port of Hamburg: what one sees of the port and its shipping are explained, virtually ship by ship, dock by dock. Cumulatively, it adds up to an insight into the vast international trade network of which Hamburg is a nodal point.

Perhaps it was an imaginative Interpreter of history with a small budget who dreamed up the 'time tunnel' – an enclosed corridor which sucks the Visitor from the twentieth century into a mysterious limbo and then projects him into a re-created past. The Scottish Crown Jewels at Edinburgh Castle are approached in similar fashion, through a winding passage lined with life-size costumed figures that gradually take the Visitor back in time until he emerges to confront the medieval treasures themselves. This is an ingenious method of crowd control, for the narrow approach forces visitors into a queue, while the tableaux provide something to occupy eyes and minds while they slowly move forward. Maybe the first person to think of this approach by tunnel had visited the ancient city of Petra in Jordan, whose theatrical facades suddenly burst on the visitor's view after a long, winding approach through a narrow passage between high rock faces.

The best order
Then there is the matter of sequence. If you visit a castle, a large garden, a museum or a nature reserve, the actual sequence of experiences can help or hinder not only the Visitor's enjoyment, but his understanding. Topography, the lie of the land, may dictate your approach. Any visitor to the island castle at Lindisfarne, Northumberland, can scarcely fail to glimpse it from the distance, perhaps across the water at high tide. Its isolated crag-top site seems romantic, while the approach to the island at low-tide, by a narrow causeway over estuary mud, raises the mild though probably needless anxiety that one might somehow be trapped by the tide, which adds to the excitement. As one walks towards the castle, its height seems to grow, and then as one ascends the path up the crag to the entrance, the long-distance views back to the mainland grow wider and deeper. No interpreter could plan a better introduction than that first imposed by the castle's builders by their very choice of site.

The inflexibility of landscape itself means that the Interpreter should plan flexibly in order to conform to it: Mahomet must go to the mountain. A museum, on the other hand, can to a certain extent control the pattern of its Visitors' experience by manipulating the indoor environment. Should the very first thing that

8:2 Atmospherics

At an open day at the Martham Farm Centre in Norfolk a few years ago, Dick Joice, producer and presenter of Anglia Television's popular *Bygones* programme, talks to a group of visitors from the top of a loaded farm waggon. The Visitors have not come expecting a formal occasion, with the presenter in a smart suit, flanked by officials, with the crowd kept at a respectful distance by a smart red rope slung between two posts. How much more fun to meet a television personality close up, in such a casual and friendly style! It is a Rural Life Museum, so it is appropriate for him to speak out of doors, perched up above the crowd on a waggon. We can see that he is not an aloof expert, but an ordinary enthusiast for the countryside. Ambience in these contexts is usually within the control of the Proprietor, the Impresario, the Interpreter. To create and sustain it, and use it positively, is an art worth cultivating.

impinges on the visitor's sight be some stunning artefact, such as the life-size silver clockwork musical swan just inside the entrance of the Bowes Museum at Barnard Castle, Durham? Or should it be vistas of enticing galleries radiating from the entrance foyer? Or should the aim be to tempt visitors with the goods in the museum shop which, it is hoped, epitomise the quality of the material in the collection?

The layout of any museum or exhibition may depend on its basic intention. Is it to offer a choice of more or less self-contained displays, which the Visitor may sample in any order (the pick'n'mix principle)? Or are the collections arranged according to a logical train of thought, perhaps chronologically (the sequential principle)? It is important that the visitor knows which, as uncertainty can cause confusion and embarrassment. The main way to make it clear is by layout. If the principle is pick'n'mix, the visitor can be offered a network of galleries without internal doors. To impose or imply sequence, the displays may be 'corridored' or numbered. To indicate free choice, titled sections within an open-plan arrangement may show that each is self-contained. Where the approach is in the control of the Interpreter, it can be made a positive part of the Visitor's experience, and be used as a kind of prologue to the Message.

5 CREATE THE AMBIENCE

The potentate's throne room (just like a director's office) has often in the past been deliberately designed, furnished and decorated to awe rivals and to put outsiders in their place. An ambassador is made to feel small, and expects to have to bow and scrape, and to walk out backwards. If his reception is to be a friendly one, then these same qualities of furnishing, the ambience of power and wealth, will enhance his sense of his own importance. In Interpretation, the Visitor and the Feature are both VIPs. The Feature is to be portrayed as of great worth, and the Visitor is to realise that he also is much respected and valued. This can be done without red carpets or the lavish use of gilt. The important thing is to decide at what level of friendliness the whole ambience is to be pitched. The rule is appropriateness: the style must suit the occasion. Many older museums are housed in splendid buildings, and can intimidate. It is up to the proprietors to make them visitor-friendly.

For a visitor centre alongside the marketplace of a certain large historic town, it was suggested that the displays (which related to local topics and were more or less self-contained) should be presented in the form of cheerfully decorated 'stalls', borrowing from the pattern of the market just outside. In a market you can always wander around, having a look at all the stalls before deciding where you will offer your custom. Art galleries and the larger museums, and perhaps the more extensive interpretational exhibitions, should recognise that this is the way that they are mostly used. It is more desirable that a visitor should look round casually, picking on one or two displays that really capture his interest and taking them in, than feel that he has to submit to being 'processed' by a sort of three-dimensional sequential lecture. Smaller museums often cram heterogeneous material into whatever showcases or surfaces they have acquired (sometimes even ancient display units donated by local shops). On a sufficiently parochial scale, there is something rather endearing about such collections: the displays themselves are actually providing a reflection and, to a certain extent, interpretation of the small-town character.

The Forestry Commission's visitor centres, and those of certain other countryside sites including country parks, have often been deliberately built of timber. In a forest context timber seems right, brick would not have the same resonance.

When an interpretion centre for the Norfolk Broads was being planned some years ago by the Norfolk Naturalists' Trust (now the Norfolk Wildlife Trust) to be built at a marshy, water's-edge site at Ranworth, the original suggestion was to drive piles down through the peat to carry it. The Trust's architects made an imaginative suggestion that resulted in less environmental damage, less expense and the perfect ambience for the display: they suggested floating the whole structure on inconspicuous concrete pontoons, and mooring it at the edge of the marsh, with a duckboard pathway leading to it through a belt of alder carr and marsh from the nearest truly dry land. The building was of timber, and it was thatched with Norfolk reed. There could be no more appropriate scenic welcome for the Visitor.

A visitor centre in the Peak District is dedicated to the story of mining. Its displays are presented in deliberate gloom, so they have to be very obviously spotlit: this ambience reflects our ideas of being underground, rather than attempting to simulate a mine. Built within it is a narrow, vertical, black-painted, chimney-like tunnel that children may clamber up to see how uncomfortably claustrophobic primitive mine shafts could be. It is not a replica shaft – it is clearly built of wood, rather in the style of an imitation rock face for training climbers in a gymnasium.

Simulating reality

Imitation timber in a forest context would be horrible, but that is not to say that there is no place for imitation textures in display ambience. There have been very successful plaster or fibreglass reconstructions of ecclesiastical stonework, of the interior of a pre-historic flint mine, and of rock faces as elements of interpretational displays. Perhaps the fact that these are just elements in displays makes them acceptable: one can see that they are artistic interpretations of stonework, chalk strata and rock, rather than a pretence of the real thing. If you do want to deceive visitors, and if the experience is to be anywhere near real, the deception must be complete.

Among the best interpretational deceptions must be the Lewis Merthyr Colliery Museum at the Rhondda Heritage Park in South Wales. Practical reasons of safety make it difficult or impossible to take visitors down through former mine shafts and galleries. At Merthyr, visitors are received by an apparent worker at the mine, who takes the party to a room at ground level where lamps and other necessary gear are issued, provides each member of the party with a safety helmet, and leads them to a formidable lift with great clanking gates. We walk in. It is rather cramped and dark. The lift wobbles and creaks and our stomachs rise within us, and the descent seems to last a long time. At last we reach bottom with an uncomfortable jolt. The gates on the other side of the lift are opened, and out we clamber into dark, damp, ill-lit mine galleries smelling of coal dust. The gallery floor is uneven, dirty, running with trickles of water, and we have to take care not to trip over the rails used by the coal waggons. We can hear the distant rumble of waggons and the occasional blast of explosive that shakes the very ground we stand on. Visitors susceptible to claustrophobia need reassurance.

It is not until we are about to be taken up to the surface again that we get suspicious. We are led to a set of waggons with seats, just a little too modern and clean to be convincing. Our hard hats (they now seem more reminiscent of party headgear – could they really protect our heads in the event of a rock fall?) are collected in, and the waggons start a hair-raising journey back to the surface. The waggon ride is a masterpiece of simulation, with scares galore and everyone holding on to the sides of their seats in nervous good humour. Back at ground level, we are let out into the daylight again. But, actually, we never left it. The simulation is so good, and the style of our guide's patter so clever, that we are half-convinced that we have experienced the reality of a working mine 4,000 feet below ground.

As for the quality of the interpretation, it seems to work. It is not real experience for there was no danger (though we were nervous enough), but we did experience that coal mine with all our senses. True, we did not know the toil, the heat, the sweat, what it was like to have our eyes sore with dust; we did not emerge with grime ingrained in our faces and bodies. But this truly was 'virtual reality' – interpretive to an extent that burying one's head in a computerised gadget could never be.

A kind of semi-simulation can be expressed through art. When visitors arrive at the amazing Living Legend exhibition on the island of Jersey, they are led into a sort of giant foyer, decorated to suggest underwater shipwreck. It is a teasing mix of simulation and art, with what look like enormous hunks of ships' hulls and engines, rusting ironwork, huge bolts, seaweed-draped pieces of rotting wooden masts or decking, lit with a sort of underwater luminosity. There are real fish, in tanks; there are nets and floats, divers' helmets; there is projected moving film of underwater scenes. You can sit down on jetsam that you imagine must have lain in salt water for a hundred years. This is not simulation so much as the generation of atmosphere, and it is preparing you for the main multi-media display that will tell the story of a small island whose trade, culture and lifestyle have been determined by the sea. Is it sculpture? Is it interior decoration? Is it theatre? Is it artistic interpretation? It is all of these, but it is not *Interpretation* (in italics). It is highly skilled Introduction, preparing the Visitor to meet the Interpreter and the Feature.

6 DRESS THE POTENTATE

Whenever a Head of State wishes to impress – whether by wealth, military power, a nation's long traditions, the size or efficiency of the court, scholarship or approachability – he or she will dress accordingly and appropriately. The reason is simple: to give the visitor the right impression. Whether the potentate turns up at the airport to welcome the visitor, or greets him on the steps of the White House, or is to be found seated on a throne in the depths of a palace – this itself sends a message. The context and the dress will determine how the visitor perceives the potentate.

A fine garden opened specially to the public on a named day will, you may be sure, have been the scene of frantic tidying and weeding, watering and possibly even surreptitious planting during the previous few days. Where fine buildings are concerned, we expect the National Trust always to maintain their properties in presentable condition. It is common today to find houses open to the public furnished not just with labelled museum pieces around the walls (though some still are!), but arranged so that they look lived in. There will be flowers in vases, books on bookshelves, pictures on walls, cushions on sofas and chairs. The old-fashioned treatment signalled the message, 'This house is a preserved shell, and these furnishings are ghosts from the past that haunt it.' The modern approach tries to signal, 'This place has seen life, and history lives for ever.'

At a bird garden in north Germany there is an open-air enclosure for shore birds. It includes an area of water and a cleverly simulated shore. A wave machine (like those at swimming pools) sends mini-breakers rolling up the sandy beach, to the delight not only of the oyster-catchers and other birds whose natural behaviour is stimulated by the waves, but of the public, who watch just because the whole scene is in motion.

It is curious how, when police uniforms are dark blue, any other person who wears a uniform of that colour tends to be seen as a law-enforcer. This may be desirable in, say, museums and galleries where priceless treasures might be at risk from misbehaviour, but to the shy Visitor it is inhibiting. It can even imply that the wearer knows nothing, nor cares, about the exhibits. Such uniformed staff tend to reinforce this image by being silent and unsmiling – partly, perhaps, as a reaction to the nervous body language of the Visitors. How much friendlier is the uniform worn by most park rangers, which tends to be an informal, not-too-military green or khaki – suggestive of expert acquaintance with trees and animals, but not formidable.

7 DRESS THE INTERPRETER

In the world of live guiding – potentially one of the most effective of interpretational methods – a simple matter such as the dress of the guide can help or hinder the interpretation process. I joined a guided walk in Hertfordshire advertised as a 'woodland butterfly walk'. Our small group of about eight people was greeted by a friendly young man dressed as informally as the rest of us, but carrying a large butterfly net and a haversack containing books, jars and appropriate paraphernalia. Instantly we knew that (a) this was indeed the leader of the walk we were looking for; (b) however knowledgeable he was, he certainly wasn't going to be stuffy; (c) there was going to be action; and (d) there was likely to be hands-on experience if we were lucky (we were). What if the guide had been dressed in rather old-fashioned naturalists' gear, game-keeper's gaiters or explorer's puttees, a deer-stalker or a large floppy sunhat? Or the Edwardian lady's equivalent? Or Ranger's uniform, with badges? The effect would have been very different.

On another walk, this time on an industrial archaeology theme, we were received and briefed by a straightforward twentieth-century young man. No sooner had our party set off and rounded the first corner, but we 'happened' upon a whiskered, quaintly dressed gentleman poking at something with a trowel – undoubtedly, a relic of the Victorian age. He looked up from what he was doing, blinked, introduced himself as a nineteenth-century engineer, asked whether we would like to be shown the old ironworks, and took over. Theatrical tricks like this should not become so much the norm that visitors either get tired of costumed guides, or else feel cheated if they do not get one. But there are times when the unexpected can heighten the excitement and the interest – so that the interpretation, when it comes, falls on more than usually attentive ears.

Interpretational literature can benefit from a consideration of this principle of introduction. A guide leaflet can appear *too* tasteful – 'above my level, too posh,' a potential user might feel. Another leaflet may seem so chummy and fun, shouting in the latest fashion of style or colour, that some readers may doubt its authority or seriousness. Yet another may look too learned – crammed with long paragraphs of academic or scientific text. Some look so obviously addressed to children that adults may pass them by (often a pity, because well-written interpretational material for children can be the best introduction for the lay adult). Styles of both script and design can be the graphic equivalents of talking down or showing off: neither endears itself to a wide audience or readership.

8 WELCOME THE VISITOR

Visitor-friendliness is a very important concept. First impressions are of great importance, whether it is the cover of a booklet, an

Llyn Llech Owain, near Gorslas, Carmarthenshire, South Wales, was rescued from possible dereliction and made into an attractive nature reserve and Country Park, interesting for its wet habitat and its birds and plants. Its 158 acres include woodland and a marshy area surrounding a small reservoir. Before its transformation it was difficult of access, while its boggy character could even have made it dangerous to explore. Besides the management necessary for wildlife conservation, a strategy had to be devised to receive, circulate and inform visitors.

From the new car park at the entrance to the site, a simple network of boarded walkways guides visitors around the park and to the visitor centre. These walkways deliberately lead people across the boggy area, enabling them to experience at close hand the nature of the terrain and its plant life, and to get views of the lake.

An attractive tower-like feature by the waterside catches the eye – reminiscent of reservoir architecture and of the fanciful tower of Castell Coch near Cardiff. It turns out to be the purpose-built visitor centre, its materials tough, plain and slightly industrial, though the general impression is of space and light. Its three floors hold an office, an interpretational display and, at the top, a viewing floor with a more or less 360-degree outlook over the water and also over neighbouring farmland invisible from the ground.

encounter with a guide, the impact of *son et lumière*, the initial seconds of an audio-visual programme, or at a visitor centre. Cultures vary in the way friendliness is expressed, so each must follow its own traditions. In Britain we are not too good at looking strangers in the eye and smiling, but genuine friendliness is a most important quality for interpretation staff to cultivate, and the best ways of showing it should be a subject for training. Visitors' perception of the friendliness of an institution may be affected by such practical things as the furnishings of a building – carpets, chairs, hooks to hang coats on, or suitably signed toilet facilities.

9 STAGE-MANAGE THE ENCOUNTER

People who enjoy showing others their local countryside or places of interest will often have their favourite approaches: 'Close your eyes as we drive round this corner – there!' First impressions can be very memorable. East Barsham Manor, a spectacular sixteenth-century manor house in 'flat' Norfolk, is revealed suddenly when approached over a hill from the south on the B1105 from Fakenham, its red ornamented brickwork glowing warmly among the trees below. I love taking passengers this way, giving no warning but slowing down gently as we reach the top, and waiting for them to exclaim at the view.

A good leader and planner of guided walks will always take presentation into account. Is the best first view of a certain feature from the south or the west? Close up, or distant? And which view speaks most eloquently of the way the lie of the land has influenced the feature's location? A windmill's power source may be best appreciated with a view from below; a watermill's often from downstream. The self-importance of a town hall or a big inn may be more obvious when it is seen from across the square. The significance of a town's location on the bank of a navigable river may be clearer if you view it from across the river, facing the former quay; or entering by its bridge, just as travellers had to do in the middle ages.

Introducing objects

Individual museum or art gallery displays will need to consider the way each object is individually introduced to the visitor. A major exhibit may require a room to itself: when the National Gallery in London acquired a celebrated cartoon by Leonardo da Vinci, they displayed it theatrically and in isolation, with nothing around it to distract attention.

I know a regimental museum with two entrances. From the main one, the visitor is confronted with an impressive set-piece, at what is really the heart of the museum: an almost life-size statuesque model of soldiers holding their regimental colours. But from the back entrance, visitors finally approach this model from behind – and the back view is almost meaningless. The visitor can experience a sense of having made a mistake, of being in the wrong place. But before this, they find themselves plunged into a replica of First World War trenches, through which they have to wind their way – accompanied by muted bangs and whizzes that provide a gentle, almost nostalgic, reminder of shells and machine-gun fire – along a safe and sanitised trench floor, of a level and dryness that no veteran of the grim battles in Flanders would recognise. It certainly makes an unusual first impression, but it fails to convince.

It is difficult to interpret real war, just as Madame Tussaud's Chamber of Horrors cannot truly interpret the horror of torture,

I saw the pyramids of Gaza early one morning, for about fifteen seconds, through the window of a military aeroplane taking off from Cairo airport. I knew how vast they are, in spite of the simplicity of their shape; but as we gained altitude their imposing size diminished until they seemed almost insignificant below us.

This aerial view pointed the contrast between the enormous scale of the human engineering achievement, and its relative ineffectuality when perceived in the wider landscape. Seeing the pyramids with this above-and-below vision was as enlightening as I imagine the more standard tourist's view must be.

and castle halls, despite weapons and standing suits of armour, cannot interpret the crude and cruel battles of the middle ages. What about modern war museums and collections of planes, rockets, tanks and field guns? One can understand why, at Britain's Imperial War Museum at Duxford, Cambridgeshire, the section that displays tanks, aircraft and other machinery of war does not include realistic sounds of gunfire (it would damage the visitors' eardrums), flashes of flame or stench of explosives. Most especially, there are no terrible cries of the wounded, no young men's corpses. Instead, the exhibits are labelled in almost clinical terms, with just a hint of pride: statistics of the weaponry's fire capacity, the barrel calibre, the range of its missiles.

I do not know what is the best ambience to build into a museum of warfare. But kinder topics can often be satisfactorily presented in appropriately chosen or designed contexts. At the pumping station at Crofton, Wiltshire, the original beam engine installed there by the engineer John Rennie can be viewed on specially announced days in summer 'in steam' – such a working engine is much more meaningful than one that has been rescued and re-installed in a museum. Interpretation is mainly in the form of friendly explanation from the volunteer enthusiasts who maintain and run the machinery. A real problem for the Kennet and Avon Canal Trust, who own it, is whether or not to put a coat of emulsion paint on the flaking walls, and whether or not to provide interpretation panels. The basic ambience (and interpretational quality) of the old industrial premises could be spoilt by excessive smartness – and yet engineers have their pride. Well-maintained machinery, but old-fashioned whitewash (even if it tends to peel) seem to provide just the right setting. If graphic interpretation boards are needed, they must be so designed that they do not detract from the ambience of such a place, or the magic will be dissipated.

10 POINT OUT THE POTENTATE

One last aspect of Interpretational practice must be included in our notion of introduction, and that is to point out features that the Visitor might otherwise miss. It would be annoying to be introduced rather vaguely to a person one doesn't recognise, exchange a few somewhat pointless words, and then discover afterwards that it was someone famous or important. It would be just as frustrating to discover that one had stood within sight of some fascinating historical or landscape feature, and not realised it was there.

In live guiding terms, the opportunities for 'pointing out' are obvious: some will be pre-planned, others fortuitous. In guiding people around architectural subjects, say, it is important to encourage people to look up occasionally – at gargoyles, or mottoes inscribed in the fabric of public buildings, or any of a host of fascinating details that the novice looker-out can easily fail to spot. In

An important point to remember in all graphic wall displays is to match the direction to the one in which we naturally read – for those from the Western world, this means from left to right. Trying to do the opposite can cause quite severe visual and mental discomfort.

woodland, it may be a woodpecker's nest-hole, a squirrel's drey at treetop height, a bird of prey soaring in the sky – yet at the same time little features at ground level must not be missed. Part of the interpreter's job is to show people 'how to see' in unfamiliar surroundings.

Guide literature, too, needs to point out features. It is not always easy for a person writing a guide to remember that his readers are starting from scratch: they probably do not know the route; they will not, unlike locals, know the names of any of the features, and as lay persons they will not necessarily know any technical terms, ecological, architectural or historical. Nor will they know where north is, so to write about 'the house to the south' might be quite wasted.

Take care, also, with directions like 'to your left' and 'at the far end of the street' – whether or not the Visitor looks the right way will depend on which side of the street he is on. The official guide of one important East Anglian town refers the reader to a building that is said to be visible from a certain spot, but it is not – the road curves just too much, and the building is actually out of sight. It seems that the writer prepared his script at a desk and failed to check it on the ground. Such carelessness can seriously damage your rapport with visitors, by quenching enthusiasm and diverting their energies into justified criticism.

Applying good principles of introduction can boost all Interpretation, and it does not usually need to be a hundredth as elaborate as in the Jersey display or at Edinburgh Castle. It can be very discreet; indeed, it is generally best when it is not over the top.

An Interpreter who points out features in print must take pains to avoid ambiguity. You could hardly be too precise if you tried.

'The fine three-storey black-and-white timbered building with the central archway, next to the Cordwainers Arms public house and opposite the war memorial . . .'

'If you stand with your back to the churchyard, at the entrance gate, and look down the lane to the left . . .'

'The date, 1866, is carved on a round stone plaque placed in the brickwork near the top of the gable (the pointed, end wall of the building) that faces the market square . . .'

Systems and signals
Means of communication

9

In the threesome of interpretation, the role of the interpreter as go-between is necessarily a dual one – with a duty to both the other parties. In language interpretation, he or she has a duty to the speaker and a duty to the listener. In Environmental Interpretation, he has corresponding duties: he owes it to the Feature to understand what it has to say, and to the Visitor to express the chosen message in the clearest possible way. Both clarity and possibility will depend on a number of factors. Communication must depend upon, and be tailored to, both the external circumstances of the situation, and the internal requirements of the message itself.

EXTERNAL CIRCUMSTANCES

External circumstances are those within or under which Communication has to be achieved (see the entry for 'Interpretation opportunity' in the List of Terms, page 9). These can vary enormously in terms of both places and people. Physically, the location and topography are major factors. The site and its Interpretation may be outdoors or indoors, at the top of a mountain or a monument, or at the bottom of the sea or a salt-mine. It may be simple or complex, direct or indirect. Features (and thus Interpretation) may vary in accessibility: they may be in publicly accessible places (streets, commons, parks, footpaths); or they may be on private property where access is controlled (museums, nature reserves, factories, farms). Features themselves will vary in size, from the tiny (a gem in a museum collection) to the vast (a landscape, a national park, an ocean, a nation). The complexity of the site may be a factor that suggests a multiple system of Interpretation: within a given site there may have to be several small Interpretation points, delivering messages cumulatively. Indeed, self-guided trails and many interpretational displays, visitor centres and museums really consist of series of Interpretation points. A site like a large national or country park may require an array of Interpretation methods – guide literature, site panels, live guiding and special events.

Safety precautions may influence an Interpretation scheme. Some sites (a working factory, a clifftop) may be inherently dangerous. In others, constraints of conservation may affect either the number of Visitors allowed – either at a particular time of year (because of disturbance to nesting birds, perhaps), or over a period of time (maybe to minimise erosion). Other Interpreted sites have to fulfil multiple functions: a cathedral exists primarily for Christian worship; the furniture in the drawing room of a stately home may be regularly used by the owners; even an ancient monument or a Site of Special Scientific Interest (SSSI) may be grazed by the land-owner's cattle.

The Visitors themselves will vary. Sometimes this is manifested in practical ways (see 'visitor pattern', page 14). They may arrive casually and unpredictably, or regularly and predictably. They may come only in pre-arranged organised parties. In some situations all visitors will arrive on foot, in others mostly in cars; in others by coach. In some circumstances there may be only one or two Visitors at a time; in others there may be crowds. They may come all year, or only in the summer; every day of the week, or only weekends; all day, or mainly in the afternoon. The visitor profile is likely to differ according to the location, accessibility and nature of the Feature.

THE REQUIREMENTS OF PEOPLE

Situations also vary in qualities relating to the Proprietor, the Interpreter or the Visitor. Relevant factors may include the aims or policy of Promoters; the skills or limitations of Interpreters, or the extent of visitors' previous knowledge.

Visitors will vary in their background and their expectations (the visitor profile). At some sites a high percentage will come because of a specialist interest (at a nature reserve, for instance, or a museum of musical instruments); at others, they will turn up out of mild curiosity; at others, just for fun, or to kill time, or to occupy the children. They may be almost entirely local, or they may be positively international. They may be mostly adults, in family groups or mainly children. And individual visitors may have problems of mobility, sight or hearing. Some sites are more accessible to those with physical disabilities than others.

Visitor motivation and background may vary according to site location and other circumstances. Some will arrive because the site happens to be alongside a long-distance walk route, or on the seafront where they are strolling. Remote sites may get a different profile from easily accessible ones. Some places cater largely for educational visits, and receive groups of children who have been brought there especially to learn. Elsewhere, adults may either include a high proportion of the well-read and broadly educated, or just a normal cross-section of the general public. Some people come seeking nostalgia, some seek exercise. Pretty few may be deliberately seeking interpretation; others may be indignant if they find none.

Each situation will have its own mix of circumstances – factors that determine how the Interpretation, and the Communication element in it in particular, will be planned. No two situations are the same – which shows, incidentally, how unsatisfactory and even ineffective it can be to try to copy what someone else has done.

The reality and relevance of this variability to the planning of Interpretation schemes is clear enough, and recognition of it will alert Interpreters to the complexity of their task. Common sense should be capable of sorting most matters out, but the variables are so many that the process may turn out to be less easy, and the solutions less obvious, than might be expected.

THE CONVENIENCE OF THE VISITOR

In situations where some kind of interpretation seems desirable, but there are no facilities for providing guide literature or live guides, information boards or panels may seem to be the answer. But such a choice should be made for the convenience not so much of the promoter (though he will, of course, have to bear costs in mind) as of the visitor. The site, its management and the needs of visitors are intimately connected factors, and will influence the means that Interpreters employ to get messages across to their audiences. It is essential to weigh systematically the pros and cons of every technique and technology you can think of.

For what we might call roadside Interpretation – out of doors, and intended to serve people who are on foot – interpretation is likely, on grounds of cost and convenience, to be provided by panels (graphics on boards). Passers-by may stop and study them if they wish.

Similar situations may be found in an open-air museum where old buildings have been re-erected; but where these sites are enclosed, and therefore all visitors pass an entry gate, it may seem better to provide personal headphones with pre-recorded sound commentaries. This has been done with great success at the famous re-created Anglo-Saxon village at West Stow in Suffolk. The scripts are a model of clarity, but if the same information had to be printed out on a series of panels the place would be half hidden by them.

A third method would be to provide all visitors with a guide booklet. This may be possible in the open-air museum context, but is less practicable for the informal roadside. Even in an open-air museum the system has limitations: it can be quite hard trying to read a booklet and study the interpreted feature at the same time; and a guide book rules out the use of recorded conversation or sound effects. On the other hand, recorded commentary does not allow the Interpretation to illustrate graphic points such as plans, artists' impressions and so on. Nor does it leave visitors with a memento, or anything they can look at again later, or use for research or to check information.

To get to the ruined abbey of St Benet at Holme, in the parish of Horning in Norfolk, is not straightforward by road – a farm track off a minor road leads to a parking space, from which visitors walk the last half mile. But the abbey site, and its stone and flint medieval gateway into which a brick windmill was built in the late eighteenth century, is a very conspicuous and puzzling landmark from the water. Hundreds of holiday-makers who take boats on the rivers of Norfolk's Broadland each year pass the site; many are intrigued by the ruins, tie up their craft and clamber ashore to inspect them. For years, however, there was not even a sign to explain what this extraordinary feature was.

A wayside interpretation panel is the outdoor equivalent of a museum label, explaining a Feature for anyone who happens to stop and look at it. Because it is out of doors, and the Feature is part of the landscape and not highlighted by being presented in a special case or with special lighting, the label itself has to catch the eye, or both it and the Feature may be overlooked. On the other hand, no one wants the landscape to be peppered with conspicuous signs, so there must not be too many of them, and their location and style has to be suitably discreet.

The Suffolk Sandlings Group, anxious that the heathlands of the east of the county have dwindled by something like 80 per cent in a hundred years, decided to point out the importance of the remaining areas, most of which are commons, by explanatory panels. The panels are sited at suitable access points, wherever possible near existing man-made features such as car parks.

Each panel has a map showing the former and present extent of the heathlands, with an explanatory paragraph; a map of the present common with a paragraph telling its story; and an illustration of some typical heathland plant or animal, with a paragraph about its habits and needs. The panels should be of interest to local residents and visitors, and it is hoped that the commons themselves will benefit as a result.

Studying an Interpretive panel at
Wenhaston Common, Suffolk.

INTERNAL CIRCUMSTANCES – THE MESSAGE

A varied and complex set of factors is inherent in the message itself, and in its relation to the physical and mental apparatus with which it is to be transmitted and received. It is with these message-related internals in mind, just as much as the externals, that the interpreter has to decide what means of communication – what media, what techniques – are the most appropriate for him to use. Some kinds of message are much better conveyed by one means than another.

For example, it is a familiar idea that some information can be conveyed in chart or diagram form more effectively than in words alone. But different forms of chart or diagram are suited to convey different types of information in specific sets of circumstances. Treasury ministers often use pie charts to demonstrate the proportions of the national income that are to be applied to different public services. The pie chart seems highly appropriate to show the distribution of something that is perceived to be 'good'. Graphs often display the rise and fall of interest rates over a period of years, with the vertical axis showing the level. There is no logical reason why the axes should not be used the other way round, but in terms of symbolism there is every good reason: the vertical symbolises rise and fall very neatly, while the horizontal represents the passage of time. Computer graphics can even indicate the passing of years by movement, with the line of the graph rising and falling before our eyes as it extends gradually from left to right. The bar chart, on the other hand, is ideal for displaying quantitative information for instant comparison – you do not even have to process figures to recognise instantly that the tall bar represents more than the short one, and in roughly what proportion. The eye takes it in at a glance.

The differences between what a place looks like today, and what it looked like a hundred years ago, can be communicated in many ways. It can be portrayed in descriptive writing. Many authors have done this, and to readers with imagination and the leisure to enjoy the descriptions, this can be very vivid, conveying not just physical change but cultural and aesthetic change as well. Good writing stimulates not just our visual imaginations, but can appeal to our recollections of touch or sound or smell. But writing is best appreciated at leisure and without distraction. A more immediate way to communicate changes in places is to present visual images of the same scene then and now: if done with drawings, they themselves will inevitably convey an appropriate period feel. The contrast may be made with a pair of photographs, but this technique should be carefully refined. The more closely the viewpoints of the photographs coincide, the better. If they can be reproduced at the same size, comparison will be easier. Perhaps the older print could be printed in a sepia colour, to signify its greater age (this is a very

'Pepper's Ghost' is a wonderfully effective method of fading one three-dimensional image (a model or a relief map, for instance) into another, for purposes of comparison. It can demonstrate changes in a particular landscape, or the growth of a settlement. The apparatus takes up quite a lot of space, and is only really suitable for installation in the context of an indoor display; but its technology is quite basic, involving special lighting and reflective glass. This spectral optical illusion was invented in the nineteenth century by an English engineer and author, Henry Dircks, and improved upon by John Henry Pepper (1821–1900), a lecturer at the Royal Polytechnic in London.

common convention, and subconsciously effective). I have seen 'then and now' photographs mounted so that the modern view was split and hinged, like a little pair of doors, to open and reveal the older view. You could look at first one, then the other, or half of each at the same time. The difficulty was that you could never have both completely in view at once; there are always disadvantages as well as advantages in any communication method.

The best way to explain a process is undoubtedly to have a live demonstration with live explanation. But this is a very labour-intensive practice (and therefore, unless you have willing volunteers, costly) and only a limited number of people can see it at once. A video film of the process is, in some ways, better. It can be edited to show close-up shots, to cut down very repetitive actions, and to show something in slow or fast motion. It can be shown over and over again almost indefinitely, so no further live demonstration time is needed, and copies can be made and distributed to different places as required. But you cannot put questions to a video programme! We can be sure that a sequence of graphics on a piece of paper or on a wall, however skilfully drawn, is by its static nature unable to illustrate a process as clearly as movement can.

Animated computer graphics can make certain points with a clarity that other systems cannot. The evolution of bone structures, fish to reptile, land mammal to whale, can be made to 'happen' before the viewer's eyes. The point may be taken in painlessly in a couple of seconds; to understand the same thing from a series of drawings would take longer and be more tedious on the eye and brain, while to learn the lesson from plain, unillustrated text would be even more difficult. Interpreters have to remember that Visitors may not always be in the mood for hard work.

THE USEFULNESS OF MAPS

Much interpretation is concerned with pointing out the relationships between things. Sometimes these are spatial relationships – for instance, the distribution of castles along the English/Welsh borders; how the former port of Winchelsea in Kent became landlocked by the silting up of the river estuary; how coal mining was distributed along the edges of carboniferous rocks; how recreational skiing is dependent on a mix of factors including latitude, altitude and weather patterns; or where the materials for a certain medieval stone building came from.

Maps or plans seem to be the obvious answer to the communication of these concepts. Essentially, they are sets of graphics representing a place or an object whose parts we need to identify in order to achieve some task – whether getting from one unfamiliar part of Dartmoor to another or assembling a piece of flat-pack furniture. For these purposes, would a recorded sound commentary make the job any easier? Or a video? It's unlikely.

At the Museum of East Anglian Life at Stowmarket there are occasional live demonstrations of traditional crafts such as basket- and barrel-making. It is impracticable to have specialist craftsmen continually on duty so, when they are not demonstrating, short video films of them at work are shown. Perhaps twenty or more people can get a good view of a video screen, depending on its size and positioning, whereas the number who can get a satisfactory view when watching a live demonstration may be only half that. The camera can also show certain parts of the process very close up, and good editing can reduce a half-hour demonstration to a ten-minute film. The video can be shown repeatedly, but it lacks the immediacy and reality of a live demonstration.

The initial cost of filming and of playback equipment may be fairly high. But once it is paid for, you have a high-quality, attractive system that requires virtually no supervision or maintenance, and can add life and Interpretation to an otherwise static display.

A map can convey many kinds of message. But not all technologies are equally good for bringing maps before the eyes of Visitors.

- **A printed map** can be clear and handy for one-person-to-a-map situations. But even two-persons-to-a-map is awkward, as many a rambling couple have found.
- **A wall map** may be helpful for making a simple geographical point, and can be studied by perhaps half a dozen people at once, but only for as long as they stand looking at it.
- **A map projected on a screen** may be viewed by dozens at once, but the individual viewer has no control over how long he can study it.
- **A map on CD-ROM** can be studied for as long as you want and printed out at will, but one viewer per screen would be a costly option for a visitor centre.
- **A map in a newspaper** may be cut out and kept.
- **A map in a book** can stimulate the imagination, but who would want to carry a heavy book round Sherwood Forest for its walk-route map?
- **Loose-leaf maps** are sometimes available for walking routes, together with a transparent wallet to hold them in.

When there is special significance in the three-dimensional quality of an image – earthworks, the ridges of medieval plough-land, the cover provided by trees or shrubs – we can sometimes offer something more helpful than a two-dimensional map. In a static situation, a relief map may convey a spatial truth more clearly than a flat image. But you cannot easily provide copies of it to take away, whereas portabilty is one of a folding map's big advantages. Better than a map, in some instances, may be a stereoscopic aerial photograph, but this has to be studied through a special viewer.

There is no space here to review the pros and cons of every symbol, technology and method of presentation available to the Interpreter. But the principles should be clear: specific types of information or message may be better conveyed by one form of symbolism than another; some kinds of symbol are better conveyed by particular technologies; and one has to choose a suitable technology according to the circumstances in which the Interpretation is to reach the Visitor, and according to the available budget.

COMMUNICATION STUDIES

The theories and principles of Communication Studies have certain things in common with those of Interpretation. To start with, both are comparatively new academic disciplines; additionally, they both embrace subject matter associated with other disciplines. Interpretation has to concern itself with matters as diverse as educational psychology, conservation and information technology: communication studies need some understanding of journalism, linguistics and sociology. The more we examine them both, the more apparent it becomes that their interests overlap. What this means for Interpretation is that a large area of its concerns is already being studied, analysed and published by other experts. For the Interpreter to ignore this – just as to ignore the wisdom latent in psychology, advertising, market research or tourism studies – would be foolish.

Communication theorists have pointed out how complex are the processes of transferring ideas and information from one person to another, and have analysed them in various ways. Such

9:3 Rousse Tower commands its island harbour

Guernsey, like the other Channel Islands, was fortified in the late eighteenth century to resist possible aggression from the French under Napoleon Buonaparte. The more accessible parts of the coast were protected by a series of cylindrical look-out towers and batteries (gun platforms).

The towers are still there, and one of them, the Rousse Tower in the north-west of the island, has recently had the woodwork of its floors and benches restored and is once again 'defended', by lifesize models of militia men. Outside, the gun battery has been equipped with replica guns; beside them, angled lectern-fashion at about hip level, are displayed reproductions of late eighteenth-century large-scale maps of the harbour that the tower and

its battery overlook and defend. Superimposed on one of the maps are the areas that the guns from this and other nearby forts would be able to cover with their fire. No enemy ship attempting to enter the harbour would have been safe.

The map chosen for this interpretation was not just any old map, but one surveyed and published at precisely the right period, whose very style and lettering evoke the time of the Napoleonic Wars. And it has specific functions: to help the Visitor locate and identify other similar towers on the horizon; to illustrate the way the arcs of fire from the different forts and guns overlapped; and to show how the landscape has changed over two hundred years.

processes can be seen from various points of view. These include physical mechanics, the transmission and reception of signals in light and sound; the meaning of words and symbols, what, why and how they 'signify' (semantics and semiotics); and personal and social development, how we learn the communication codes of our particular society. Such matters as tone of voice, facial expression, deliberate gesture and unconscious body language are important factors in human communication, but may vary from culture to culture.

Communication Studies have their own models by which communication processes can be analysed. A basic one might read something like this:

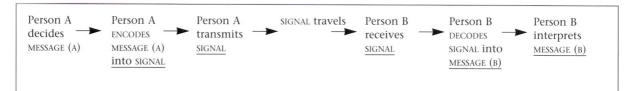

| Person A decides MESSAGE (A) | → | Person A ENCODES MESSAGE (A) into SIGNAL | → | Person A transmits SIGNAL | → | SIGNAL travels | → | Person B receives SIGNAL | → | Person B DECODES SIGNAL into MESSAGE (B) | → | Person B interprets MESSAGE (B) |

In the basic communication model (above), note that at each of the five underlined stages human or mechanical error can cause distortions. MESSAGE (A) as intended by Person A may become something different – MESSAGE (B) – in the mind of the recipient, Person B.

Here, MESSAGE (A) is what Person A wants to communicate; the ENCODING represents the symbolism or convention by which the Message can be transmitted as a SIGNAL and presented to the receiver by the medium of sound (spoken words, noises), visuals (written words, signs, symbols, gestures) or something else (moths can communicate by smell, and most animals, including humans, by touch). Encoding is the translation – deliberate, unintentional or both – of a Message into a Signal in some Medium. Decoding is the reverse process, which elicits a Message from the Signal.

The significance of this kind of analysis is, first, that it distinguishes between the Message, the Code and the Signal; secondly, that it highlights the independent existence of the Signal – that part of the process when the encoded Message has left the sender but has not yet reached the receiver; and thirdly, that it reminds us that these Coding and Decoding processes (the working of the mind) may result in imperfect communication or interpretation of the intended Message. Success depends largely on the skill of the Encoder, but partly on the experience, knowledge and skill of the Decoder. MESSAGE (B), with any luck, will approximate to MESSAGE (A); but under certain circumstances it may not.

It is not difficult to transfer these concepts to Interpretation, and to expand them a little in the process (see facing page). As an example of Message, Technology, Technique and Code, let us imagine that we want to communicate to visitors the significance of some ruined walls at the site of a medieval castle. The Message[1] may be 'These ruins are the remains of the gatehouse that guarded the entrance.' The Form in which the Interpreter frames his message could be a direct statement, or even a question: let us suppose

1. Used here in the Communications sense of the meaning to be conveyed by a particular signal. If used in the general Interpretation sense it would indicate the wider concept of what the Interpreter has chosen from all he feels that the Feature has to say.

The Feature and
physical
circumstances

The Interpreter: how
he devises and passes
his message

Visitor patterns
and profiles

Conceptual

THE MESSAGE
that the Interpreter selects
from all that the Feature seems to say

↓

THE FORM
in which the Interpreter decides to express
the chosen message (the rhetoric)

↓

THE MEDIUM
by which the message, in chosen form,
is to be received by the Visitor
(i.e. sound, sight, touch, smell, taste)

↑

Technical

↓

THE TECHNOLOGY
by which the message is to be
transmitted by the chosen medium
(e.g. direct speech, print, film/video, audio
cassette, computer screen, etc.)

↓

THE TECHNIQUE
by which the message is encoded for
transmission to the Visitor by the chosen
technology (e.g. written text, pictures with
captions, cartoons, computer database,
live drama, etc.)

↓

THE SIGNALS
(encoded) that travel by the chosen medium
to the senses of the Visitor

↓

DECODING
in which the Visitor does his best
to recreate the original message
from the signals that his senses receive

The diagram (left) is a simplified model, in which arrows indicate continuous logical flows of influence rather than any time sequence.

Not only will the MESSAGE and its FORM influence the choice of CODES, TECHNIQUES and TECHNOLOGIES, but vice versa. Implicit in this tangle of interactions is the fact that the nature of the Message partly determines how it is to be communicated. The software, we might say, helps determine the hardware; while the hardware may impose constraints on the software.

It will be noted that the Interpreter has choices to make at every stage; and that any single interpretational presentation may involve a variety of technologies and techniques.

that in this instance he chooses to use a self-explanatory drawing rather than the written word.

The Technique by which the message is encoded might be an artist's impression of the gatehouse as it was when in use, showing the drawbridge down, human figures passing through and guards on duty. Other Techniques would be to have a cut-away drawing that shows the floors and rooms within the gatehouse; or a drawing labelled to identify different features of the building. Cut-aways and labels are generally recognised conventions or Codes that can be carried by two-dimensional graphics. The Technology might be a reproduction of the drawing, placed on a low-level panel so that the Visitor may look from the panel to the Feature with the minimum of discomfort.

For the Interpreter who often has to communicate at a remove from his audience (by means of permanent graphics or video film, for instance), the separation of Message, Form, Technique, Technology and Signal is a crucial concept, for his whole aim and intention are, at each step of the process, at risk. At each step he may unwittingly weaken or distort the original Message. At the point where his control ends, the Code and the impersonal Signal travel alone, to be received by the senses of the Visitor: will the mission be achieved or not? The same process, of course, occurs when one is communicating directly. The moment may be infinitesimal, but even a word or gesture becomes a signal in light or sound, and for a fraction of time it travels on its own, and cannot be called back.

RHETORIC: GIVING MESSAGES 'FORM'

The effectiveness of a script (in the old-fashioned sense, the written words of a book or a play) has long been seen to depend not just on the actual words the writer uses, but the Form of his work. Shakespeare communicates with us by philosophical verse (his sonnets), narrative (his early poems) and drama. Within his drama he uses reportage; soliloquy; conversation; comment; songs; spectacle (actors fulfilling his stage directions), and humour. Interpretive scripting has this important element of Form too. Different Forms are available for describing, informing, explaining, analysing, surprising, challenging, delighting, amazing, testing, comparing, recommending. These ways of giving Form to the gist of a message are what used to be called Rhetoric – the skills that all writers, public speakers, barristers and Interpreters need to study and practise. Here are some of them.

Simile and comparison. These may seem the same, but simile expresses subjective notions of likeness, while comparison is more precise and analytical. Similes can simply add to our ability to visualise a scene ('His goats grazed, scattered about the hill, their great udders swinging like bagpipes beneath their bellies'[2]), but they can also add to our understanding ('The English identity was like a rope

2. Gerald Durrell, *My Family and Other Animals*, Hart-Davis, London 1966, p. 41.

which depended for its strength upon the many strands of regional culture'[3]).

Comparisons may be visual and artistic;[4] or intellectual rather than imaginative. The coastal pastureland to be found in Cumbria and Lancashire at places around Morecambe Bay can be compared with similar landscape near the ancient town of Dol on the north coast of Brittany. Comparison is not only able to reveal similarities, but can just as well point out the significantly dissimilar, and explain contrasts. The cob walls of Devon and the clay lump farmyard walls of East Anglia are both built of unbaked clay, but the techniques differ – the Devon walls are protected from the weather with a little roof of tile or thatch, while the East Anglian walls are normally rendered with plaster and painted with tar. Fens and bogs are both waterlogged, but strictly speaking fens are alkaline, and bogs acidic. Comparison points out the differences, and the differences then need explanation in terms of why and how.

Posing questions instead of making statements can provoke Visitors to think, to become aware of dilemmas, to solve problems and to admit feelings.

Story-telling illustrates a point with an anecdote or parable.

Cumulation builds up evidence, arguments, points and lists.

Demonstration shows how something is or can be done.

Naming can give immediacy, reality, individuality and particularity. Characters may be obscure and previously unknown to Visitors, but naming them helps to 'personalise' information: 'In 1742 William Grantley was hung from a gibbet erected at this spot, for demanding money from travellers on a stage coach.' Similarly, to tell visitors that in a certain fen grow 'marsh pea, yellow rattle, fleabane and spotted orchid' is more vivid and informative than a vague generality such as 'several interesting marsh plants grow here.' Such naming must of course be accurate, for knowledgeable specialists may read the sign, too, and it should be used with moderation, and only to embellish statements that are significant in their own right.

Media other than words have their own techniques and conventions. Mime has its own; so do cartoons, in single frames or strips (with different degrees of abstraction in the drawing and uses of captioning); so has film. Even in still photography there are subtle differences in what may be communicated by different angles of shot, lenses, lighting and proportions in the format of the print itself.

Each Technology has its own Techniques. Some Interpreters may become masters of one or two of them. Not everyone is strong on live guiding, scriptwriting *and* display design, but all Interpreters should recognise the principles, and wherever necessary seek specialist help to achieve particular communicational objectives. Aim for the best: second-rate work always shows up.

3. Richard Muir, *Shell Guide to Reading the Landscape*, Michael Joseph, London 1981, p. 23.

4. See the lovely book *David Gentleman's Britain*, Weidenfeld and Nicolson, London 1982.

TECHNOLOGIES OF COMMUNICATION

Signals vary enormously in kind according to the technology involved, and encoding has to be different in each. Can you imagine trying to communicate, to a person who does not know your language, the notion of climbing the stairs of a lighthouse? You may start by resorting to the code of gesture or of mime. It might be easier to use the comparatively high technology of paper and pencil, encoding in two-dimensional graphics – but even that may be difficult!

If, on the prairies of North America, your technology consists of a smoky open-air fire and a blanket, your code is going to be made up of the patterns you can make in the rising smoke, and you can only communicate with someone else in this way if you yourself have the necessary technology, techniques and knowledge of the Code to send a message, and if they have the necessary knowledge to receive it.

If your technology includes a simple electric circuit, you can break the circuit at one end of the wire with a switching mechanism in such a way as to make a light or a buzzer go on and off at the other, in patterns that stand for letters of the alphabet – the code devised by Alfred Vail for the communication technology invented by Samuel Morse in the 1830s. But if either you or the person at the other end is weak on Morse code, if they cannot spell or do not know how to switch the receiving machinery on, or if you happen to speak different languages, your attempt at communication is likely to fail.

The very phrase Information Technology emphasises the multiplicity and complexity of modern methods of communication. We can transmit sound by cable (telephone) or radio; we can store it on magnetic tape, or in microchip (solid state). Visual images, which until quite recently were confined to stills in two dimensions (drawings, photographs) can now be transmitted in motion (by film, radio waves or cable) and will soon, no doubt, be presentable in three dimensions. Storage of such images can be achieved through film and electronic means including magnetic tape (video) and solid state.

The origination of visual images has a varied technology of its own, including photography, video and computer generation. These technologies are widespread and evolving so fast that a decade can bring a communication revolution. To become literate in new systems may mean learning a range of new technologies, techniques and codes. As part of the population makes a point of doing so, others, to varying degrees, are left behind. The Interpreter wants to communicate with the whole of society, not just the technologically updated. Sophistication brings its own problems.

During the Second World War, British citizens quickly learnt that a siren sounding a note with alternatively rising and falling pitch gave warning of an impending air raid, and they took precautions accordingly. When enemy planes had left, a continuous note with a level pitch announced that the danger was – for the time being – over.

CODES AND SYMBOLS

Smoke signals, Morse, shorthand, air-raid sirens and the world's alphabets all show how codes are devised for different technologies. Language itself is a system of codes – a different set of sound symbols in speech and graphic patterns in writing for every language. Letters are really symbols that represent sounds made by the human voice – i.e. they are symbols of symbols. We have to remind ourselves that they can be displayed as three-dimensional objects, projected by a beam of light through a transparency, transmitted by radio waves to be reconstituted on a visual display unit (VDU), or transformed into the raised bumps of Braille.

The Signals by which we communicate must be definable in terms of the senses of the receiver: the Sender, whatever technology and coding he may use, has to channel the Message through the sense organs of the Receiver. There is no other route, and Interpreters who want to communicate their messages must always keep the physical, social and mental situations of their Visitors in mind.

Many kinds of symbol other than words can be transmitted visually or in sound. Graphic symbols are commonly and internationally used to convey warnings or instructions, processes or identities, emotions or information. The symbols used to represent topographical features on a map are appropriately known as 'conventional signs',[5] reminding us again that their meaning has to be agreed between the map-maker and the map-reader. Computer operation is increasingly simplified by the use of arbitrary icons. Musical notation is similarly 'conventional' – and not everyone is able to read its conventions. Every representational drawing or painting is a symbol – marks applied to a two-dimensional surface to represent an external, three-dimensional reality, at a given moment in time. A black-and-white landscape photograph is a mere convention: it needs to be reinterpreted by the brain in colour, and in three dimensions.

Living with conventions and symbols all around us, we become so familiar with those we use that it is easy to overlook the fact that other people may not understand them. Not everybody is aware, for example, that the abbreviation '4to' means quarto, which in turn refers to a book whose leaves consist of sheets of paper folded twice. Mathematicians, chess-players, knitters, physicists, doctors, choreographers – they all use their own formulas, meaningless to those not in the know.

Communication has to be done through symbols: there is no other way. But it is useless – probably even counter-productive – to express something in a code that your audience does not recognise or may misunderstand. Interpreters need to choose symbols that, as far as possible, are familiar to everyone, and that are best calculated to carry the particular nuances of the Message to the audience intended – that is, that are best suited to their Circumstances.

A person watching an old film for the first time may be puzzled when a character falls asleep in a chair, the image wobbles and fades, and the character suddenly reappears in a different situation and in different clothes. The viewer has to recognise and add to his schemata this early screen convention to signify a dream.

5. The word is derived from the Latin *conventio*, agreement.

10 Particular cases
Limitations and possibilities

It would need a bigger book than this to consider all the possible situations in which interpretation may be offered and received. Is anything that we encounter in our natural, historical or cultural environment not worth understanding? The opportunities for sharing such understanding must be infinite; and even if the means of communication available to us are somewhat less than infinite, at least there is scope for experiment and imagination. On occasion our commonplace repertoire of leaflet and information board may seem predictable and uninspired.

It may be helpful to pick out a few interpretation opportunities, various situations and means of communication, and to consider what their limitations and possibilities really are. The interpreter, when exploring possibilities, should be something of an original, even a lateral, thinker. Most importantly, he must always keep his eye on the ball, and not allow himself to be diverted from his main aims, those we have tried to expound in earlier chapters.

ASSOCIATIONS

I use the term here in the way that second-hand booksellers use it of books, to indicate that a main interest of a particular copy is its association with some interesting person or event. Wall plaques on buildings often commemorate associations, but are they interpretation? Some are and some are not, just as some have more public significance than others. Information, or the manner in which it is presented, can sometimes carry overtones that may be of greater significance than the statement itself. The secondary, covert or incidental message may be as important, or even more important, than the primary, overt or intended one.

The village of Eyam in Derbyshire is known for deliberately imposing a quarantine on itself at the time of the great plague of 1665–66; by their heroic deaths, the inhabitants prevented the plague from spreading. Many houses and cottages in this village carry simple signs saying, for example, 'During the plague in this cottage John Wood died in March 1666; Francis Wood died July 1666.' No elaborate inscription could convey to the twentieth-

> Associations might be termed the QUELSH factor: Queen Elizabeth Slept Here. Just how many buildings survive in which Queen Elizabeth I spent the night during her 45-year reign (1558–1603) has probably not been calculated. There are certainly very many: the QUELSH factor would have more rarity value if she had stayed at home more or died younger.

century traveller the extent of the village's stoical suffering more movingly than this series of brief statements, almost identical but for the names and dates they list. These signs do not interpret the village as we see it – the architecture, the ground plan – but perhaps they help us understand how important an element community solidarity was in our ancestral past.

AUDIO-VISUAL PROGRAMMES

Some communication media, we may hope, will never die. Surely, books with leaves will never be entirely displaced by hand-held VDUs, will they? Writing and printing are likely to survive a while yet – graffiti on walls, scribbled notes pinned to the door, receipts and theatre programmes should last another generation or two. Even the old-fashioned lecture and the discussion group (favoured by Socrates and the frequenters of Academe in ancient Greece) are still in use. Conversation is not likely to become obsolete.

Innovations in technology do not necessarily invalidate earlier systems of communication. The slide-tape programme is the most basic prerecorded sight and sound medium, yet it is highly effective and versatile. The skill in preparing such a programme is to get the balance right between visual image and spoken commentary. The mind of the listener/viewer tends at any moment to be concentrating more on one than the other, so to overcrowd either the images or the text is to waste one of its virtues, the mutual reinforcement of messages received.

> *'On this site', stated a plaque in Norwich, set on a large blank wall, 'stood the pre-Conquest church of St Christopher destroyed by fire in the late 13th century.' Our appreciation of the brick wall is not in the least enhanced by this information. The statement appears at face value to be non-interpretational, but has this plaque an oblique message? Perhaps: 'This city is mighty old, and it once had even more churches than it has now.'*

10:1 Information that entertains, but scarcely interprets

'From the above window on November 22nd 1772', runs the wording on a cast metal plaque on this old house in Newcastle, 'Bessy Surtees descended and eloped with John Scott, later created Earl of Eldon and Lord Chancellor of England.' 'So what!' the spoilsport visitor might remark. Perhaps we could read into the text the moral 'Don't be afraid to be unconventional – you may still become a great man.' What was the thinking behind the erection of this quaint memorial? Perhaps the city fathers, or the owner of the house, or a descendant of the protagonists of this little incident were just having a quiet boast. In a way, it does not really matter, because the story cannot fail to generate some pleasure and a smile. But it is hardly Interpretation.

Meanwhile, we are left wondering how this extraordinarily fine, half-timbered, obviously old house comes to remain standing near the Newcastle riverside, in what appears to have been until recently a busy industrial and commercial area. It can also be argued, of course, that it is more fun to come across these architectural puzzles as a

surprise, rather than always find that someone with an improving mind has got there first!

And it is rather disappointing to discover, if you look up Lord Eldon in a biographical dictionary, that this free-thinking young man grew up to be 'a poor statesman, opposing reform and religious freedom'.

Two virtues of this medium are its self-imposed quality control (it comes over as good as ever each time it is presented); and the fact that good photography, tight scripting and sensitively read commentary can make every image, every word, reach home to the audience. Not a moment, even a moment of silence, need be wasted: the system can convey a message more efficiently, in terms of words and time, than even a good speaker showing slides manually. A good way to present such a programme is for an expert to introduce it personally; then run the audio-visual programme (perhaps just ten or fifteen minutes long); and then give a personalised talk to the audience and answer questions. This pattern enjoys the best of all interpretational worlds – variety, conciseness, immediacy, participation.

It is sometimes said that people want a moving image these days. This is not always so. The static image can be savoured in a way that a moving image cannot. It can be quite hard eye-work to keep up with a movie, and it is easy to stop listening attentively to the voice-over in case one misses something significant in the momentary images on the screen. Where the moving image wins is in the depicting of how things are done, how objects are made, how tools are used. In explaining manufacturing processes, for instance, film or video may even have the advantage over personal demonstration, since a long process can be shortened, or the craftsman's hands shown in close-up.

BATTLEFIELDS

Battles are often important and influential events, though the ordinary person – as opposed to the military historian, the partisan enthusiast or those who love war games – may find it difficult to get excited about them. Some people sanitise warfare by interpreting battles as if they were games, like chess or football, in which we can admire the skill of the general as he makes his moves, or the teamwork of the side we support. Others see only the glamour of war – shining armour, clashing swords, Laurence Olivier promising that his soldiers would be for ever proud to have fought at Harfleur on St Crispin's Day. There are those who get a vicarious thrill from victories won by their ancestors many generations ago; while the descendants of the defeated, by brooding on the long-past event, can keep political or racial hatred glowing even in the present.

What exactly is our experience of a battlefield? An Englishman can gaze over the green fields of Bosworth, or an American walk along the Battle Road at Concord, Massachusetts, or Europeans visit the site of Waterloo, and there is not a thing to be seen (except signs, plaques or visitor centres) that needs to be explained in terms of the battle for which the site is famous. We see the countryside as nature has since reclothed it or as man has adapted it. The landscape in which the battle was fought cannot be interpreted by the manoeuvring of the foot soldiers, the placing of the artillery, the movements of the cavalry some centuries ago. The truth is the other way around: the manoeuvres, the artillery stations, the cavalry charge, could, on the day of the battle, be interpreted in terms of the landscape.

The Feature to be interpreted at a battlefield is not in fact the site at all, it is the story. The site's relevance is merely that something significant happened there, which was influenced by the lie of the land. The battle did not make the site but, in a sense, the site influenced the battle – and thus the legend that is part of our heritage. The Trojan War, the wooden horse and the exploits of Ajax, Achilles and Helen are elements in the interpretation of culture, not landscape (even if Hermann Schliemann did correctly identify the site of Troy).

The stories of Culloden or Bosworth or Concord are part of national history, and national history is part of national culture. The facts of history are material that can be used in interpreting the culture we experience today. A battle site is yet another place whose significance is association – a reminder of history, not a product of it.

COMMUNITY PROJECTS

Community projects come in great variety; as well as encouraging social cohesion, they can do much to enhance a community's sense of place and history. An adult education class that tackles an exercise in local history will properly include fieldwork as well as documentary research, and should lead to a presentation of the group's findings for other local people to share. Some such exercises have resulted in publications, some in exhibitions, some in Parish Maps (see page 133). From the Interpreter's point of view, these presentations can be a little too specialist, perhaps because the class has learnt a good deal about how to decipher documents, but little about how to recognise what can be made significant to less academic people.

Mini nature reserves are another bright idea. Communities find (or beg from a local landowner, or are bequeathed) small spaces that may be managed for wildlife and public amenity. I know one such reserve in a former garden, and another in an odd corner of a field that abutted on a village street. In many of our cities are other examples, tended by enthusiasts on former wasteland. Creating and maintaining such a reserve can involve the local parish council, the local school and youth club, and many volunteers. Because it can be visited and enjoyed by all, it can provide an intensive and continuous interpretive experience for a large number of people. Once again, its interpretational value will inevitably depend on how the scheme is promoted, led, managed and publicised.[1]

1. The County or District Planning Department and the county or city Wildlife Trust may be able to help with aspects of such a project.

A redundant and partially ruined church has been looked after and restored by local enthusiasts. Practical conservation work in woodland or marshland, the restoration of a village pond, bird and insect surveys in town parks, hedgerow surveys in country parishes, preparing a new church guide leaflet or planning a series of walk routes or archaeological digs (authorised and with expert supervision, of course) – all of these, arising out of neighbourhood conditions, can stimulate the interest of local communities.

There are at least four key qualities for such projects, if they are to be interpretational.

Openness. A scheme should not become the almost private hobby of a self-selected few, but deliberately welcome and involve all. Anyone who has taken part in community schemes will be aware of the inevitable hazards, hassles and heartaches, but if it is intended to provide an interpretive experience, then the more who are involved and learning, the better.

Expert input is a second essential quality – it is important to have someone who knows and will explain the why and the how. He or she can suggest alternatives, discuss, be patient, give time and trouble, laugh and be sociable, and inspire.

Being seen is the third essential. This is another way of ensuring that the benefit of the activity is spread around the community. Hold open days, come-and-help days; report to the local press; raise funds by jumble sales or whatever; maintain interest; arrange an open meeting to launch the scheme, and another later to report on progress.

Ensuring on-going benefit is the fourth essential. It is a shame to wind up a scheme by depositing a single copy of a report in the local history library, and then letting all the effort be forgotten. Some accessible memento of the project should remain – a publication, a natural history or local history club, a physical monument (a nature reserve, a parish map, some permanent display in the local church, an interpretation panel). Let the know-how and the understanding be passed on to another generation.

LIVING HISTORY

We have considered battlefields. What about the value of re-enacting battles in period costume and with period equipment? The interpretational worth of historical re-enactment can be no better than the extent of its realism. Mercifully, you cannot re-enact a battle with full realism, whereas you can reconstruct work on a Victorian farm, or even the running of a watermill, with minimal risk to life and limb. Like a period play or film, staged activity enables visitors to experience something in replica that can no longer be experienced in reality. What you are doing is creating a 'virtual reality', by which the lost reality of the past can be explained and interpreted.

At the Chiltern Open Air Museum, Chalfont St Giles, Buckinghamshire, there is always something happening. Medieval peasants are here going about their chores (above), while one of them takes time off to chat with a twentieth-century child. How authentic their costumes and implements are, and their activities, is a matter for experts to determine. Obviously, shortcuts have to be taken – but how can the visiting public be persuaded that what they see is an accurate enactment of the past?

It may be easier to impress small children, who will more readily accept the idea of being able to chat with folk from a past age, and who will marvel at procedures so different from what they see at home. Adults will need convincing that they are watching something more than pleasant play-acting with not-quite-authentic props or dialogue. Did people really cook and carry on domestic crafts outdoors in the middle ages? What did they do if a sudden shower came on?

It is fascinating to watch a skilful lace-maker or wood-turner, or to see butter being churned or fabrics dyed, because although we have often seen the finished articles, we are nowadays hardly ever present when these crafts are practised. Interpretation by demonstration is as much a comment on our remoteness from manufacturing processes today as it is on the occupations of our forebears.

Many readers will have experienced some kind of interpretation by costumed guide, or visited an old house where verisimilitude is provided not only by period furniture but by people in period costume. Does this 'interpret'? One of its functions may be to enhance the visitors' sense of period: the experience leaves a strong visual image in the mind. For example, folk in Anglo-Saxon dress doing Anglo-Saxon things certainly reinforces one's appreciation of the reconstructed village at West Stow, Suffolk.

Further south in the same county is Kentwell Hall at Long Melford, where the owners have built up a deserved reputation for the way the Hall and estate are peopled, for the benefit of paying visitors, with Elizabethans or Jacobeans – according to the year that is being reproduced at the time. The enthusiastic volunteers who take part have to make their own costumes from natural materials from head to toe, with no anachronisms – no twentieth-century glasses, no wrist-watches, no plastic buttons on the doublets, no trainers peeping out from beneath the gown. Each person is allocated a name and a role, and throughout the exercise must live that role continuously. All participants are briefed about the news current at that date – is there an Armada scare? Is there news of Mary Queen of Scots? And, most difficult of all, they must, even in the face of enquiry by visitors, refuse to know about anything outside their own period:

'Do you come and dress up like this every year?'

'Aye, Madam, I have lived near here since I was a child.'

'No, *really*, I mean.'

'Upon my honour, Madam, I speak truly.'

Butter is made in the dairy, wool is spun and woven. All is done well, and it is the thoroughness of the commitment to near-authenticity that is its virtue. Quite apart from what is learnt by the paying visitors, think what insight into the period must be gained by the dozens of volunteers, some of whom spend two or three weeks on the job. When you visit Kentwell during the re-enactment season, it is worth letting your mind willingly suspend disbelief – don't spoil things by wondering where all these Elizabethan characters sleep, where their cars are parked, or whether they drink beer out of cans when the visitors have left!

MAPS

Maps can be helpful tools; but just as a carpenter needs several chisels to do different jobs, so maps, if they are to be really helpful, need to match each task for which they are intended.

Maps on outdoor panels have very limited functions. On some district council boards, they can illustrate quite complex patterns of footpaths. Unfortunately, the ability to memorise a map is a gift possessed by very few; most of us may think we have memorised it, set off boldly, then after a hundred yards hesitate, and have to go back to check up. Providing a map on an outdoor board in the hope that the mere memory of it will guide Visitors round a two-mile route is a waste of money and effort.

What can a map on an interpretation board usefully do? If so designed, it can make the point that a certain area has many varied habitats. It can indicate general features to be encountered within, say, a country park – a lake, some woodland, the former mansion house, a maze, a tumulus – though on its own it will not be able to get the visitor there (that is a job for footpath signing). A map can also illustrate the relationship between features that cannot be appreciated from any one point at ground level – for instance, how a castle is sited both to guard a road route, and to use a river as part of its defence.

For finding one's way on an interpreted route, a specially prepared map may be a great help. I once lost my way, however, using a countryside trail guide whose designer had drawn an oversimplified map on which the route was indicated by a thick coloured line without enough other features by which to check one's position. Luckily, the local footpath network was well signed and it was possible to get back on track.

The Parish Map concept is very different; like so many other community-based projects, its benefits consist largely in the creative experience of working together. The aim is to produce a map, in any medium, that expresses a community's current vision of itself and its territory. Such exploration, research and discussion, and the discipline of having to express the results in a publicly accessible form, could hardly fail to be an eye-opener for those who become involved (see appendices D and E).

ENTERTAINMENTS IN PERIOD STYLE

Medieval banquets can be great fun, but the ones I have attended were only minimally interpretive. I now know what it is like to eat off a wooden plate, and I have tasted mead, but I am little wiser about life in the middle ages, medieval halls (one 'medieval' banquet, by the way, was held in a Victorian Gothic banqueting hall), the constraints that determined one's manners at manorial banquets, or even the evolution of cutlery. False experience can never really enlighten. To appreciate the way a medieval banqueting hall operated, you would need to know what the kitchens were like, and where they were sited. You would have to appreciate the function of the high table, and of the two doors that so often can be seen today at the back of ancient halls. A medieval banquet at which everyone – apart from an over-mirthful 'host', a jester and the serving wenches – wears twentieth-century holiday clothes is no more than a good laugh. A pair of minstrels who sing *Greensleeves* to the accompaniment of a guitar, and follow it up with *Annie Laurie* and *Old Macdonald had a Farm*, or a jester whose performance is the set patter of a twentieth-century stand-up comic provide little insight into medieval entertainment. It is all simply good fun, and not intended to be educational.

There is no reason why a meal should not be interpretational, though. A themed meal could have a printed menu that included comment, rather like a concert programme with notes on the works. A 'wild food' supper, with comments on the species; a 'Shropshire dinner' with notes on the county's traditions of food production; a 'Mrs Beeton' menu with the original recipes reprinted. Novelties such as roast peacock, braised alligator, seaweed and moose milk could all have their taste and texture appropriately interpreted.

As for entertainment, why settle for clumsy modern pastiche when the very plays, music and dances of the period are known to us? We can be fairly sure that not everyone would much enjoy *authentic* medieval entertainment (the dances tend to be monotonous, and the plays not always easy to understand), but presented interpretationally in smallish chunks, it could be a fascinating challenge.

What actually might an Elizabethan entertainment be interpreting? The only reasonably sound answer is 'our heritage of Elizabethan culture'. If we believe that a Feature should be more concrete than that, and that Interpretation should be seeking the why and the how, then we might hope to demonstrate or learn something as unexciting as the functions of the minstrels' gallery, or the service passage at the back of the hall – so long as the event was held in authentic premises.

NATURE TRAILS

Nature trails, the novelty of the 1960s, became the interpretation cliché of the decades that followed. They sprang up at a time when nature conservation was beginning to enter popular consciousness, evidence of the synchronisation of the naturalists' concern to interest the public with the public's readiness to be interested. Guide booklets listing all known English nature trails were issued, followed soon by handbooks on how to set them up.

It is interesting now to consider what the users of nature trails were hoping for – and, indeed, what they hope for today. Apart from the pretext for getting out into the countryside, and the convenience of having someone else to suggest a starting point and a route, a nature trail offers the hope of seeing wildlife, and of having animals or plants identified for us. These hopes, however, can be frustrated and end in disappointment. The nature trail has its limitations, caused by the changing of the seasons; the furtive mobility of wildlife; our own lack of experience in looking, and the very severe difficulty the novice has in identifying species.

Naturalists know that what you are likely to see in summer you are less likely to see in winter; what you may hear in spring you will not hear in autumn. Flowers have their seasons to bloom and die back; seasonal migrations mean largely different bird populations at different times of the year. Animal mobility means that even if a wood abounds in deer or squirrels, nuthatches or white admirals, you may still be very lucky to see one in half an hour's walk. Species cannot be easily identified until you have acquired a basic repertoire of the commoner species – especially if all you have to help you is a line drawing of a woodpecker on a board that you passed a hundred yards back, or that you won't encounter until you are a hundred yards further on. Even if you carry a guide leaflet with some illustrations, the chances are that the species you spot are not those shown in the leaflet.

The two strategies available to the provider of nature trails are to recognise these limitations and try to overcome them; and to try a different approach altogether. You can try to overcome limitations by providing different information season by season. This might mean having two to four different sets of noticeboards, or ensuring that at least some of the boards have seasonal alternatives. Specially designed fixing methods might be needed to enable changes to be made easily. The animal mobility problem might be overcome by concentrating on plant species only – and even then you might have to plant some appropriate specimens surreptitiously along the edge of the path.

As for how to look, you can always offer hints: don't talk; walk slowly; keep your eyes peeled, especially when you enter new spaces; try sitting down and waiting for twenty minutes, and watch and listen carefully; experiment by examining detail – look under leaves, peer into holes. Your guide text could refer only to features that are conspicuous (trees, hedgebanks, areas where plant species are massed), and make it extra clear where to look for them. This, and the rudiments of species identification, are always much better achieved through live guiding than by means of print.

The second strategy, to try a different approach, requires imagination and perhaps some lateral thinking. Why always a nature trail? If a certain route has other elements of interest (former land use, archaeological features, farming practices), why not mention them, too? Very often such things interact with the wildlife anyway. Would a general guide leaflet with a footpath map be better than interpreting at fixed stopping points? It might be supplemented by a live guiding system at peak visiting periods, or occasional special events or open days with interpretation built in to the programme.

The important thing is to recognise visitors' problems, and then deal imaginitively with them. As in all interpretation planning, think creatively – and do not automatically do the obvious.

SPECIAL EVENTS

This generic term describes one-off happenings that include some kind of Interpretation (see the List of Terms, page 13). Instead of having something permanently available on a small scale for people to visit (such as an outdoor interpretation panel, or a semi-permanent indoor display), you gather together dozens or hundreds or even thousands of people on one day – a context in which Interpretation may be offered either to more people than usual, or in a form whose expense is only justifiable because it is experienced by people in large numbers.

The Broads Authority in Norfolk and Suffolk has experimented with Interpretational riverside puppet shows. Conservationists take stands at county agricultural shows. Two or three times a year, the Chiltern Open Air Museum invites groups that specialise in period re-enactment. English Heritage mounts performances and displays that are intended to enhance appreciation of the historic and cultural background of the houses, castles or monastic ruins in their care. On late summer evenings *son et lumière* (a modern descendant of the old-fashioned pageant) tells the story of buildings with narrative, music, silent action and lighting effects. Country parks, museums, farms, visitor centres, town halls, factories, nature reserves and lifeboat stations may all announce open days. Special events must offer entertainment, but they can easily and justifiably be used as vehicles for Interpretation. Interpreters may mount their own events, with Interpretation as a prime objective, or they can take a stand or a spot at someone else's. The advantage in both cases is the chance to grab the attention of more people than usual, in a special context with special opportunities.

Large numbers of the public are attracted to county agricultural shows because they know they will have an interesting and varied day out. Anyone who has manned a stall at such an event knows that of the many thousands of visitors present, maybe two hundred may visit your stall, and only ten may take much interest. Success is measured by the results of the interest of those ten. This may seem a small and uncertain reward for all the effort involved – but how else would you have the opportunity to address two hundred people in one day that you have not met before?

Other special events may be more focussed, and the audiences more truly captive. A *son et lumière* performance may involve two hundred people watching and listening to your programme for an hour or more. It is probably the closest that Europe gets to the camp fire setting of Interpretation so popular in American national parks.

Making the most of such opportunities needs careful thought and, as ever, an appreciation of the nature and mood of the likely audience. These will differ according to the type and location of the event. A vintage car rally will attract a different audience from that found at a falconry display, and the spectators' interest will have to be engaged by different means. Clearly, if a theme is specialised, a significant proportion of the audience are likely to be already interested, though others may be present out of intelligent curiosity. Any element of Interpretation should be relevant to the general theme.

TOUCH SCREENS

These interactive retrieval systems can be great fun. If you know what you want, you can dig out in a matter of seconds information that might take twenty minutes of searching in a library – provided it is programmed in! Or – what most users at high-tech interpretive displays seem to do – you can 'surf' them in a spirit of serendipity. A display on the history of one London borough has a whole bank of such screens, backed up by sound. The material available at the touch of a finger includes not only statistics and information, but stills and clips from old film that illustrate selected themes very effectively. All this will mean more to local residents than it can do to visitors, who are unable to relate the images and names on the screen to the place itself.

It is now becoming more usual to find this kind of equipment installed in museums to interpret their collections. The touch screens at the Sainsbury extension to the National Gallery in London are really an illustrated, high-quality database, and they are housed in a special room. But at the Manor House Museum at Bury St Edmunds each room is equipped in this way, so that it is possible to move the eye directly from a display case to the screen and back. It serves as a sophisticated museum label, but one that offers whatever kind of information you ask it – and much more information than any label could carry. The extent to which such information is truly interpretive will depend, of course, on the nature of the programming.

AUDIO CASSETTE

Audio cassette interpretation can be splendidly effective in the right contexts, and there are some things it can do superbly. As with the slide-tape programme, the script can be refined and improved until it reaches something near perfection in choice of subject matter, skill in exposition and clarity of wording. Secondly, each user, having personal playback and control of the switches, can move at his or her own pace without missing anything. Even better, you can rewind and listen to a section a second time if you want. Thirdly, the recorded message can easily include instructions about where to look, which way to walk, when to switch on or off, and so on.

Good audio guides (such as those to the island of Jersey, for example) will ensure that the user crosses roads safely, and is always on the right side of the street to see the feature under description. But the content of some of the Jersey tapes sound like readings from local newspaper articles – and an audio text needs to be written in quite a different style.

The limitations of audio guiding by personal stereo are, first, that it is rather isolating – you cannot immediately share your experience with a friend, because after a few minutes you will be

138

10:3 A guide that does not rush you

Several years ago Stephen Weekes, owner of Penhow Castle, Gwent, South Wales, thought up a new way to show visitors around his home. He created audio guides to be played back in portable cassette players. These were not just guide books read into a recorder, but were devised as a fresh art form, using the opportunity to mix in, where appropriate, music, dialogue and sound effects. The very first thing the Visitor hears when he switches on are simple instructions about to use the equipment, and where to begin the tour (left).

This kind of sound guide is quite common now, though because it requires equipment and cassettes it is largely restricted to sites with a controlled entrance and exit. Its advantages include ensuring that the user uses the route the proprietor has chosen; offering a carefully and professionally prepared script that never falters; the capability of providing dramatic or other interesting effects; holding the attention of the listener very closely indeed; and allowing Visitors to follow the route at their own preferred speed. Guide cassettes to towns or other uncontrolled sites may also be available for playing on the Visitor's own equipment; they can either be bought outright, or hired with a refundable deposit to ensure they are brought back.

I still remember the excitement of the first time I switched on the hired headphones at Penhow Castle. Instead of the old-fashioned guidebook language I expected to hear, read in a 1950s newsreader voice, my ears were filled with a thrilling fanfare of trumpets and drums. The experience was exhilarating, even before the commentary started.

listening to different parts of the commentary, and you cannot talk to each other and listen to the tapes at the same time. Secondly, you cannot ask questions, which is all the more reason why the script must be perfect and the performance of it clear and unhurried. Poor scripting, poor commentating or poor recording quality can spoil the experience. Scriptwriters may be tempted to imitate the style of radio plays, with regional or period voices, ambiguous background noises, music. To produce good audio interpretation requires specialist experience – professional advice, scripting, reading and studio work will almost certainly be needed. And even radio professionals are not experts in interpretation.

The latest audio guide development consists of hand-held solid-state units with keypads – keying in numbers will summon up commentary on whatever aspect of the Feature you want, even in a choice of languages. Personal miniature video handsets may soon be available, though there must be few situations in which such a facility would be the best interpretational medium.

VISITOR CENTRES
Visitor centre, like nature trail, is a term we are now familiar with. The name does not necessarily imply, however, that its aim is interpretation any more than the provision of tourist information, or

of shelter, rest, refreshment or an opportunity to buy souvenirs. Some are equipped to offer all these facilities, as well as a base for staff, while others may just be outlets for propaganda or places to sell entrance tickets or recruit supporters. The interpretive value of every place that calls itself a visitor centre cannot be taken for granted. In Britain there has been a rash of such centres over the past two decades, some really excellent, others poor. Some may have been established for prestige reasons or because funds or grants happened to be available, and may now be regretted by their proprietors because of the cost of keeping them open.

Since a visitor centre meets only those needs of the Visitor that the proprietor chooses, it is hard to say what constitutes a good one, except that the range and standard of its provision should be appropriate. It is easy for a centre to offer too much, too little, or something in the wrong style. If it offers interpretation, then it is better that it be pitched modestly and well than extravagantly and poorly. The other vital element in a good centre is what we might call visitor-friendliness. A large, silent interior – with no sign of human presence except for a closed door with 'Office' on it – is less effective than a small one where a friendly warden or ranger looks up from a table and smiles as you come in.

A visitor centre should be able to act as the hub of a range of interpretation activity – walks, demonstrations, events – which brings the visiting public into direct relationship with staff who can introduce them to the Feature. Face-to-face interpretation can be much more effective than any other: visitor centres should ensure that staff and Visitors do actually meet.

If a centre has an interpretational display – and most do – then it may as well take advantage of being indoors, and try to engage Visitors' interests in several different ways. These should not be just written statements and pretty pictures, but some three-dimensional material as well; something interactive, however simple; something living, perhaps; models, a relief map, or a table with chairs so that you can sit down and flip through a reference book or an album of photos. It may be possible to provide a simple two- or three-minute video or slide-tape programme, or a closed-circuit presentation if there is anything interesting nearby that moves, such as a mill-wheel turning, birds nesting, or a craft or industrial process that can be watched.

There is, of course, little point in showing on screen what Visitors could perfectly well see by stepping out of the door. If aspects of the Feature to be interpreted are within sight of the centre, then ensure that they can be viewed and explained from a window. If elevation is needed, consider an upper floor or a viewing platform. Such variety of media must be selected primarily to convey appropriate messages: any advantage they bring in maintaining the interest of Visitors is a bonus.

11 The entertainment factor
Interpretation and fun

'Five minutes to go before the show!' yells a uniformed commissionaire. 'A thousand years of kings and queens!' Where is he drumming up his public? A theme park? Madame Tussaud's? No – this is Westminster Abbey, and he is calling them in to the Westminster Abbey Experience. *This real-life scene was filmed for a programme presented by the playwright Alan Bennett on Boxing Day, 1995. Such showmanship itself becomes part of the 'experience'. For some, such an introduction is just what they need to stimulate interest. But mood, atmosphere and ambience are significant in people's appreciation of an experience, so there may be a few visitors who leave the abbey feeling that they have discovered something new and disappointing about humanity in the mass rather than the significance of one of the world's famous historic buildings. Bennett, by careful comparisons and juxtapositions of images, and a commentary characteristically low-key but flavoured with inferences and allusions, was actually offering an interpretation of human behaviour.*

Fashion and ideas affect the business of Interpretation just as they affect so many others. Some years ago the slogan was 'The fewer words the better': an exhibition that consisted solely of visual images made, it was believed, few demands on the Visitor, and demonstrated the virtuosity of the Interpreter. More recently, the favourite has been 'Interpretation should be fun.' At first hearing, both seem to demonstrate a Visitor-friendly approach, but both maxims (as is usual with generalisations) were hopelessly, even disastrously, misleading advice for any would-be Interpreter not in the habit of thinking much. Imagine what Dr Joad would have made of the second of these. 'It all depends', he would have said, 'what you mean by "interpretation", what you mean by "fun", and what you mean by "should be".'

Presumably interpretation in this context is the visitor's experience of encountering INTERPRETATION – the Interpreter and his whole set-up; rather than *interpretation* – the process of enlightenment. 'Fun' is more difficult. Does it, in this context, denote satisfaction or amusement, enjoyment or hilarity? Is it meant to include or to exclude the word's common overtones of party frivolity? In the television sitcom series *Hi-de-hi!*, the 1950s holiday camp host instructs his novice assistant comedian: 'You'll get thrown into the pool about four times a day – we've got to keep the fun going . . . It's fun and laughter all the way.'

Is fun more to do with the sense of satisfaction after an experience, or the sensations during it? Does it include the emotional fears of the bungy-jumper, the physical agonies of the long-distance runner, the mental frustrations of the researcher? No doubt they all enjoy what they do, or they would not go on doing it. 'It's good fun,' they might say, even though the activity does not double them up with laughter. If it is fun to be with friends and family, is it 'non-fun' to be enjoying oneself alone? Does fun depend on having some kind of jolly leader?

As for the phrase 'should be', it is important to know whether this is to be read as a plea from the Visitor (in which case we must admit that many Visitors would probably insist that 'fun' is the wrong word); or a rule for Interpreters (many of whom would, I suspect, regard the statement as a partial and occasional truth rather than a constant one).

Visitors are not all the same, and do not always meet Interpreters in similar contexts or approach them with similar motivations. Age, degree of interest, who they are with, their reasons for being here, the nature of the place – all affect the kind of fun, enjoyment or satisfaction they are seeking. The basic division is perhaps between those who hope to learn something, however informally; and those who come for different reasons, but might welcome intellectual stimulation in the guise of entertainment.

ENJOYING THE AGONY

Taking part in sport is fun. But it can be exhausting: you can limp off afterwards, bruised, sweating and tired out. Even within the field of the arts there is hard work and pain. The concentration and teamwork involved in a drama production or a quiz competition, playing in a band, singing in a choir or performing in a ballet can be a trial of endurance, making demands both physical and mental. But it can also be great fun. And what is more, you do not participate in these activities without commitment and preparation. Some demanding forms of interpretation can be enjoyable; conservation work – digging ditches, clearing scrub – can be interpretive even if blistering. Research or study can be mentally exhausting as well as interpretive.

Yet most Interpretation offered is deliberately undemanding. Visitors are not expected to have prepared themselves, nor is any commitment required. They are probably seeking some kind of stimulus, and it is to be hoped that they will become involved, apply their minds and enjoy themselves. But all this can be true without invoking some imprecise notion of 'fun' as a prime element – that only confuses the process. Idealists will hope that the true experience of interpretation will be a profounder joy; realists will be generally more modest in their expectations.

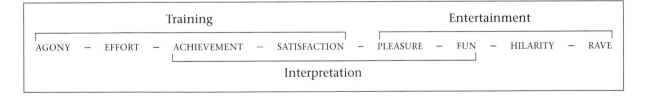

'Agony', 'effort', 'satisfaction' – the very words are imprecise, and their meanings and overtones grade into each other: the list (above) forms a sort of continuum. The first half probably concerns earnest trainers, and the second half light entertainers. Interpreters inhabit mainly the middle territory – bridging the gap between training and entertainment, but not needing to offer their wares

11:1 The annual Mud-In

Young people, such as these members of a young naturalists' organisation, usually have plenty of energy to expend, and also like to be involved in anything a bit crazy. Digging mud in order to create banks for retaining shallow seawater after each tide, so that waders and other birds may feed, satisfies both requirements. Members of this group regularly devoted their August Bank Holiday weekend to the annual Mud-In, digging all day, sleeping each night on the hard floors of a nearby hall and finding time to prepare their own food as well. Each year they would volunteer to come back and do it again. It was fun.

But they were also serious naturalists, learning about habitats and plants, birds and other animals. They observed, they kept records, they wrote up their results in their own newsletter. They organised most of their own activities, calling from time to time on parents or other well-wishers to transport them to and from their meeting places, and on adult naturalists whenever they wanted advice, demonstrations or introductions. Their activities were self-supporting, with the local education authority youth service staff giving practical help. A number of these youngsters went on to play active roles in nature conservation as adults.

under the name of either. Certainly, on the one hand, understanding may sometimes have to be achieved with effort; and, on the other, the pleasure of learning can often be considered fun. Effort and laughter are not mutually incompatible.

Not everyone can sustain non-stop hilarity, just as most of us do not want to exert non-stop effort. We tend to seek different contexts in which to sweat and to laugh: we do not expect to be doubled up with mirth the whole time we are in a museum, stately home or coalmine, any more than we expect to be constantly and uncomfortably challenged. The occasional chuckle is as welcome as the occasional puzzle, but an Interpreter would need to be very clever and charismatic to do effective work in an atmosphere either of agony or extreme mirth.

Rather than trying to define 'fun', it may be easier to agree what 'non-fun' is. I would suggest that the opposites of fun include: boredom, pomposity, pedantry and lack of humour. Those are qualities that anyone who wants to be listened to should avoid.

WHAT GIVES ENJOYMENT?

It is not difficult to separate out some of the elements that contribute to enjoyment in the context of Interpretation. These are not quite the same as the elements that 'grab' (see chapter 7), though there are similarities.

1 Novelty

To children especially, novelty tends to enhance an already enjoyable experience. Adults are essentially no different, but have seen more of the world. They may reach a stage where the familiar is most enjoyed, and novelty has become a little threatening, or at least discomforting. If you offer senior citizens novelty, you may have to find ways of wrapping it within the familiar – for example, by having a friendly interpreter chat them through the experience step by step.

To most of us, to experience the latest technology is entertaining and gripping just because it is the latest. How many exhibitions of three-dimensional holograms have there been in the past decade? As a technology becomes commonplace, so its power to attract lessens. Touch screens are now familiar, so their intrinsic novelty is wearing thin. But because they enable our fingertips to summon up the unexpected, their attraction and usefulness will no doubt continue.

What is the future of 'virtual reality'? As an entertainment it is splendid, so long as its improvement can keep ahead of people's rate of disillusionment. As an instrument of interpretation, I would suggest that it is unlikely to be of any more value than other tools that are suited well to perform specific tasks but that cannot be of much use otherwise. Interpretation is concerned with interpreting reality. Simulated reality (such as a photograph or drawing) can be a useful tool to help explain something, but you need to define and experience the genuine thing, too. In Interpretation, virtual reality may prove to be a useful aid, but should never be considered a substitute for real experiences.

2 Participation/interaction

I have suggested that the fun of interactive technology wears thin as familiarity grows. But while the technology may cease to amaze, the potential for interaction lives on, and much of the fun in that remains. Being able to do something, to interact, can in itself be satisfying. Watch the process, and see how people will wait their turn just to pull a lever or press a button. Observe behaviour at the big London museums of Natural History, Science and Geology. Observe children (and adults, once they have overcome their self-consciousness) at some of the recently created science parks or discovery centres. Some children will simply rush from one game to another, operating levers and switches indiscriminately. This is not surprising: physical discovery is satisfying them more immediately than mental discovery. Running around operating things is fun, even if you do not learn much more than the fascination of exercising manipulative power.

Participation does not have to be high-tech, and can be at its most useful and effective in face-to-face situations. Farm open days

A few years back, a folk museum was looking for ideas to update its presentation and interpretation. Someone had seen, at another attraction, a three-dimensional 'talking head', which was obviously fascinating a crowd of viewers. It was decided that the museum's new scheme must incorporate the idea, in order to 'attract visitors'. Whether it would enhance visitors' understanding of the museum's holdings, whose head it should be, and what it should talk about – these things were not yet considered. Since the museum was at a site already much visited and associated with other famous features, the likelihood of its drawing greater crowds on the strength of possessing a multi-thousand-pound hologram was an irrational dream. Novelties tend to have a short shelf-life.

11:2 Rapt attention and happy smiles

Among the countless hands-on opportunities at Eureka!, the interactive museum for children in Halifax, Yorkshire, is a television studio complete with cameras. The whole purpose-built complex and its contents are dedicated to education through discovery. Here, if anywhere, Interpretation is fun. 'Eureka!' ('I have found it!') – the exclamation of Archimedes of Syracuse echoes cheerfully down the centuries. A museum for children? Yes, but see the delight of the adults, too.

Most of what is called Interpretation is site-based – that is, it explains a specific object or place. This is a sound principle, but we also experience phenomena other than places, and it would be a ruthless purist who refused to allow the term to be applied to more ephemeral experiences, such as music or dialect, or more general and pervasive experiences, such as weather, human behaviour or science. Is it not the immediacy of the experience, the revelatory quality of the explanation and the personal sense of discovery that add up to Interpretation?

Testimonials to Eureka! include:

'Our visit to Eureka! was brill. I do hope that we can visit again because it is the best idea I have ever heard of.' (Katie, aged 9)

'Two words – ABSOLUTELY BRILLIANT! I have just spent such an enjoyable afternoon at your museum with my four children. Both my children and myself are so excited by all the hands-on, the dressing up, the role play, the layout and the whole set-up.' (Parent, from Stockport)

and zoos often provide opportunities for visitors to touch animals, or feed them. Some raptor centres not only display falconry, but encourage the visitors to let the birds of prey come to their wrist, to feel the grip of the talons and the weight of the bird through the leather glove. I have visited a demonstration smithy where the smith chats to his audience as he works. He also invites them to join him at the forge, to hammer the red-hot iron and to feel how heavy the hammer is, and what energy is needed to wield it.

Exponents of living history often encourage their audiences to interact with them, to ask (or answer!) questions, to handle a fabric, to hold a horse by the reins, to taste the cheese they have just made. Wildlife trusts may invite the public to come and spend a day in some form of practical conservation work. Some guided walk programmes have built-in audience participation – picking mushrooms, looking for beetles, recording bird-song.

3 Interest

This has to be included, in case we forget that enjoyment is not just a matter of mood or externals. There is enjoyment to be got from learning and understanding. For very many visitors, that is what they will remember with the greatest delight.

4 Variety

A theme park will promote itself by advertising how much there is to do. Already popular venues advertise each year what new attractions they have to offer. Such promotions make sure that their print advertising – the typestyle, the colours, the capital letters and exclamations marks – shouts 'Have fun!' A theme park on today's pattern will probably not be truly educational or interpretive, however much it would like us to think so.

But there are visitor attractions that try to mingle interpretation with entertainment – rare breeds alongside a children's assault course; a folk museum and a talking head. These can either be primarily commercial money-spinners with a touch of education, or primarily interpretive with some entertainment back-up. In the former category, the public are being drawn entirely by the entertainment, while mildly interpretive panels or displays accompany some of the exhibits. A touch of educational purpose can help a venue to attract grants.

In the second category are venues that are primarily interpretive but that have decided – especially if their viability depends on visitor numbers – to exploit the pulling power of variety. If you want entire families to spend an hour at your visitor centre, you must make sure that there is enough to keep the children happy while the adults at least get a chance to learn something. This is stating the principle in the crudest terms. A good interpretive display will itself employ a variety of presentation to sustain both children's and adults' interest.

5 Quality

It is not always easy to recognise why a particular interpretational experience gives satisfaction: one elusive virtue is what we may call 'quality'. If a place that we visit is excellent and appropriate in every way – setting, ambience, facilities, interpretive presentation, friendliness, high-standard texts and visuals, graphic design and follow-up – then the sheer appropriateness, how well it is all done, will impress. This is not the same as lavishness, let alone extravagance. It need have nothing to do with carpets on the floor or the provision of high-tech units or expensive designer whimsy – it is user-friendliness and appropriateness that I mean. This kind of quality will occasionally be achieved by amateurs, and occasionally missed by professionals. Generally, however, all-round quality will depend on professional advice – modest but expert, sympathetic but imaginative professional input should always be sought.

6 Games

We all play games whenever we exercise our skills (physical, intellectual or social) merely for the pleasure of it. Some games are highly structured, with complex rules (cricket, Mah-Jong); some are simple in structure, even if quite hard to play well (lifting up a chair by the leg with one hand, solving an anagram). Yet others have no structure – situations just seem to invite us to respond ('Who does that policeman remind me of?'; 'What system shall I use today to pick lottery numbers?' 'I wonder if I can cut five minutes off the time it usually takes to drive home?'). Faced with a simple opportunity to 'play', we will often join in. Consider how willing most of us are to try and solve a crossword clue for someone else, or to take up the challenge, 'I bet you can't do so-and-so.' In interpretation, games can come in all these forms.

Highly structured games require time, and a suitable context, to get people to play. An invitation to come forward to learn steps from an Elizabethan dance, or the simulation of a town or country planning exercise require the structure of a special occasion, pre-planning, staffing and the bringing together of motivated participants if they are to succeed. If outdoor war games are interpretive, then they come into this category, too. So do organised safaris;

WANTED!

Assistant on a missing person case.

YOU

could be the private eye and ear needed to help
Polly Chrome, private investigator, solve

THE REDCLIFFE CAVES MYSTERY

*In just two hours you could find the missing
architect and help uncover a plot to threaten the
unique environment of Bristol.*

*This mission, should you decide to accept it, lets
you take part in the first cassette guided tour of its
kind in the U.K.*

*Equipped with crime-solving personal stereo and
tape, your urban adventure will lead you on a
trail through the dockland of Bristol.*

REWARD

*Resident of Bristol or visitor, you will learn so
much about change in the city environment that
an urban stroll will never be the same again.*

11:3 An invitation to play

The Bristol Civic Society (affiliated to the national Civic Trust), with support from Avon County Council and British Telecom, dreamed up the idea of interpreting aspects of their city by means of a sophisticated kind of treasure hunt. Members of the public were invited to set off, equipped with an audio tape and supporting documents, on a sort of themed architectural sleuth trail through the streets of Bristol, searching for a missing architect, Norman Moulding. It was suspected that he had been kidnapped by a rogue developer who proposed to demolish some listed building in order to erect a supermarket.

Those who took part had to search and observe architectural detail, apply their minds to process the information supplied and use it to 'solve' problems inherent in the buildings they visited. The whole interactive scheme was cleverly devised to attract the attention of the general public (leaflet, left), and to engage them physically and mentally in exploring the city, the why and how as well as the what of Bristol's buildings.

Like all interpretational methods, it had limitations: how many people would be willing to commit themselves to such a time-consuming game? Even servicing the few who did kept the staff of the local tourist information centre pretty busy. But operated for, say, a couple of months, with volunteer back-up, an enterprising and imaginative scheme like this could add a new dimension to local interpretation, and perhaps reach an audience that more conventional means might not attract.

See Heather Tarplee, 'The Perilous Plight of Norman Moulding', *Interpretation Journal*, no. 51, 1992.

ornithological, botanical or historical cruises, and holidays. You can even sign on for a holiday crossing the Arctic ice-cap with husky dogs.

Occasionally, Interpretation has been deliberately planned in the form of a complicated game for people to play individually. One splendid example was a detective story adventure devised by the Bristol Civic Society, based on the treasure hunt principle and entitled 'The Redcliffe Caves Mystery'. In terms of standard Interpretation methods, this ingenious experiment shared elements of a guided walk and a special event.

More simply structured games would include quizzes, commonly presented today by touch screen. Any simple, hands-on, try-how-it-feels exhibit in a display comes into this category. We tend to assume that a game that handles intellectual material must automatically engage the intellect of those who play it. Chess, yes – there is little physical or visual excitement to be gained from the moving of the pieces, and it is the long gaps between moves that constitute the nub of the game. But a jigsaw of a half-timbered cottage teaches us nothing about vernacular architecture, because the play that the jigsaw offers is simply the challenge of assembling the pieces. The pleasure is physical and visual, testing the capacity of the eye and the brain to match shapes and colours.

Educational card games have been in use for hundreds of years – some enterprising educationist in the eighteenth century was offering historical playing cards exhibiting Roman history, and an arithmetical game with a sum worked out on every card.[1] There are many card sets with tabulated information in the shops today. But the card game designed to interpret rather than just to supply information is probably yet to be invented.

Many would-be educational games are based on the principles of snakes and ladders or Monopoly™: 'Oil seeps into river, miss two throws.' The trouble is that these games, however dressed up, are still essentially snakes and ladders, and are scarcely more exciting for being disguised as ecology. The Royal Society for the Protection of Birds had, for many years, a travelling 'Birdbus', which journeyed from place to place providing a novel display (the very idea of a display in a double-decker bus is a novelty to most people) and for the Society a mobile recruiting office. One element, intended for children, was a bird migration game – an ornithological snakes and ladders. I watched two small boys hurl themselves into it, throw the dice two or three times with mounting restlessness, then scatter the pieces and rush on to see if they could find another game. They exacted what little physical and mental stimulus they could, but applied no intellectual effort – which is just what one might have expected. Earth Education, however, is a programme that is moderately highly structured. Developed by Steve van Matre, it enables people (usually children,

At the Norfolk Wildlife Trust's Visitor Centre at Ranworth Broad was an exhibit made of two old-fashioned rotary kitchen whisks, set into the lids of glass sweet jars. In one jar was clear river water; in the other was water with a thick sediment of organic mud. The visitor turned the handles to see how the whisk in the muddy water whipped up the sediment even though it did not quite reach down into it – thus simulating the effect of motor-boat propellers disturbing the river bed. So many visitors played with it, however, that the sediment was kept in perpetual suspension and half the point of the exercise was missed! Almost all interaction, in this sense, is a species of game.

1. R. J. Mitchell and M. D. R. Leys, *A History of the English People*, Longmans, Green and Co., London 1950.

who are less selfconscious) to appreciate the outdoors at first hand. To the children, it appears as a series of simple, organised games.[2]

Structureless games are the third category, like finding images of things in the patterns of the clouds or in the flames of a log fire. I-Spy is almost structureless, or games where you say a name, and the other person has to say another name that starts with the letter yours ended with. There are spot-the-difference games where you have two drawings with half a dozen or so small differences. This sort of game can be played anywhere with minimal equipment and scarcely any rules – but it keeps the mind exercising. Some interpretational display techniques invite this kind of intellectual play – showing a series of similar artefacts, for instance, which sets the Visitor making comparisons almost unconsciously. Or presenting a before-and-after pair of photographs – the village before motor traffic, and the village today; a scene in summer and the same view in winter; or a woven basket beside a bunch of willow stems straight from the withy bed.

7 Wit and humour

It has been said that humour consists in subject matter, and wit in the skill with which it is expressed. Few of the matters we treat as Interpreters – certainly not the basic principles of how the world works – are essentially funny, so in Interpretation wit may have a bigger and more useful role than humour. This is interestingly borne out by the use of cartoons. There are humorous cartoons and witty cartoons.[3] A humorous cartoon exists just to be funny – the traditional seaside postcard sort of funny, a fat man lying in a fragile deckchair, or a drawing with a caption involving a *double entendre*. A witty cartoon makes a point, maybe quite a serious one, in a clever way, a way that is revealing or thought-provoking.

Most interpreters are not comics, and amateur humour can be positively embarrassing – though it all depends how far you go. Unless you can get unbiased critics to agree that you do it brilliantly, you may be wise to leave the more extravagant forms of wit and humour to the professionals.

2. See Steve van Matre, *Sunship Earth*, Acclimatization Experiences Institute, Illinois 1979.

3. And very solemn cartoons, too – among the very best are the political ones drawn by Bernard Partridge for *Punch* in the 1930s and 1940s.

I once attended a supreme demonstration of teaching through humour in the USA, among professional interpreters. It was advertised as an Ornithology Lecture by Professor Avian Guano (alias Denny Olson) from the University of Bird-lin. A crow-like person entered, wearing a black gown and a large white false nose. Nervously darting his head backwards and forwards rather as apprehensive chickens do, he made his way around the floor. The climax of the slapstick was when he stood in the middle of the floor and a carefully contrived gadget in the ceiling plopped a dollop of white stuff on his head.

Then came the lecture. It was a brilliant exposition of bird ecology, illustrated with superb colour slides. It was still delivered in the crow character, but it came over with the greatest clarity as a revelation of principles demonstrated by facts. It would have been first-rate interpretation even delivered straight: set in this matrix of wit and humour, it was a tour de force.

8 Glitz and razzmatazz

Carnival time is probably not the most suitable moment for interpretation. Uninhibited fun can be marvellous – so can fancy dress,
the finales of musicals, Las Vegas, fireworks displays and wild
parties, even the more extrovert political rallies. Interpretation
requires a more thoughtful mood, though not necessarily a solemn
or an exclusively conscientious one. Its context does not have
to be tranquil and purely intellectual. Understanding can be
accompanied by emotion – joy, laughter or even sadness – but it
does, as the word itself suggests, have to have an intellectual
component.

What of the Disneyland factor, that larger-than-life, mind-
blowing showmanship that is now part of the world's cultural
vocabulary? At the risk of sounding like a spoilsport, dare I suggest
that our understanding of the world is best fostered in situations
where the mind is not 'blown', and where experiences are the genuine size of life rather than inflated parodies of it? Some visitor
attractions, professing to be interpretational, draw their crowds by
sheer extravagance of concept, by lavish trappings and vast expenditure on current state-of-the-art technology. They may well succeed in repaying the millions of pounds invested in them, and in
bringing in tens of thousands of visitors to spend their money
locally. But it will be interesting to see how they are rated for their
interpretational achievement, in a few years' time and with hindsight. It is possible that much more modest enterprises may interpret more effectively. The tourism industry might say that this
comment misses the point, but here rival philosophies will beg to
differ.

'Interpretation should be fun'? The four-word slogan is far too
vague and emotive to be helpful. 'Interpretation should be enjoyable', if you like. The Interpreter is not concerned with amusement
that does not instruct, but knows better than to provide instruction that does not amuse. Perhaps James Jennings got it more or
less right in 1829 with that 'amusing and instructive lounge' (see
page 30).

(see page 30).

149

*Some visitor-attraction complexes
cheerfully and shamelessly mix,
in their promotional material,
what appears to be inter-
pretation with sheer showground
excitement, as though one might
pause in the midst of a ride on
the ghost train to expound the
ecology of spiders.*

**'Enjoy the wonders of Wookey
Hole; Britain's most
spectacular showcaves'**

*The slogan employs an
interesting term for a geological
phenomenon.*

*'Fairground memories; traditional
paper-making; the Witch of
Wookey; an absorbing collection
depicting the 50,000-year
history of the caves, with sections
on geology and archaeology;
Magical Mirror Maze.'*

*These are phrases selected at
random from an advertisement
in the Somerset Mendip holiday
brochure for 1997. Whether the
educational and interpretational
messages get through
successfully, among the heltering
and skeltering, would be an
interesting subject for study.*

12 The business angle
Implications for management and finance

I have emphasised that providing Interpretation is not just a matter of learning mechanical procedures or following sets of instructions, like pruning a rose or replacing a washer in a tap – it is an art as much as a craft, and cannot be satisfactorily undertaken without some understanding of theoretical principles, and the exercise of creative imagination. But we must also face the fact that Interpretation always has to be carried out in the harsh context of everyday life. To work, it has to be compatible with the realities of logistics and economics.

Just as some Interpreters are essentially practical people, never happier than when manipulating the nuts and bolts of communication techniques, others may be essentially visionaries, artists whose temperaments are most at home with ideas and concepts, words and images. Similar divisions of skill can be observed in the world of music, for example. Composers, performers and impresarios are all needed when it comes to putting on a concert.

The world of Interpretation can be organisationally just as complex, though there is almost infinite variety. Certain situations that are simple, such as going for a country walk with a knowledgeable friend: this is the equivalent, perhaps, of a pianist inviting a few friends round to listen to a sonata or two. All that is required is to choose a date and a place, remember to practise beforehand, and hope that your friends turn up.

On the other hand, there are Interpretation's equivalents of celebrity concerts in the Hollywood Bowl or the spectacular entertainment at the opening of the Olympic Games. An Interpretational entrepreneur may be considering a multi-million-pound visitor centre to occupy hundreds of Visitors at a time with a mix of all the latest computer-coordinated electronic tricks. The books must be balanced, and the more complex the situation the more daunting the financial risk.

These are imaginary extremes to emphasise the point. They may serve to remind us that the person we call the Proprietor or Promoter is a very important contributor to any interpretational set-up. Someone has to initiate every new scheme; someone has to finance it, to accept legal liability. Who is to provide the money for the multi-million pound project? Rarely the Interpreter, for sure! Who owns the stately home, the cathedral, the nature reserve? Always, someone stands to gain or lose – whether it is their money, their time, their job, their comfort or their reputation.

The owner or trustee of a Feature is rarely also its Interpreter, though there are exceptions. Examples I know include a blacksmith who has opened his village smithy to the public; he is expert at explaining his work as he goes about it, and has even adapted the building to make it safe for visitors. The second is a family that runs a mixed farm; concessions to visitors' comfort or fastidious-ness are minimal and the interpretation is primitive – you must take the farm as you find it, muck and all. The third example is at Kentwell Hall, Suffolk, a superb sixteenth-century house whose owners, as well as restoring it structurally, have developed to a high pitch of expertise a system of interpreting it to the public by means of period re-enactment of daily life (see chapter 10, page 132). How-ever, even these simple exceptions reinforce the point that as soon as you offer Interpretation to the public, you have to cope with the consequences. These include hard work and inconvenience, team leadership, legal responsibilities and financial risk.

RESPONSIBILITY FOR SAFETY

The blacksmith could find himself in trouble if a visitor got burnt, the farmer if someone slipped in the muck and hit his head on a piece of machinery, the house-owner if someone put a foot through a floorboard and twisted an ankle. As well as being careful, they must also be insured.

If a local authority runs a guided walk programme, it will ensure that the guides employed (including volunteers) are briefed not only to be aware of the dangers of crossing a road at the head of a large group of people, but also to know what to do if a child cuts a hand on barbed wire while climbing a stile. On a well-organised guided walk, the guide or a colleague will be carrying a simple first-aid kit. They will have instructions about what to do if it pours with rain, or if someone announces, half way round the route, that they cannot walk another step.

If something goes wrong, someone is legally responsible. Any risk must be minimised, by attending to at least three important things: always put safety considerations on the planning agenda; get expert advice as appropriate – from the Fire Service, Ambulance Service or Health and Safety Executive, for example; and ensure that all staff, whether full- or part-time, paid or voluntary, are trained and briefed about safety and first-aid procedures. The local surgery telephone number and the whereabouts of the nearest tele-phone should be displayed in all buildings to which the public have access. The back-up, in case you do have an accident in spite of careful preparations, is appropriate insurance cover.

The business angle   151
Implications for
management and finance

152   The business angle
Implications for
management and finance

Even recommending routes for a self-guided trail, offered to the public in leaflet form, has its risks. The route that leads users to the edge of a quarry so that they can see the rock strata might be the cause of someone slipping over the edge. To point out the architectural detail on a building high above a busy street could result in a scream of brakes and an ambulance siren.

It should go without saying that any permanent indoor exhibition or display must be planned to observe fire regulations. This may involve providing and signing an emergency exit; providing fire extinguishers; ensuring that the route out is clearly visible; limiting the number of people who use the facility at any one time; and ensuring that the materials of which the display is built are fire-resistant. The local Fire Service should be consulted.

Temporary exhibitions or one-off large gatherings (special events) need just as much care. The larger the gathering, the more likely it is that at least someone will fall ill or get hurt, or a child get lost. Perhaps the St John Ambulance Brigade or their equivalent should be asked to be on duty. Provision should be made for access by vehicles of the emergency services.

PROVISION FOR THE HANDICAPPED

Another responsibility, now widely accepted, is to make facilities as far as possible accessible to those with physical or other handicaps. Those who have sight or hearing problems will obviously not be able to benefit from all media – it is worth bearing this in mind, and trying to mix media accordingly. A presentation that includes both sight and sound will be at least partially accessible to those with impaired vision or hearing. Designers need to be briefed on this matter: people with impaired sight may find it impossible to read text in very small type, or to cope with certain contrasts of colour and tone. Those who are hard of hearing can find the spoken word unintelligible if it is backed by even moderately loud music. Live guiding can be more flexible and responsive to the needs of individuals, but guides will need advice on the best ways to communicate with handicapped visitors.

Wheelchair access is a purely physical matter, though the designer's thinking should go beyond the provision of ramps, lifts and extra-wide doorways and spaces. Other factors to be considered are the height above ground of graphics and display material. Much good practical advice has been published, and Interpreters should have it to hand.[1]

COPYRIGHT: A MATTER OF MORALITY AS WELL AS LAW

Copyright is a matter on which good advice is desirable; Interpreters, as communicators, may want to quote or at least rely on what others have done, said or written. The legalities can be quite complex. The basis of the law is that while facts are common

1. See appendix E and page 172.

property (deemed to be in the public domain), the form in which they are expressed may not be. Creative writers or artists are entitled to the benefits of their own skills, and anyone who tries to exploit their productions for gain is, in effect, stealing someone else's personal property.

Essentially, authors, artists and designers or their assignees are automatically protected by law against anyone making unauthorised use of their work until seventy years after their death. Even if you write a letter to a friend, it is you alone who have the right to the form of words you have written – not the recipient.

Morally, the worst offence is to lift chunks of text from another person's work, and to incorporate it into your publication as if it were your own. The original may perhaps be out of copyright, and thus beyond the protection of the law, but a self-respecting writer will never steal a phrase or even a sentence from another author and pass it off as his own.

It is perfectly acceptable to quote from someone else, even if copyright has not expired, so long as it is made clear that the words are someone else's; the source is acknowledged; and permission is given by the author (if still alive) or his or her literary assignee or heir. Permission will not be needed if the quotation is very small – say, just the title of a book, or a phrase – or where a short piece of text is quoted just in order to prove or disprove a point, or so that you can comment on it. But wherever a sentence or a passage or some lines of verse form a quotation that stands in its own right – that is, if the original author's words are used just to enhance the value of the new work – then permission must be sought. Quite apart from the law, good manners require that we err on the side of being conscientious about this.[2]

Where an intended quotation is fairly short – say, a paragraph or two – permission may, if you are lucky, be given readily and free of charge (acknowledgement must always be made). But the holder of the copyright is entitled to refuse permission, or to ask a fee. Equally, you may then exercise your own right not to use the quotation after all. Generally speaking, an acknowledged quotation will do the original author no harm, and may even encourage your reader to go and buy his book.

Permission is best sought via the publishers, who will, if they are able, tell you where the copyright lies. But publishers do sometimes close down, get taken over, or fail to answer letters – pursuing the matter may become tedious, but it has to be done.

The design aspect of making acknowledgements is sometimes awkward. It is particularly difficult in the context of exhibitions and displays, where permissions and credits can be hard to accommodate without distracting from the main messages. It may be best to incorporate a separate announcement at or near the end of the display. It is probably within the law to make such acknowledge-

The business angle   153
Implications for
management and finance

2. If in doubt about the legal position, consult an up-to-date book on the subject, or the appropriate chapter in the current *Writers' and Artists' Yearbook*.

154 The business angle
Implications for
management and finance

ments in small type, but moral duty demands that they should be seen, not hidden.

Reproducing illustrations is subject to similar restrictions – and this includes photocopying text from books or any other printed matter for republication. It must be remembered that a fresh printing, even of an out-of-copyright work, is itself subject to reproduction restrictions; so that you may not photocopy for publication or display even a poem by Shakespeare from a recently printed edition of his works (though it is long free of author's copyright). Having text reset by a typesetter may be the best solution – that particular setting is then your own copyright, and you could start suing those who photocopy it without your agreement!

Copyright protects Interpreters

Interpreters have the benefit of copyright too, of course. When scripting, illustrating or photography is done by an employee for his or her employer in the course of employment, and with the employer's equipment and materials, then the copyright rests with the employer. Whenever such work is done by an independent person, then it is his responsibility to ensure that provision for copyright is agreed to his satisfaction at the time any contract is drawn up, or before handing such material over to another party. This matter is often overlooked, but it can lead to embarrassing confrontations if it is not clarified at the outset.

It is not uncommon for clients of Interpreters to try to insist that any copyright in their work is to be vested in the client for any future use whatever, rather than be restricted to the purpose for which it is designed or written. The Interpreter (writer or artist) is entitled to insist on retaining the copyright, while the client pays only for the right to use the work in that specific display or publication.[3] If the client draws up what the Interpreter thinks is an unfair contract, then the latter should either dispute it (at the risk of losing the job!) or claim a higher fee for forgoing copyright. If the client's concern is the perfectly reasonable one that the material should not be used by anyone else, it may be possible to agree in the contract that the author/artist will not re-use or re-sell the same work elsewhere; but that if the client were ever to want to re-use, alter or sell it, the author/artist should have the right to be consulted and either forbid it, or be involved in its re-editing and negotiate fresh payment for it.

INTERPRETATION'S SHORT SHELF-LIFE

Interpretation has to keep moving, and certain forms of it can quickly become out of date. The more expensive forms of presentation – visitor centres, indoor displays and outdoor panels, for instance – carry with them certain problems of maintenance, updating and decommissioning.

> *I once walked into a riverside pub and found that it had made up a display about the adjacent waterway by means of large (but poor) photographs of an exhibition that I and two other professional colleagues had created for a voluntary organisation. To add insult to injury, they had reassembled the various bits of the exhibition in a haphazard collage, so that its sense and ability to communicate was quite spoilt.*
>
> *Since copyright in the material had been reserved by us, we could have sued the charity, who had apparently given permission to photograph our exhibition for re-use in the pub's display. We did not sue, but I had the satisfaction of seeing the secretary blush.*

3. This could be important to the author, who might want to insist that he be credited with authorship (as is his legal right); and who might be reluctant for the client to be able to chop his text about, alter it and re-use it, possibly in inappropriate contexts, with the author's name still attached, for further gain.

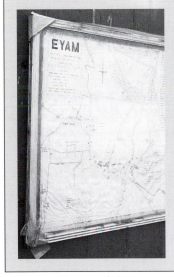

Interpretive panels showing signs of weathering.

It is usually easier to find money for interpretation hardware – say, one-off grants or sponsorship – than it is for administration or maintenance. This must account for the shabby look of some outdoor panels. The one shown above has now been removed, but for many months it stood as a reminder that signboards are vulnerable to weathering and vandalism. No sooner is one erected, than it starts to need care and attention, and the reputation of the provider is on the line.

Mildew and mould

Information presented on paper cannot be protected from weather by covering it with Perspex or polythene for more than a few days or weeks – atmospheric damp always intrudes. Better materials and technologies have been devised in recent decades. It pays to get expert advice on the matter, and to spend a little extra for materials that will endure. And arrange from the start who is to be responsible for regularly inspecting and cleaning the panel.

Few interpretation signs should stay in position for more than five to ten years anyway. Most will begin to look worn, or to fade; and the style of display, and even the information itself, is likely to become dated. The danger is that, after many years, no one may feel responsible for a panel's removal or replacement.

Outdoor panels have to be resistant to weather and vandalism. Even the toughest and most expensive may have to endure not only graffiti and scratches, but ultra-violet light (which fades colours and degrades certain plastics), rain, frost and heat (which damage different materials in different ways), atmospheric pollution (which results in the deposition of dust and sometimes greasy dirt), and algal and mossy growth (wild nature, albeit on a small scale, gaining a foothold in any cracks, gaps or ledges). If the panel happens to have vegetation nearby – grass, weeds, shrubs or trees –

156   The business angle
Implications for
management and finance

these will grow much more quickly than one imagines, until the approach becomes barred by brambles or nettles, branches block the view, or wet leaves drape the whole of the panel like a soggy patchwork quilt.

Indoor displays are just as vulnerable in their own way. Glue unsticks, corners curl, fingers press and rub the graphics, sweet wrappers, chewing gum and cigarette ends are poked into crevices, and dust settles so insidiously that you do not notice until someone draws a face in it.

The content and style of interpretation also date surprisingly fast. So much time, effort and money can go into a major Interpretation scheme that those who promote it can be forgiven for imagining that it really is a once-for-all job, there for the public to enjoy for all time. Not at all. And there are few things so glum to behold as a display that was created to attract, inspire and inform, allowed to survive until it repels, depresses and misleads. Publications also suffer from the passing of time. Any Interpretation material that looks or reads as if it is more than ten years old is probably already losing its power to communicate.

The mid-term budgeting for any scheme involving interpretive hardware (a display or outdoor panels) should reckon on a sum of, say, one-tenth of the original cost to be available each year for a regular programme of replacemement and renewal. This would enable displays to be updated or replaced as part of a rolling programme of improvement to keep visitors happy, and would ensure that virtually everything could be renewed within ten years. Any organisation that undertakes an interpretation scheme must anticipate such needs, and make financial and practical plans to meet the costs. Such plans should be written into the Interpretive Plan for the scheme at the outset (see chapter 13).

INTERPRETATION AND MONEY

We could classify Interpretation schemes into three classes, according to their financial strategy. First, let us consider those that are to be provided as a free service to the general public – by local government, a commercial organisation, a charity or an individual. In these cases, the promoting body will earmark from specific funds or budgets monies to provide interpretation. These monies will consist of capital invested in hardware such as information boards, printed material, audio-visual equipment or a visitor centre; and regular funding to maintain the scheme and, where relevant, to pay staff. If the scheme is to remain a free service, the administrative costs will have to be provided on the same basis as the initial capital outlay, and covered from local taxes or by the provider. The scheme will be seen as an amenity provided for the public's free interest and enjoyment.

A second category will be schemes that are intended to be self-

> *One major Interpretation scheme I knew fell into disuse. It once consisted of dozens of outdoor panels over an area of more than 2,000 square miles, and a series of printed guide cards to about 60 different sites. The panels gradually deteriorated until they looked appalling, to the shame of the organisation responsible. In many cases, local people took the matter into their own hands and prised them off their posts or walls and threw them away. In one or two instances unknown benefactors looked after them, and have done their best to prolong their usefulness, but they will never be replaced. Most of the remaining guide cards – which had cost thousands of pounds in charitable and other grants – went into store, deteriorated, and had to be destroyed.*

The business angle 157
Implications for
management and finance

supporting. This implies that the promoters, however they raised the initial capital, intend that the scheme should earn enough money to maintain itself, even to be extended or improved. Educational and conservation charities have been doing this in Britain for some time. The National Trusts are good examples: Interpretation is subsidiary to their main aim of preserving historic buildings and significant countryside, and not strictly essential to their secondary aim of providing public access, but it is properly seen as reinforcing both. The Trusts would never provide Interpretation for its own sake, since that would be beyond their charitable aims and intentions. But insofar as it enhances the public's enjoyment and appreciation, and encourages more people to visit Trust properties and to take up membership, they are glad to provide Interpretation. In one way or another, Interpretation earns its keep.

This principle can be extended to the component parts of an Interpretation scheme. The addition of a new item to a range of publications may be acceptable in the hope that it will pay its own way – it should make sufficient profit to cover the cost of reprinting when the initial supply runs out. With similar intentions, one might instal a coin-operated video or slide-tape programme.

The self-supporting principle is always at the mercy of national economics. Whenever the public 'feel good' factor operates, and so long as transport is inexpensive, schemes that are on the borderline of viability may succeed. One imaginative educational and interpretational project that regrettably went under is featured overleaf.

Many council-owned country parks in Britain have visitor centres. They often double as headquarters for the ranger staff, who may have responsibility not only for providing direct services for the public, but also for maintaining the essential qualities of the park through conservation management. The visitor centres will include Interpretation, usually of the conventional two- and three-dimensional display sort, but will also be places where the public can meet the rangers face to face, and from which activities such as guided walks or open days may radiate. In this context, Interpretation can seen both as a service to the public and a mechanism for enhancing management. No cash may change hands, but in a sense it pays its way. This indirect contribution to the management of a site or project is hard to quantify in financial terms, but must be evident to those involved.

The third category must be those Interpretation schemes that are intended to make a profit for someone. There is a fine distinction between Interpretation schemes that make money, and money-making schemes that exploit Interpretation. But there is no reason to object in principle to the idea that an interpretational amenity should provide a modest living for its Proprietor (see chapter 2). We may urge that if any Proprietor of a visitor attraction

An Interpretation Centre was created at a certain privately owned country park largely because it would add one more simple attraction to enhance a family's day out. It cost remarkably little to set up, because there was a suitable farm building available to be converted for the purpose, and a skilled estate staff with the equipment and materials to convert it. The first display was produced at a budget price, and lasted at least five years, though by then it was beginning to show signs of age. Unfortunately, the Proprietor had to be careful in balancing the park's books and there was just not enough cash in hand after five years to afford a good-quality replacement.

Bodmin (left) is a steel narrow boat which used to work on the canals of the English Midlands. Some years ago she was bought by an enthusiast who repaired and refitted her virtually single-handed, and who set up a charitable trust to enable her to cruise the western end of the Kennet and Avon Canal with a travelling display explaining historical and wildlife aspects of the waterway. Visitors would also be able to peep in to the cabin and imagine what domestic life on such a boat must have been like.

To fulfill these educational aims, the trust sought and received grants. A number of little cubicles, each with a desk and seating, were built in to the boat, and two sets of interpretation panels were commissioned and fitted, and all seemed set fair. This facility was designed primarily for schoolchildren, though *Bodmin* would be able to receive members of the general public at weekends.

The viability of the scheme was to have been underwritten by a busy programme of school visits. But its launch coincided with a poor period in the British economy, which gave rise to restrictions on school spending. There were too few bookings: a delightful and imaginative project had to be abandoned, and the boat was sold.

makes part of his living in the name of Interpretation, then his Interpretation should be well presented and genuinely educational.

Interpretation on its own hardly ever pays for itself entirely. When costed out carefully, it is almost always found to be subsidised somehow. It can be underwritten by an educational trust, by national or local government or by business, or it can be pursued by private individuals as a hobby or as an adjunct to some other profit-making concern. Sometimes it is supplied by a corps of volunteers; but mostly it rides on the back of entertainment or sightseeing, and appears as a function of tourism.

Every projected Interpretation scheme needs to have a secure financial foundation. Whether the strategy is to make a living for the Promoter, to cover a proportion of Interpretation's own costs within local government, or just to make the optimal use of resources provided by a charity, careful calculations will have to be made.

The business angle   159
Implications for
management and finance

FINANCIAL VIABILITY

The main mistake to avoid when assessing the financial prospects of a new scheme is over-optimism. It is much better to under-estimate income and over-estimate expenditure than the other way around. The temptation is to try to convince oneself (or one's bank manager) that one's ambitions are realistic, by massaging the esti-mates. There was a time, in the 1970s, when entrepreneurs would assert: 'Nowadays you only have to advertise some new visitor attraction for the public to start flocking in.' But those were the days of apparent widespread affluence, and of far, far less choice of destination for the family's day out. Anyone intending to set up a tourist attraction today, even on a modest scale, should get some realistic figures from someone else already in the business. Ask them some questions:

- How long do your visitors stay on your premises?
- Where do they come from?
- Do you get many making repeat visits?
- How much do you charge?
- What proportion of the visitors are in family groups?
- How do they actually spend their time on your premises?
- What proportion of visitors seem to want refreshments, or the chance to buy something?

The answers to these questions, taken together, should shed light on the intrinsic popularity and basic value for money of the attrac-tion, as the visitor sees it.

Other questions may indicate the value of the return on capital investment and running costs:

- How many visitors do you need to pay for admission on any one day to make it worth opening?
- What days of the week, in which months of the year, do you get that number of paying visitors?
- What times of the day, in which days of the week, do you get enough visitors to make it worthwhile to be open?
- How many visitors (including repeat visits) do you have in a year?

Other questions may reveal what are the real sources of income:

- How much a year do you take in entrance fees?
- What is your annual profit (net of staff costs and other over-heads) from any sales counter or shop?
- How much net profit do you make on refreshments (if any are provided) in a year?

Yet other questions will reveal running costs:

- How many staff do you need on duty while the attraction is open?
- How big is your annual staff bill?
- Do you employ a cleaner? How much does cleaning cost you in a year?

160 The business angle
Implications for
management and finance

- How do you promote your attraction, and how much do you spend on this each year?
- What are your electricity or other fuel expenses in a year?
- How much do you spend on security, insurance, etc.?
- Are you paying business rates on premises that form part of the attraction?

The next thing to do is to prepare an imaginary, but pessimistic, estimate of the same kinds of figures for your own project. True, visitor numbers will have to be estimated, but items such as profits on sales should be itemised as closely as possible; it is easy to over-estimate the proportion of the money passing over the counter that actually ends up as profit.

In this early, 'guestimate' stage it may be helpful to prepare three financial scenarios: a pessimistic one, a reasonably calculated one, and a slightly optimistic one. This will reveal what the possible range of viability might be. But the important thing – if you are to go ahead – is to ensure that you will be able to cope even if the pessimistic one turns out to be true. Anyone thinking of starting up such a business without previous experience should certainly attend a business management course, or seek expert advice.

PUBLISHING GUIDE LITERATURE

Consider the implications of deciding to print a colour guide to a house open to the public. First, the capital outlay. You may have calculated that you will get your money back once 10,000 copies are sold. But how long will that take? Five years, you hope? Can you afford to lock money away for so long, while inflation or interest rates may rise or fall? Where will you store 10,000 copies? Is there a risk that the furniture described so carefully in a stately home's guide booklet, room by room, may have been moved about a bit, or other important changes made, before five years are up?

Anything you publish, in print or on tape, is liable to become out of date. If a local council officer suggests printing cheap guide leaflets to local small towns, claiming that they will easily cover their printing costs if they sell at 15p each, let us hope that some councillor will be bold enough to ask where they will be sold; who will ensure a regular supply to the outlets, and how; who will collect the money; who will handle the accounting, and who will be responsible for reprinting. It would be easy to spend twice as much as the originating and printing bill on paying people to distribute the publications, and as much again on handling the money. The exercise could prove an administrative and financial fiasco.

Planning the production of publications is curiously difficult, for the following truths have to be accepted, and the options balanced and juggled until the best possible formula for your particular production and situation is reached. This 20-point checklist should help.

There is a fine old house, now run as an excellent museum by a local authority, where a sound guide had been prepared. For £1.50 the visitor could hire an audio cassette and a personal stereo player, and explore the house with the audio guide. We asked to use one, and were warned that quite a lot of the exhibits had been moved since the tape was scripted. Frustratingly, it was a well-prepared programme – just as long as everything mentioned in the script was in place. 'On the wall to the left of the fireplace,' it might say, 'you can see a portrait of the 3rd Lord Mountebank by Reynolds.' You would look up, and there would be a picture of someone in a satin dress – strange people, these Mountebanks!

Presumably no one, at the time the programme was scripted, had envisaged that the exhibits might have to be re-arranged. The cost of updating the programme, re-scripting and re-recording, had not been considered, nor the waste of money invested in the equipment if this interpretation system were to come to a premature end.

1. The more copies you print, the cheaper the production costs are per unit.
2. The more copies you print, the longer it will take to sell them, and the more space you need to store them.
3. The longer it takes to sell a stock of booklets, the longer your capital is tied up, and the more likely they are to go out of date.
4. The cheaper the production cost per unit, the more percentage profit you might dare to seek on each copy sold.
5. The more you charge per copy, the fewer you are likely to sell.
6. The bigger, brighter and better illustrated the booklets are, the more the public will want them if the price is right.
7. The bigger, brighter and better illustrated they are, the more it will cost to produce them.
8. A stiff, glossy, colour cover helps sell booklets – they appear to be better value for money, if the price is right.
9. Glossy, colour 'stitched' (stapled) booklets are much more expensive to produce than single folded sheets (leaflets).
10. You might make more profit selling 20 glossy booklets than you could on 100 leaflets, but that might leave 80 people without any interpretive literature at all.
11. So you might decide to stock two types of guide: a glossy booklet and a cheap leaflet.
12. Then you would have two publications to invest money in, and to store.
13. The simpler the booklet or leaflet, the cheaper to produce, and so the more you can print for a given outlay.
14. The cheaper the sale price, the more likely it is to sell if the quality looks acceptable.

162 The business angle
Implications for
management and finance

15. If it is cheap enough, the public may buy it even if it is obviously produced on amateur equipment (for example, your own computer), but only if it looks reasonable, and the public think they need it in order to understand the place.

16. If it is *that* cheap, your profit on each will be limited, but at least you should not go bust.

17. But effective interpretation needs good quality graphics, illustration and scripting, which will probably require professional input.

18. You may not be able to afford professional input until your sales have made sufficient profit to invest in your next publication.

19. If your product is attractive enough, you might be able to sell copies through retail outlets (shops, tourist information centres).

20. But this will mean time, trouble and expense in ensuring that the stocks are kept up; and you will see much less profit on each unit.

The only way to balance all these factors is to juggle them, setting up hypothetical scenarios of quantity, quality, printing and selling costs over various periods of time; and costing each one realistically. To find out production costs, discuss several options with a friendly printer. For information on selling prices and quantities, talk to your local tourist information centre. If you can afford it, an Interpretation consultant may be in a good position to advise, and to prepare sets of figures for you.

STAFFING INTERPRETATION SCHEMES

Some Interpretation schemes are very labour-intensive, while others require almost no staff time at all. Highly specialised kinds are among the most intensive. A battle re-enactment might involve hundreds of participants, all suitably attired and equipped. Such groups are mostly amateurs and take part in a number of events in a season; they have to be hired, for their expenses may be considerable. Other specialists would be those who work with art or drama, or who demonstrate crafts. Such skills usually have to be bought in for one-off occasions, special events. At the lower end of the labour-intensity scale are the more permanent outdoor signs. They may cost hundreds of pounds to create, but once installed should require no more than an occasional check-up and a wipe with a damp cloth, or perhaps waxing and polishing.

In between, come such useful systems as live guiding, visitor centres and publications. The man-hours required for a system of live guiding will depend on circumstances. At popular attractions – such as a stately home – it may be desirable to have a regular team of guides, whether volunteers or part-time paid, who really get to know the story of the place. But remember that maintaining a

This leaflet details a host of outdoor activities, devised and run by leaders who are familiar with the area and eager to help you discover your local environment.

 The Theme Walks look closely at different aspects of the environment - many are led by local experts.

33   Sunday 23 March, 2 pm - 4 pm
HISTORIC HADLEY

Another chance to discover the history of the area on a 5 km ramble (moderate) with Barnet Leisure Services. We'll include a stop where Edward IV secured his crown in the battle that was to end the Wars of the Roses. *Meet at Bakers Hill car park at the bottom of Bakers Hill, Hadley; grid ref 262 971.*

40   Sunday 27 April, 4.30 am - 9 am
DAWN CHORUS WALK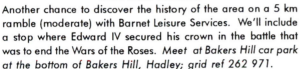

See the world wake up as you spring off to a good start with this 6 km walk (moderate) along the Stort Valley followed by a barbecue breakfast. *Meet the CMS Site Ranger at Pishiobury Park car park, off the A1184 between Harlow & Sawbridgeworth; grid ref. 476 139, (167).*

Donations welcome

41   Sunday 27 April, 10 am - noon
CHORLEYWOOD CHILDREN'S CHOICE

Fly like a bat or leap like a squirrel - it doesn't matter how you get here as long as you come! These nature games are **BOOK** aimed at 6 - 11 year olds, who must be accompanied by an adult. *Ring the CMS on 01707 650041 to find out more and book a place.*

43   Sunday 27 April, 2 pm - 4 pm
WHY CONSERVE?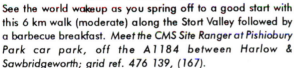

Barnet Gate woodland has been left untouched for many years .... but now a five year programme of work is underway to restore the ancient woodland to prime condition. Staff from Barnet Leisure Services will explain the work taking place on a 3 km walk (easy). *Meet at Moat Mount car park off the A1 southbound, one mile south of Stirling Corner; grid ref. 211 942. Bus - 292.*

44   Sunday 27 April, 2.30 pm - 4.30 pm
HIDDEN WILDLIFE OF THE OLD RAILWAY

Don't miss the chance to visit Mill Hill Old Railway Nature Reserve, normally closed to the public. There's a little walking and a lot of looking - staff from the London Wildlife Trust will help you identify birds, butterflies, flowers; keep an eye out for early slow worms. Ring Ann Brown on 0181 346 5011 for more information. *Meet at Deans Lane entrance, between Hale Drive and Dryfield Road, Edgware; grid ref. 202 917. Bus - 305.*

Among the biggest and most imaginative programme of guided walks in Britain must be Walks and More, arranged by Hertfordshire County Council's Environment Management Group, a partnership between the county and district and borough councils. It currently coordinates seasonal programmes totalling over 150 walks a year, each led by an experienced expert in some relevant topic – landscape history, wildlife, local buildings, or just rambling! The administration requires about half a day's office work a week. In addition, training is provided for walk leaders, some of whom are countryside rangers, and for the other volunteers. No fee is charged to the public for the walks.

It is not easy to test the cost-effectiveness of various forms of Interpretation ('effectiveness' itself is difficult to define, let alone measure), but a programme of well-guided walks is probably among the most worthwhile. Most participants come hoping to experience and learn something new, and face-to-face interpretation is acknowledged to be the most effective form. What is more, the investment in hardware is nil, and the administrative costs comparatively small. Those schemes that do take a fee from the users probably more or less cover the costs of the necessary publicity.

Items from a leaflet promoting Hertfordshire County Council's Walks and More programme.

roster of guides is itself very time-consuming, for it involves time-tabling, frequent phone messages in and out, emergency substitutions, training and monitoring performance, and continual on-the-spot supervision if everything is to run smoothly. The importance of staff training is considered in chapter 15.

Visitor centres will normally need to be staffed whenever they are open, especially if one of the main aims is to provide person-to-person contact with the visiting public. How many staff are needed at any one time will depend partly on the size and layout of the centre, and partly on its contents (are they vulnerable or valuable?). If there is a sales counter, it must be staffed (and staff time will be required for buying goods and keeping accounts). Refreshments will need staff with specialist skills (buying, preparing and accounting as well as serving). The centre will need regular cleaning and general maintenance (light bulbs, towels, squeaky hinges, minor damage, touching up paintwork, repairing the surface of the car park, removing litter). General management (including readiness to receive phone calls, supervision of other staff and so on) could take many hours a day. The annual patterns of visiting will probably mean that some of the centre staff will be seasonal part-timers. Once again, briefing and training, maintaining a roster system and coping with staffing emergencies will take up more time than might at first be guessed.

Publications may seem at first sight to be free of staff implications. Not so. Even a leaflet dispenser has to be checked and re-filled frequently. If leaflets are offered to the public free, then staff time can be cut considerably. But if they are to be sold, then the distribution of each single one requires a cash transaction and accounting. Distributing publications in small quantities to ordinary retail outlets takes time and – unless it can be done on foot or by bicycle – fuel. Many such outlets will only accept very few copies, and then only on a sale or return basis, which necessitates further journeys to keep the supplies topped up, and to collect what cash there may be. Almost certainly, such cash will not cover the cost of going to fetch it, even if you were fortunate enough to find volunteers to do the job. The distribution of publications is a highly competitive business among middlemen who deal in bulk quantities of a wide range of titles.

The only sure formula for making a hefty profit on a publication is to run a highly popular visitor attraction which visitors can enjoy fully only if they buy your exclusive guide. That way you may sell hundreds in a day from your own ticket office, earning 200 per cent over and above the cost of printing, with minimal overheads!

Strategies to suit situations
Planning Interpretation projects

13

It is axiomatic that no two Features, however similar, are the same. The mere fact of geographical distance makes places and their contexts different, and it follows that their interpretation must be different too. Even if two artists in different parts of the world were by some miracle to paint identical pictures, the pictures would have to be interpreted differently. They could not be explained by identical factors, nor would we expect them to be viewed by the same visitors.

This means that every time an interpretational exercise is planned, both the general strategy and the detailed presentation have to be worked out from scratch. True, the interpreter may have at his disposal techniques of communication that have been tried and tested elsewhere; but the decisions about what messages to highlight, and in what terms and by what media to communicate them, must be worked out afresh. There can be no such concept as off-the-peg interpretation.

This is both the trouble and the joy of Interpretation. It is trouble only insofar as it means work, and work means spending skilled time and therefore (usually) money. But the work can be a joy, and the fact that every scheme has to be thought out anew means that it should never be boring or repetitive. What is more, the outcome – the resultant scheme and message and the visitor's experience – should be fresh and stimulating every time. If the Visitor feels, 'I'm sure I've been through all this before,' it must be the Interpretation that is stale, not the Feature.

There are many different aspects of what we may call an Interpretation opportunity, or situation. There is the Feature itself, its size or extent, its value and vulnerability, its location, its 'story'. Then there are the intended or probable Visitors, their numbers, their age, their expectations, their likely length of stay, their kind. There is the Proprietor. Someone has decided that there should be interpretation: why? What does he want to achieve? What are his resources?

The assessment and analysis of such factors is usually called 'interpretive planning': the term originated in the US, but has been accepted by those concerned with Interpretation around the world.

It is a methodical planning process, which systematically considers all relevant factors, and then proposes appropriate action, with all necessary explanations. These considerations and proposals are spelled out in an Interpretive Plan.

Because situations vary so enormously in scope and size, Interpretive Plans may come in various sizes, too. They might cover just a couple of sides of A4 paper, or consist of hundreds of pages and require several volumes. Generally speaking, the contents, however they may be sub-headed in the Plan, will be found to be comprised in eight main categories: introductory; social and political; strategic; academic; communicational; administrative; financial; and procedural.

WHAT INTERPRETIVE PLANS ARE FOR

To begin with, in many situations there are so many factors to be considered, often at first sight seeming rather trivial, that it is easy to overlook some of them altogether during the planning process. What time of day a certain site may be busiest may seem of little relevance – until problems of staffing, the maximum capacity of an audio-visual theatre, or the feasibility of organising separately guided groups of visitors all come into play. Whether or not there is an active local naturalists' club or historical society could have an important influence on the task of researching the story of the Feature, on the pattern of guiding, site maintenance or relationships with the local community. Interpretive Planning is a discipline that ensures that nothing that matters is overlooked.

Secondly, different factors, when they are combined, often have influences that one might never appreciate if they were only considered singly. A classic example is the matter of producing guide leaflets discussed in chapter 16. The way visitors will use them, the style, the cost of printing, the number required in a season, storage space, distribution methods and procedures for handling cash are only some of the interacting factors on which a decision about a leaflet system will be based. Unless all the relevant factors are identified and considered together at the appropriate moment, a poor decision may result.

The third benefit of an Interpretive Plan follows from the second. The decision-makers who have to approve a new project need rational explanations for all the recommendations put before them, some of which perhaps they would not have thought of themselves. It is not necessarily their job to identify the factors – their role is probably to study the proposals critically with the help of information gathered by others. Having the facts tidily presented and the reasoning spelt out step by step may enable them to authorise the go-ahead – or to spot flaws in the thinking.

Fourthly, a good Interpretive Plan will be so thorough, and will have examined the implications of a scheme so carefully, that if it is approved it will serve as a blueprint to be implemented over a period of months or years. Many plans will go so far as to recommend priorities, sequences, time-scales, staffing implications and financial budgets. If the plan is consistent and coherent, then its reasoning and recommendations can be followed through even if several parties are involved in the scheme's implementation, or if the staff change during the process.

Fifthly, a well-prepared Interpretive Plan is a demonstration of responsible forethought and reliable management. When sponsorship or grants are to be sought, potential backers will be the more readily convinced that the scheme is sound and the proposers are to be trusted, if they are presented with a carefully thought-out plan.

A CHECKLIST FOR INTERPRETIVE PLANNING

It is helpful for the planner to have a checklist; the one I offer below is only one of many systems that have been devised (appendix B gives just the headings, as a quick reference). The items here are not suggested titles for use in any final document, but are processes and procedures that must be completed as appropriate by the planner. The results of these processes will then be recorded, with whatever headings may be chosen, in the final document.

Introductory

1. Identify the site or feature, and its location, ownership and present management.

The plan document may well be read by some people who do not know the site well, or at all. A single paragraph may be all that is needed to put them in the picture. If it is an outdoor feature, then it is a good thing to provide a six-figure Ordnance Survey map reference.

Sample Plan statement for point 1

Clutteridge Hall is a spectacular ruin of brick and stone, standing among overgrown woodland on rising ground on the northern edge of the 128-acre Clutteridge Country Park; on the south side of the A9999, it is about half way between Bagstone and Glumbury. The surviving structure, now a roofless shell, dates from the end of the seventeenth century. It and the five acres that surround it were bequeathed to West Loamshire District Council by the late Col. Dawkins in 1994 as an extension to the Country Park which his father Sir Richard Dawkins donated for the enjoyment of the public in 1951. The Hall (map reference NP 404128) is a grade II listed monument, and in recent years has been securely fenced with corrugated iron and barbed wire to prevent unauthorised access.

Sample statement for point 2
The Council proposes to consolidate the ruins of the Hall and clear some of the trees and other vegetation so that it may be made visible as a feature of the Park. This plan for the possible interpretation of the Hall and its outbuildings has been commissioned from StoryLine Ltd by West Loamshire District Council.

2. Tell how the site or feature comes to be the subject of the proposed interpretation.

This and item 1, as they may appear as an introduction to an Interpretive Plan, are really just to put the plan in context – to identify and explain the document's subject and origin.

Social and political

3. Determine the underlying motive for suggesting an interpretive scheme at this place.

The scheme at Clutteridge, for example (see boxes, left and previous page), may have been proposed in order to transform an otherwise unwanted ruin into a public amenity; perhaps the ruin is already being broken into, and misused, and the council feels that any use is better than none; maybe the Colonel left an endowment to ensure that the site was looked after, and his executors are insisting that action is taken. Perhaps the council's chief executive has a sentimental interest in the site. The answer to this question of basic motive does not necessarily have be made public – it need not appear in the Interpretive Plan. But the person preparing the plan must be admitted to the Promoter's confidence in this matter, or his proposals may miss the real target.

Promoters will often claim that they have a number of objectives. The Interpretive Planner will have to take them all on board, and then assess (and hopefully get the Promoter to agree) which objectives are really fundamental, and which are secondary (see also item 7).

4. Predict local reaction.

This is a factor easy to overlook. Will local people be delighted or enraged? They may not feel too strongly about Clutteridge Hall, but they could be genuinely anxious about, say, the increased traffic that a new attraction on the edge of the village might generate. Rate-payers may declare that a certain scheme is a waste of council money. Local people may sometimes resent the prospect of a piece of woodland or heathland being taken over by a wildlife organisation, when they and their dogs have had access to it for years. Some new schemes can provoke political wrangles. Even over the future of Clutteridge Hall, the local press might carry letters complaining that trees are to be cut down in a country park, and demanding to know how the council can have the nerve to pretend it is concerned for conservation. To assess local reaction, enquiries may have to be made specially for the preparation of an Interpretive Plan.

Depending on the feature to be interpreted, and the possibility that new estate management practices may have to be adopted, there may be specialist local groups whose opinion ought not only to be canvassed, but respected. Will the scheme affect ramblers,

One Interpretation scheme made a faux pas when it invited a television company to film the official unveiling of an interpretation panel, and omitted to invite a representative of the local parish council. The council expressed 'regret', and quite rightly too. Interpretation should encourage local interest and participation, not short-circuit it.

riders or fishermen? Will it be of interest to local historians or naturalists? Might it in any way affect local farmers, landowners or other householders? In towns or villages, residents may be anxious about increased traffic or kerbside parking; or they may not like the idea of the appearance of their common or green being spoilt by an outdoor panel.

More positively, are there ways in which local people may become creatively involved? Local experience, wisdom and skill could enhance a new scheme, and provide a helpful input into its planning. The town or parish council, the school, the churches, the chamber of commerce, the police and the youth club may all have relevant views. If a major change of use is intended, planning permission must be sought.

Consultation such as this need not be very formal or unnecessarily extensive, but it must be conscientious and methodical. Personal interviews with chosen representatives of local interests may be of greater use than distributing questionnaires (it may be just too difficult for respondents to imagine what the scheme will really involve) or public meetings – though on occasion a public meeting, intelligently devised, can be helpful.

The amount of space allocated in the plan to reporting on this may vary from none at all (if local opinion really is irrelevant) to a quite detailed report (if major issues are at stake). Often just a few summarising sentences will do.

5. Investigate the pattern of tourism locally, and predict visitor pattern/use for this site/feature.

It will obviously make a big difference whether a proposed site or feature is utterly off the tourist beat, where visitors are hardly ever seen or access is difficult; or, at the other extreme, is in a place already teeming with numerous tourist attractions competing for too few people's attention. There are some places – small towns, perhaps – with a single attraction that brings in visitors but occupies them only for a short time. Visitors may then ask what else there is for them to do. Here is scope for even a modest interpretational entrepreneur.

It may be useful to estimate the population resident within, say, a 45-minute journey of the proposed project. It seems right to work towards patterns of tourism that rely more on public transport than on private cars, but at the same time interpretive planning must be realistic. In Britain, public transport systems are much less relevant to most people than they used to be. Rail and bus services – and, for that matter, cycle routes – may not have a noticeable effect on the pattern of visiting. And only in very few places are there real walkers in any significant number.

In most situations, the pattern of visiting will vary not only seasonally, but also according to the days of the week or the hours of a day. It may theoretically be possible to modify such patterns, but it will be hard work. A proprietor ignores habitual visiting habits at his financial peril.

Patterns of visiting may even influence the very Interpretation media to be used. Whether or not an outdoor panel will be an effective medium of communication will depend largely on how many people pass that way on foot, and whether or not it tends to be the same people week after week. In a much-frequented situation, a panel may expect to be read by ten thousand passers-by in a year; in other situations, it may be lucky to attain a readership of a hundred. Only by some kind of survey can the potential readership be estimated. Many surveys have been published on patterns of visiting (see also chapter 15).

6. Predict the types of potential users, and their attitudes, expectations and behaviour – the expected visitor profile.

This is not something that can be done with any precision, but in certain situations the visiting public may include a high proportion of people with identifiable characteristics. In some places a majority of visitors may come as families out for the day, requiring freedom, variety and nothing too intellectually demanding (though this may be more to do with the pressures of parental responsibility than with mental capacity!). Another situation may attract a high proportion of school parties or foreigners. Some will expect a majority of specialist enthusiasts, or country-lovers or (if the place requires a lot of walking) energetic young adults. Experienced Interpreters soon learn to 'identify' types of visitors.

If a new scheme is located close to or among other attractions, then it is likely to attract visitors of similar kind: study, therefore, the visitor profile of your neighbouring rivals. If the new provision is just an extension of an existing scheme, then you will perhaps know your visitors already.

Strategic

7. Define official aims and objectives.

This is not quite the same as point 3, which may be partly an enquiry into the attitudes and personal hopes of the Promoter. Here we are looking for a definitive official statement or policy guide, which will spell out the more direct objectives that will become the basis of the interpretation strategy.

It may be necessary or politic in some instances to cite in the plan two or more layers of policy and objectives – at Clutteridge, for instance, the district council's general policy for its country parks, and its particular policy for Clutteridge Park. If stated aims are many, then it may be necessary to quote only those likely to have an obvious bearing on the plan. If there are no official stated aims, then it may be a good idea to draft, with the Proprietor or

---

> **Sample statement for points 5 and 6**
>
> *Clutteridge Country Park attracts its visitors mostly from the neighbouring towns of Bagstone and Glumbury, and the adjacent housing estate at Wreaking. Many are frequent visitors. Since both the main access point and the sports and play areas are at the south end of the park, most visitors tend to stay near there. Others walk their dogs or take exercise by making a circuit of the park. We do not expect that opening up the Hall grounds will make a great difference to the pattern of visiting, nor to the visitor profile.*

Promoter, a suitable statement expressing hitherto unwritten intentions.

8. Assess the nature, quality and conservational needs of the site or feature to be interpreted.

This is an exercise in identifying those general qualities that will have an effect on the strategy. The size, extent and possibly the shape of the Feature may be among them – I have had to prepare Interpretation for features as varied as an English county, the bare brick shell of a former postmill roundhouse, and a 95-mile long waterway. Note, too, where relevant, the general pattern of roads or paths by which the public may reach and explore the feature. In these assessments, the object is to identify aspects of the site or feature that may influence the strategy for interpretation.

General categories of interest should be listed – historical, geological, archaeological, landscape, wildlife or whatever. Is the feature interesting because it is typical, or because it is rare or unique? If there are any old buildings, are they listed or mentioned in available county guides? Is the feature, or any part of it, within an Area of Outstanding Natural Beauty (AONB), a Site of Special Scientific Interest (SSSI) or a nature reserve? How are the site's or the feature's value and importance rated by experts – such as English Heritage or English Nature, or their Scottish, Welsh or Northern Ireland equivalents; the county museum or archaeological unit, or a wildlife trust? Will conservation requirements affect any provision for public access or interpretation?

9. Note any external constraints that might affect management and Interpretation.

External constraints are those over which the Proprietor and Interpreter have no control. Perhaps the site is classified as an SSSI or an ancient monument, with consequent restriction on building or management – even on whether or not one may dig a hole in the ground. Or perhaps there are unconditional public rights of way. There may be dangers that cannot be eliminated – a river bank; a crumbling cliff; an unsafe but listed footbridge; old mine shafts; or severer hazards still, from glacial crevasses to alligators. A space otherwise apparently suitable for an interpretational display may not get the approval of the fire safety officer. A potential display room may be of an awkward size or shape, or have windows in the wrong places or not at all. A house to be opened to the public may have only one staircase suitable for visitors – will this make circulation difficult? Imposing stone steps at the entrance to a building or narrow doorways could cause major problems of access for the disabled.

If in outdoor terrain the ground is rough, or the site is cut in half by a river with only one bridge, or if an interesting feature

13:1 Removing unnecessary barriers

Visitor-friendliness means accessibility in every sense of the word. Here John Dever of Insite, an Edinburgh-based visitor care consultancy (see appendix D), teaches staff at the Glasgow Royal Concert Hall about building good relations with wheelchair-users (above).

Any Interpretive Plan must consider ways to make the Interpretation available to as wide a range of the general public as possible. Sometimes this will involve constructing surfaced footpaths, stiles and direction signs; elsewhere it may be a matter of providing a wheelchair lift to an upper storey, or transport around a large site, or tactile signs. It may mean making a raised platform so that children can see an exhibit, or offering written or audio information in three or four languages. Such matters should be addressed at the planning stage and built in to the scheme, rather than dealt with later in a series of modifications.

The skills and attitudes of staff can play a significant part in helping those with mobility, sight or hearing difficulties, or those with limited understanding of the language. The twin principles of suitable facilities and staff training can be embodied in an Interpretive Plan.

requires a steep one-and-a-half-mile climb to reach it – record the facts. Equivalent factors in indoor interpretation might be the size, number or visual appeal of artefacts to be displayed; their vulnerability to atmospheric moisture or daylight, and ambient noise (quite a severe problem for the hard of hearing trying to make sense of an audio interpretation). In a nature reserve, visitor access may have to be limited to certain seasons. The interpretation of a popular feature may have to be conditioned by the fact that it is over-visited. All these and similar factors will impose limitations on the Interpretive Planning, and should be identified before the strategy is worked out.

10. Note any constraints imposed by the Promoter/Proprietor. Theoretically, the Proprietor could be argued out of constraints, but he has the last word. Perhaps part of the site is to remain inaccessible to visitors, or be closed entirely from time to time, for reasons of conservation or of privacy. There may be constraints on alterations – no new footpaths, outdoor panels or false ceilings, perhaps. There may be constraints on management (is an area of woodland to be managed for forestry, wildlife or a compromise between the two?); or an insistence on shared use. The Proprietor may wish to reserve or grant specific rights in shooting or fishing, or want a certain space to be shared with other activity groups.

On these and similar restrictions the Proprietor may have the right to insist.[1] If an entirely new idea is suggested, some problems may not become apparent until discussions are well advanced. These constraints must be mentioned in the plan. Working under constraints is part of the game – it is amazing how difficulties can stimulate imaginative responses that positively enhance a scheme.

11. Assess the Promoter's/Proprietor's resources – manpower, skills, experience, materials, premises, finance, storage, etc.

This is not just a matter of money, though that is obviously of major significance. There is all the difference between 'Spare no cost' (this must be rare!) and 'We start with an empty budget.' There may be other resources in kind – knowledge and documentation to contribute to the research; a building that can be used for a display; estate staff able to lay paths or erect fences; a pool of volunteers; artefacts or other material that may be used in a display. Is there already a system for keeping accounts or paying wages? Resources in kind, skills and manpower should be listed in the plan document.

12. Note the relationship between the new project and any existing scheme of Interpretation administered by the same Promoter/Proprietor.

In some circumstances, a new Interpretation project launched by a Proprietor such as a conservation trust or a district council, a museum or a waterways board, will have to integrate with existing schemes. This may be just a matter of ensuring that a 'house style' is maintained in any signing or publications, or it may extend to pricing policy or administration by an existing secretariat. The Interpretive Planner will have to find out to what extent this may inhibit or determine aspects of the new scheme. I once prepared plans for a display at the request of a national organisation, only to discover at a comparatively late stage that all the typography was expected to conform to a centrally determined pattern – regardless of whether or not it was appropriate in any particular instance.

1. If the scheme is to be partly funded from outside, the backer may have certain requirements as well – that is to say, the Proprietor himself may be constrained in some respects. For instance, a financial grant may be conditional on a prescribed level of public access.

13. Propose an outline strategy based on or consistent with all other factors envisaged in this checklist.

Such a strategy must offer a logical, reasoned framework for Interpretation in the situation under review, taking into account all the major factors identified in the processes described above. It will serve as a framework for an interpretation scheme, and must be proposed clearly in the plan, but not at too great a length (detail is not needed at this stage). It may be desirable to spell out the options, in order to show why you recommend one in particular.

It will be noted that the sample strategy shown in the box (below) is largely concerned with logistical matters arising out of practical considerations. Any Interpretation strategy that ignored these could turn out to be wasted effort: the actual Interpretation

---

Sample statement for point 13

A strategy for interpreting Clutteridge Hall must clearly be integrated with other interpretation and visitor facilities in the Park, since the stories of the Hall and the Park are closely interwoven, and responsibility for administration of any new scheme will logically be assumed by the Park staff. A second factor of great significance is the risk of injury to the public, or of vandalism at the Hall site unless it is to some extent supervised.

Options appear to be:

(a) to create a new Visitor Centre in one of the Hall outbuildings, coupled with a major new access point near the Hall at the north end of the Park, thus moving the administrative centre of the Park from the southern to the northern end; or

(b) finding some other use for the outbuildings, such as leased craft workshops or a County Council nursery garden that would provide a constant supervisory presence at the Hall site.

If Option (a) is chosen, then the interpretation of the Hall and the Park would best be provided by an entirely new display at the Hall site; while a subsidiary staff office would be maintained in the existing Reception Building at the southern end to deal with the supervision of the playground, boating lake and sports facilities. Simple interpretation would be provided at or near this office so that visitors arriving at the south end of the park would be made aware of the Park's history and the existence of the Hall and the Visitor Centre at the northern entrance. A new car park would also have to be located in the Park near the northern entrance. Simple leaflet guides to the Park, with a map showing the footpath routes and the main features, could be made available at both entrances.

Option (b) would require an updating of the Reception Building at the south entrance, and the incorporation there of a new display interpreting the Park and Hall. Access from the A9999 (the north entrance) could either be restricted to the staff of the workshops or nursery at the north entrance, or be allowed to serve as a second main access to the Park. Appropriate parking arrangements would have to be made in either case. Since, according to this option, the main interpretation would be at the Reception Building at the south entrance, it would be desirable in the north of the Park to interpret the Hall from some viewpoint from a suitable pathway. If it was felt necessary to discourage walking among the Hall ruins, it would be possible to fence them off with, say, a decorative iron fence which would minimally detract from the view of the Hall as a landscape feature.

Our preference is for Option (a) since, although it may involve more expense, it seems more appropriate to identify the Hall site with the main entrance. Furthermore, a new public entrance from the A9999 would relieve traffic on minor roads, and make access easier for visitors from Bagstone and Glumbury. From the point of view of interpretation, it is more logical to start at the Hall, and to introduce the Park as a major element of the estate of which the Hall was formerly the focus.

is intimately bound up with the logistics. Note that proposals for Interpretation are very basic at this point: this is not the place for discussing details of media, though it would be very much in order to introduce the question of a choice of theme for the interpretation here if it seems likely to influence the strategy itself. Otherwise, the theme might well be presented as a logical outcome of the next main section, academic.

Academic

14. Research the site or feature, and record the findings.
There are two elements here. First, the actual resource and its component parts and qualities, a catalogue of which will form what has often been called an inventory of the site's resources. The list may be very short if the Feature itself is small or simple; or it may be quite lengthy if the Feature is large. An Interpretive Plan for the Kennet and Avon Canal had an inventory section many pages long, and included discussion of bridges and locks, aqueducts and wharves, industrial buildings such as pumphouses (complete with pumping equipment) and warehouses, public access points, canal artefacts and a wide variety of documentary, archive and illustrative material, including the engineer John Rennie's surviving notebooks and drawings. The canal's wildlife was an extra resource.

The second element is what we might call story research (see chapter 6). It is unlikely that the Interpretive Plan document will have space to record the story research findings in full. A summary of the most significant information may be offered as a contribution to the thinking behind the proposals for a strategy; or, if it seems important to record a substantial amount of such information, it could be presented in the form of an appendix.

15. Catalogue the documentary sources used and/or available.
Such a catalogue, which is bound to be useful to future managers or interpreters of the site, should be produced whether or not it will be included in the printed plan.

16. Study the context (geographical, historical, cultural) of the site or feature.
This has been already discussed in chapters 6 and 7.

17. Draw out the messages of the site/feature and express them in simple, single-sentence form.

18. Select possible main themes for the interpretation.
In the Interpretive Plan document, discuss these and recommend which should be chosen. A single theme is desirable; what at first appear to be rival themes may in practice be made into subsidiary stories that enhance the main theme.

> *Sample statement for point 18*
> *The possible topics from which to draw a theme for the Interpretation of Clutteridge Hall and Park include:*
> - *County families*
> - *Gentlemen's pleasure grounds*
> - *Sheep farming*
> - *Stone and brick.*
>
> *A theme to link them all would be 'Several generations of a county landed family created this landscape', since the other topics can all be used to illustrate it, right down to the time the Park and Hall were given to the Council – upstairs reconciled with downstairs, as it were.*

Communicational

19. Select appropriate media to communicate the theme, messages and stories.

Proposals for these will form an essential section of the Plan. It will be superfluous and too time-consuming to record all the reasons for suggesting particular media, but the Interpreter should bear in mind the principles expounded in earlier chapters of this book. When it comes to committing his proposals to paper in the document, he should explain his thinking whenever he thinks that to do so may help convince those who study it.

Sample statement for point 19

We suggest that the former stable block of the Hall (now used only as a store for Parks Department materials) should house a Visitor Centre with a small display about the Dawkins family and their long association with this estate. We think that the Hall's location near the proposed north entrance will encourage visitors to enter the Centre on arrival and discover the combined story of the Hall and Park.

It should be possible to open the Centre almost every day of the year, especially if an adjoining room can be provided as a Ranger's office. The Centre should require comparatively little maintenance over and above what is already required for the present Reception Building. We calculate that the the display could occupy some 42–55 square metres of floor space, with graphics panels on the windowless walls. It should be planned to include a variety of presentation, with sections treating:

- *the Dawkins family since 1302*
- *the old and new Hall sites*
- *the Black Death*
- *the demise of medieval Clutteridge in the fourteenth century*
- *local architect Horace Wilkinson's new Hall of 1692*
- *the landscaping of the Park in the eighteenth century*
- *the military exercises of the Loamshire Yeomanry in the Park in the nineteenth century*
- *the gifts of the Park and the Hall to the Council in the twentieth century.*

A simple new extension to the south of the stables would enable us to incorporate a five-metre viewing window. A little gardening would open up a fine view, not dissimilar to the one that would have been visible from the drawing-room windows of the Hall down towards the lake and the portion of parkland that shows the remains of medieval ridge-and-furrow fields and provides a glimpse of the deserted village site. We suggest that a portion of that grassland should be newly fenced so that a small flock of sheep may be kept on it for many months of the year. This would add interest and significance to the view.

It should be possible to incorporate a schoolroom or meeting room in the stables, which could be used for evening meetings or special exhibitions and would make a more satisfactory headquarters for the Park Rangers than the present cramped Reception Centre. See our proposed plan for the conversion of the stables in Appendix II.

Toilet facilities would have to be installed: there is already a mains water supply, but we think that a new drainage system would be required. There would be scope for creating a refreshment room and kitchen in due course if the number of visitors, especially in the summer, were ever to warrant it.

[Further paragraphs on the provision of outdoor panels, guide leaflet and special events might be included, but at this point no details of wording or design are needed.]

---

20. Draft a provisional script for the Interpretation, including suggestions for illustrative material.

At what stage in the planning this should be done may depend on the circumstances. Sometimes a requirement for scripting may be included in the instructions or contract under which the Interpretive Plan is being written. Otherwise, all that may be needed are samples indicating the way the communication is to be approached – perhaps a few draft paragraphs of text, with examples of illustrations and designs. If the plan document is to include a large quantity of such script, then it may be best to present it as an appendix.

21. Consider general ideas for design and style.

Design and style are so tied up with Interpretation scripting that ideas on them should be presented alongside – almost as part of – the script. In the document, design ideas will certainly require a paragraph of their own, if not a whole section. The Interpreter may well bear in mind that, while he may have constructed his own image of how interpretation of a certain place will look, the readers will need help. Artist's impressions and sketches of proposed display panels or covers of guide literature may be useful – as would 'dummy' material of a quality good enough to be exciting.[2] This need not form an integral section of the plan, but may be provided as a supplement, while simple explanations for the recommended style and design should be given in the text of the plan. General suggestions about style and ambience should come under this heading. Very often the design ideas proposed in the plan will form the basis of a brief for a professional designer.

> **Sample statement for point 21**
> We suggest that the general style of display for the new Visitor Centre in the stable block at Clutteridge Hall should be simple, in keeping with the rough-textured white-washed interior walls of the stable block and outhouses, with a discreet hint of Victoriana in the typeface and ornaments. The stable floor will have to be levelled and resurfaced. We recommend using dark blue-grey paving brick, which provides an easily cleaned surface and, with its slightly bevelled edges, is somewhat reminiscent of old-fashioned stable flooring.

Administrative

22. Consider and suggest how the scheme will be administered.

23. Assess the staff time and skills required.

The importance of fully thinking through the implications for staffing was stressed in chapter 12. This thinking must be presented in the plan in precise and business-like terms – man-hours, levels of skills or qualifications required, wages or salaries, possibly even job descriptions. If sales or admission charges are part of the plan, consider who will be expected to handle cash and account for it.

2. A 'dummy' is a full-size, full-colour simulation of a publication, done by paste up, hand-painted or computer-generated – it might be a leaflet, a poster or the graphics for a panel. A dummy booklet would have the full graphic treatment on the cover and perhaps a few sample pages, with the rest of the pages blank – the general appearance, size, weight and 'feel' should be as realistic as possible. Professional design help may be needed to achieve this.

13:2 Bespoke designing

The unusual lidded interpretation panels at Pensthorpe Waterfowl Park, near Fakenham in north Norfolk, were specially designed (left). Simple, inexpensive panels were needed that (a) could carry colour identification drawings; (b) have the contents replaced whenever the occupants of a particular pen were changed; (c) were weatherproof; and (d) were not obtrusive or unsightly.

The answer (devised by Bill Makins, the proprietor) is a panel angled slightly out of the horizontal and at a level low enough for wheelchair-users to read, with a plain wooden hinged lid. This conceals and protects the graphics when not in use, but can be raised with one hand by any Visitor who wants to refer to it. Admission to the Park is by payment at entry, and it is well supervised, so damage or theft is very rare.

24. Consider the need for, and recommend in detail, any necessary supporting provision such as structural alterations, car parking, toilets, signing, advertising.

In the written plan, some of these matters may be raised as elements in the strategy. But there will also be a section devoted to specific proposals under separate headings.

Sample statement for point 24
Car parking

If the former entrance to the Hall from the A9999 (now bricked up) is to be re-opened as a new main entrance to the Park, then parking will have to be provided in the vicinity of the Hall. We propose that an area of about 850–1,300 square metres should be cleared, levelled and landscaped in the now semi-derelict area to the west of the Hall outhouses, to take perhaps 50–70 cars. There would be scope for extending this at a later date if it proved necessary. We assume that the exisiting car park at the south entrance (capacity 60 cars) will still be much used, especially as it serves the sports facilities at that end of the Park.

---

25. Estimate ongoing maintenance requirements.

These include all regular or occasional work needed to keep the proposed Interpretation system operating. The more complex systems (visitor centres and guided walk programmes, for instance) may require a considerable amount of continual administration.

Other schemes (special events, in particular) need a gradual build-up of teamwork and activity beforehand, intensive team activity on the day, and quite a lot of winding up immediately afterwards.

All equipment needs maintenance and eventual replacement – whether mechanical, electrical or electronic. Other schemes may need constant updating. Publications and other sales need updating, reprinting, distributing, stock-taking, selling and accounting. Outdoor and indoor panels need a certain amount of maintenance and cleaning, and eventually renewal. Car parks may need supervison, with signs and waymarks needing touching up, repair and occasional replacement.

The Interpretive Plan will have to suggest the shelf-life of various forms of display, publication and equipment, and systems for monitoring their smooth running.

Financial

26. Estimate the capital costs.
This cannot be done by guesswork, only by detailed costing, item by item, based on quotations and estimates from potential contractors and suppliers. This will require reasonably precise specifications for every aspect of a new scheme – hardware, software, professional input, building alterations, landscaping. These expenses will represent the cost of the proposals made as a result of consideration of points 19–25 above.

27. Consider sources of capital finance, if relevant.
This may not be the Interpreter's responsibility, but in some situations he or she may be more aware of possible grant sources than the Proprietor/Promoter. Even an Interpreter working within a large organisation may have a better chance of getting ideas accepted if it can be shown that they can be funded without too much strain on the firm's resources.

28. Estimate the running costs.
See chapter 17. Every Interpretive Plan must treat running costs thoroughly. Any conscientious committee member, superior or potential backer will be surprised or suspicious if the document does not give a realistic and detailed assessment of such costs.

29. Estimate any income to be generated by the scheme itself.
There may not be any income in some cases, but where a proposal includes sales or admission fees, realistic figures must be suggested, with estimates of visitor numbers and proposals for charges. To be convincing, these should include patterns of seasonal and daily variation. It may be useful to prepare two sets of figures based on optimistic and pessimistic scenarios for visitor numbers, sales, entry charges and retail prices of any publications.

30. Estimate the likely costs of eventual replacement of Interpretation material, for long-term budgeting.

It may be useful to calculate this (according to the nature of the scheme) as an average annual requirement over a period of, say, five, ten or fifteen years. In the plan, all this financial material will have to be presented partly in the form of a detailed budget, and partly by comment on the figures. It may be wise to discuss any draft budgets with the project's treasurer or equivalent before the plan is published, so that the Interpretive Planner does not find himself solely responsible for the estimates presented.

Procedural

31. Consider the need for any further consultations.

Such consultations, for instance with specialists – perhaps an architect, researchers, designer, interpretation consultants – may have already taken place as part of the preparation of the plan. But it is very likely that once it is approved, further more detailed discussions or commissions will be necessary, depending on the nature of the scheme. Liaison with other bodies – such as the local planning authority, or potential sponsors or grant-aiders – may be needed.

32. Propose a time schedule and phasing.

Many clients – whether the Interpreter's superiors in an organisation or, say, members of a committee or working party – will be sailing in unfamiliar waters, not at all sure how to proceed. The plan could make it clear what decisions now have to be made, what are the procedures for taking the scheme forward, and in what order its proposals need to be carried out. It may be helpful to suggest two or three stages into which the implementation of the proposals could be broken down, with appropriate target dates, starting from whenever authority may be given to proceed.

Note that many of the headings in this checklist assume that the Interpretation is site-based. Most is, but there are other valid forms – for example, screen presentations (film, video or computer) and books and articles – which will have similar procedures for their preparation.

THE INTERPRETIVE PLAN AS A DOCUMENT

The written form that an Interpretive Plan will take must depend on the size of the scheme, the factors operating in the particular case, and the nature of the group or groups to which the document is to be addressed. Most recipients will be grateful if it can combine the contrary qualities of brevity and comprehensiveness – no one wants to wade through pages and pages of boring text, but it will be criticised if important factors seem to have been overlooked.

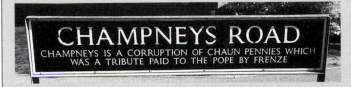

It was a good idea (whose, I wonder?) to give some significance to the street names of the Norfolk town of Diss. The success of these 'interpretive street signs' seems to be mixed, however.

Champneys Road is a real riddle, which must leave visitors to the town quite baffled. What is a 'chaun penny'? And is 'frenze' local dialect for 'friends'?

Fitzwalter Road: we need not doubt the truth of the statement here, but may reasonably enquire what is the connection with the town of Diss.

Skelton Road commemorates the eccentric John Skelton; there will be visitors who have at least heard of him, but have not associated him with Diss. No wonder the town wants to celebrate his memory, though probably few visitors will spot this street sign.

Whytehead Gardens: many a local worthy has had his or her name immortalised in a street name. There is something touching about citizens taking the trouble to explain to later generations who Whytehead was.

The Skelton Road sign is, alas, the only one to use lower-case lettering for the explanation. It is easier to read, and instantly expresses the difference in function between the street name and its explanation. If the Champneys Road sign had been presented in the same style, we might just have been able to guess the fact that Frenze is a hamlet in the parish of Diss.

One possible way of getting the best of both worlds is to preface the document with a one-page summary, to help anyone who has to rush to the committee meeting unprepared. This can be followed by a contents page that shows the headings of all the sections and sub-sections, with their page or paragraph numbering. It is essential for a document of this kind to be logical in the sequence of its sections, and to display frequent clear topic headings to enable those reading it to find their way about it quickly.

Some matters may be best conveyed in diagrammatic or tabular form. These could include:

- location of site (a map)
- location of nearest centres of population (stylised map with population figures)
- comparative visitor figures at other nearby attractions (table)
- site plan
- exhibition layout
- walk routes (map)
- production costs, wholesale and retail prices for range of publications (table).

The Interpretive Planner may want to discuss a number of the recommended points with the Proprietor before drafting the plan, and/or to submit the draft for approval prior to having it copied and circulated. In other situations, it is best for the plan to reach the Proprietor as an entirely independent proposal.

I have tried to include almost everything that Interpretive Planning may have to cover, and not all the points listed here will apply in every situation. But the principles will. Every project, however complex, however simple, from a strategy for a National Park to the preparation of a museum label, deserves the same quality of careful thought in its preparation. Without care, schemes may end up with only moderate success, or even fail – often through overlooking quite simple and, with hindsight, obvious factors.

The style of language in an Interpretive Plan should be clear and simple – plain English with a minimum of jargon. Aim for clarity of thought and expression: these are what convince, not fashionable catch-phrases. Include brief explanations of specialist concepts for the non-specialists who are likely to read the document. Respect the special interests of those who are involved – if they are farmers, recognise the concerns of agriculture; if they are businessmen, show that you are businesslike; if they are educationists, stress learning.

Above all, an Interpretive Plan must be realistic. To produce over-ambitious or over-optimistic proposals, or to recommend schemes that are not soundly based on experience, is a disservice. It could result not merely in disappointment, but in financial disaster and job losses. It is partly for these reasons that Interpretive Plans are often commissioned from independent consultants. Clients who commission such reports are time and again surprised not just by the fact that the consultant has raised unexpected questions, but by the thoroughness of a good plan. Interpretation consultants are not always right, but they must not be afraid of saying if they have doubts about the viability or the effectiveness of their clients' ideas. Better for a consultant to fail to get the job than to go along with ideas in which he has no faith – and better, too, for the client to have an honest, independent opinion.

The academic perspective
Assessment and evaluation

14

Interpretation has clear aims and a number of more or less standard procedures. One would think, therefore, that it should be fairly simple both to check that the procedures are based on sound principles and to assess whether or not the aims are being achieved. In practice, the second of these matters turns out to be not so simple; while, for the first, it is so generally taken for granted that the procedures are adequate, that their soundness often receives very little critical examination. There are two aspects of interpretational achievement to consider: the general and the particular. Is Interpretation as a whole an educational force to be reckoned with? And has your effort actually helped anyone?

EVALUATING AN INTERPRETATION EXERCISE

Let us start with the local and particular. We must ask ourselves how much we really care whether we are communicating anything useful, so long as visitors keep coming and seem to enjoy themselves. If Interpretation is seen just as a factor in attracting tourists or entertaining them, the communication question may seem irrelevant. But you could not get away with such an attitude in the advertising industry. There, your business client has a message to get across, and he will monitor his sales figures closely. If he cannot measure a significant improvement, he will assume that the message has failed. He will drop the campaign and possibly his advertising agency as well. You lose the job. This takes us right back to the question of aims and motivations considered in chapter 2. Only if you really care about the educational function of Interpretation should you claim the title of Interpreter – and if you do, your effectiveness will be of prime importance to you.

The USA National Parks believed from the outset that Interpretation would modify the attitudes and behaviour of their Visitors. That their provision of visitor services has been beneficial they would not doubt, but how much of that benefit derives from structural provision and how much from education is less easy to discern. Even education has two distinct elements in it – the voice and the message. A friendly, dedicated, even charismatic park ranger who urges visitors not to pick wild flowers may achieve his

A range of facts about
Interpretation's visiting public
can be discovered by systematic
enquiry. A simple survey undertaken in Ipswich about people's
use of the town's fine public
parks provided quasi-statistical
data,* showing which parks were
the most popular for what kind
of activity, and how often
individuals used them. There
were very interesting differences.
As frequently happens with this
kind of enquiry, the results
reinforced what the Park
Department's own staff might
have guessed – but instead of a
subjective hunch, it became
quantified fact.

*'Quasi-statistical' because the
sample of people was not large
enough to satisfy the strict criteria
for statistical validity.

or her aim as much through personality and leadership as through providing insights. If we are hoping to embark on some kind of programme of assessment, we must be clear what kind of achievement we want to measure, and what particular elements in our work we want to test.

The effectiveness of structural provision should not be too hard to assess. Whether a new path succeeds in encouraging visitors to keep away from a vulnerable area of a nature reserve can be determined by observation. Whether signing that indicates how long it may take to complete a certain trail route encourages people to walk it, is again a matter of observation. It may be backed up by a simple survey of walkers to find out whether the signing has been helpful to them – this basic kind of enquiry is not to be despised, for visitors do not often get a chance to tell providers if they are pleased or frustrated. No formal questionnaire may be needed – just a friendly member of staff trying to speak to a target number of visitors about a simple matter, and jotting down the answers. To the visitors it may seem very casual, but to the enquirer it should be a disciplined exercise with the responses tabulated or otherwise noted. We all find it difficult to recall comments from even twenty people with any accuracy, and your survey should probably aim to involve at least a hundred. If such data, however simple, are to be compared with the results of other surveys, something better than general statements will be required. Even if your sample is small, a well-conducted survey can produce results of significance. Where data are to be used for scientific comparison they must, of course, meet rigid standards to have statistical validity.

When it comes to assessing the effectiveness of Interpretation as opposed to structural provision, we are in the realm of the intangible. If Environmental Interpretation is comparable to language interpretation, then it is effective only when the Visitor understands the message that the Interpreter translates for him. So it is the Visitor's comprehension that needs to be assessed. This is tricky – it is not merely knowledge that matters, but understanding. Interpreters are involved in an educational process with members of the general public, but have no formal procedures for testing what visitors have learned, let alone what they have understood.

It is at least possible to observe whether Interpretive provision is being used. If the public are buying a certain guide leaflet, sales figures may give you a clue to the extent of the demand for it. It is time-consuming, but not difficult, to observe at a certain site whether visitors are using the guide, and how thoroughly. If audio cassette guides are available, you should be able to check how many people return the player with the tape only part-played; more sophisticated audio guides actually record data about their use.

If you interpret through outdoor panels, it is possible to observe visitors, and categorise and quantify what proportions of them pass a certain panel and:

(a) do not apparently notice it

(b) obviously notice it, but do not stop to look at it

(c) go up to it and read a little, but give up

(d) appear to read it right through.

This exercise can bring to light extraordinary contrasts between the public use of apparently similar panels at different sites; and can suggest certain patterns of use that vary with the location of the panels and the nature of the sites. A panel in a very much frequented street, for example, might have many hundreds of passers-by a day, of whom only a small percentage stop to read it, while another in a remote situation might have only two or three visitors a day, but would be read in its entirety by all of them.

The only way to find out whether or not visitors have really learned anything is to subject them to some kind of examination. This obviously cannot often be done – not only is it an inconvenience to the visitors, but a big undertaking for the examiners (whether the Interpreters themselves, or an independent organisation). Assessing what people may have learned is itself a professional skill – most of us attempting this without training would ask the wrong questions in the wrong way, and end up with results that were almost worthless.

Some quiz-type questionnaires that have been used by teachers or museums show how shallow such approaches can be. A teacher may expostulate that the function of a quiz sheet is not really to test, but to provoke children to read the display texts. Quite true – it is a low-tech alternative to the Interpreter's ploy of providing touch-screens in the hope of enticing visitors to interact with the information offered. But some teachers, when they get the children back into the classroom, will concoct tests of this quality just the same.

A survey was conducted among those using two very differently sited car parks at Marsh Farm Country Park at South Woodham Ferrers, Essex, alongside the river Crouch. It consisted of counting, on various days of the week and at regular intervals during the day, the numbers of cars parked, and the number that arrived or left during the ten minutes following the count. This was backed up by speaking to the occupants of the first car to arrive immediately after that ten-minute period, and asking them a few simple questions. These were designed to allow visitors to comment in their own words if they wanted.

Two unexpected things clearly emerged. First, a surprisingly high proportion of visitors had not set out with the intention of visiting the park, but had seen signs to it along their journey and decided to have a look. Secondly, among those who had set out specially to visit the park there was a strong feeling of apprehension that developments might spoil what to them was an idyllic riverside and marshland scene. Both these discoveries must have been important to Essex County Council's management of the park.

The least troublesome way to test visitors' recall of facts is to quiz them as they leave an interpreted site. This has been tried many times but, as far as I know, it provides little encouragement. Even immediate recall is much less than the producers of interpretive texts would hope. This should not surprise us, for a typical display of about a dozen panels may well carry some two hundred facts – many of which may have been entirely skipped by the visitor, others passed over as not particularly significant, and others just plain forgotten. Is it, then, a better strategy to confront visitors as they walk out of the exit and ask them, more openly, 'What, if anything, do you actually remember from that display?' This has also been tried, and what one tends to find is that respondents are a little embarrassed and say something like, 'Well, now you ask me, I can't actually recall anything – oh yes, there were those fossils or rocks or something, weren't there?'

'I shall always remember Venice . . .
For wasn't that the place
Where Mrs Mason hurt her foot,
And mother bought the lace?'
From J. B. Morton, The Best of
Beachcomber, William
Heinemann, London 1963.

A colleague and I once tried asking those people whom we had seen reading panels if they would be willing to be sent a questionnaire in four weeks' time. The idea was to test recall after a time lapse. The first disappointment was the small percentage of those who actually returned the stamped addressed envelopes. It was somewhere in the region of 15–20 per cent of those who had agreed to receive the questionnaire. Scarcely any respondent could recall any factual information at all; one or two even said they could not remember the occasion or the place where they had read it and met us.

Of course, visitors probably stop to read panels not because they are interested in the feature, but because a notice is a notice, and human curiosity wants to find out what it is all about. Furthermore, people may read dozens of panels, or visit several gardens, stately homes, cathedrals or nature reserves in the course of a week's holiday – how can they possibly remember what they saw when and where? I am a little wiser now, and have no illusions about interpretive scripts being consciously remembered. I, too, can enjoy an informative book, but a week later will have forgotten virtually all the facts.

1. Psychologists skilled in study techniques have attempted to devise ways of testing whether or not visitors, after experiencing interpretation in particular situations, have grown in understanding. They are able to suggest what kind of messages, presented by what means, seem to be most readily understood. Many investigations have been undertaken into how Visitors behave, how people learn in informal situations, and how Interpreters have sought to modify their methods to match Visitors' known needs. Results are published in a variety of tourism and museum journals, and in publications of the Society for the Interpretation of Britain's Heritage or the Centre for Environmental Education (see appendix D).

It is the same with displays in Visitor Centres. You can visit dozens and perhaps retain clear visual images of most of them, and definite impressions of their interest and quality, but you do not remember the facts. If this is a general phenomenon, then any test of factual recall after an experience of interpretation may be misleading. However, even if the visitor cannot answer the direct question 'What have you learned?', some of the information offered may have subconsciously reinforced or modified his understanding.[1]

Interpreters who have great faith in the efficacy of what they themselves are doing are in danger of resenting or resisting attempts to test their work; negative results might shatter their enthusiasm and result in disillusionment. People from so many professions are involved in Interpretation that individuals tend to become somewhat defensive when ideas are offered from outside their own speciality; but a greater willingness to regard educational or cognitive psychologists as helpful colleagues could only do good.

LEARNING FROM OTHERS

It is probably best to leave studies of cognition (how and under what circumstances people learn) to the experts – but we may call upon them for help in designing specific studies. If interpreters are approached by academics for help, they should cooperate. Anyone wanting to explore the world of educational psychology as it relates to Interpretation could contact training institutions (see appendix D) or the Society for the Interpretation of Britain's Heritage. They may be able to recommend relevant books or articles.

Advertising – whether we love it or hate it – may have a lot to teach us both about targeting messages to specific audiences, and about techniques of communication both audio and visual. Advertisers may not entirely understand what Interpreters are about, but Interpreters would do well to try to understand how advertising works its magic in the mind of the consumer.

Many universities and colleges offer courses in aspects of communication: media studies, media production, communication studies, semantics. Not every Interpreter will have time or opportunity to study these subjects in depth, but Interpretation as a profession must learn to recognise their relevance, and benefit from them.

For skill in carrying out surveys, consult experts in consumer research and statistics. But do not be bewitched by academic jargon: not all academics are bright, imaginative or capable of lateral thinking, and Interpreters may have to exercise discernment.

ASSESSING ONE'S OWN WORK

Interpreters can, and should, undertake certain elements of self-assessment themselves. If you run a visitor attraction or some kind of centre, keep a daily record of visitor numbers and the yearly pattern of visiting. This will either encourage you, or make you consider whether a promotional drive may be necessary, or a change of programme or display, or even a systematic enquiry as to why the public do not seem interested (you might need professional help with this last option).

Watch visitors – carefully but unobtrusively observe how they behave. What elements in a display do they seem always to skip? What panels do they look at, but obviously not read through? What, if anything, holds their interest, or regularly has several people gathered round? If you can discover what it is that makes some elements in your display boring and others popular, you may be able to make appropriate modifications. If you or your staff can

14:1 'Keep up the good work!'

Well done!
I like it
Very educational
Excellent!
Very good
Most interesting
Radical
Very well done. Good
Well done
Interesting collection.
Super!
Keep up the good work.
Great
Well worth visiting.
Fascinating.
Very Interesting
Most informative.
Very informative.

How difficult it is to express one's feelings in a visitors' book! There is usually only room for four or five words, and you are often slightly flustered – it's time to go, someone else is waiting for the pen and, anyway, you have not had a proper chance to sort out all the thoughts running through your mind. So you just write 'Very interesting' or 'Well done,' which is pleasantly imprecise and appears to be positive. But it is hardly the stuff that surveys are made of.

What the book does show, of course, is the geographical distribution of where visitors have come from, which can be a matter of interest and importance. It also gives people a chance to express themselves, to register their presence. A visitors' book needs no staff supervision and little maintenance (except for deleting the occasional obscenity). And even vague, kindly remarks are probably sincere. What are the alternatives?

- no canvassing of visitors' opinions at all
- occasional, carefully structured, labour-intensive surveys
- a comments and criticisms box, with pad and pen provided, which might receive the occasional helpful complaint or suggestion as well as hoaxes
- some staff time devoted to chatting informally to visitors and noting down their reactions immediately afterwards.

It is important to seek information that you can actually use to make improvements.

Comments from the Kennet and Avon Canal Trust visitors' book, which is kept near the door of the interpretational exhibition at The Wharf, Devizes, Wiltshire.

follow up the observation by talking in a friendly, casual way with visitors to draw out their reactions to the display, you may learn something to your advantage. As soon as a conversation has finished, make a note of what was said, and by what kind of person – whether it was a teenager, a young couple or an elderly man. It is methodical observation that accumulates useful data, just as in beetle-watching.

Other rather more disciplined enquiries may shed new light on who your visitors are, or how they have turned up at your premises. You may discover what proportion responded to a recent press advertisement, saw a poster in a hotel or at a caravan site, heard a recommendation from friends, or had never heard of you until they happened to see a sign and turned off the road to investigate. This may seem irrelevant, so long as enough people keep coming – but in fact it can tell you a lot about what people are actually looking for. You may discover that your promotional efforts are ineffective, or that your Interpretation is aimed at a kind of audience that you are just not reaching.

THE VALUE OF INTERPRETATION

I suggested at the start of this chapter that enquiries into the effectiveness of interpretation may concern themselves either with the local and particular, or with the general and universal. We have considered the first of these categories: now let us look at the latter. It is not often done. Is Interpretation, as a whole, really worthwhile? How can we find out? If individual acts of Interpretation do sometimes provide pleasure or enlightenment, then all the acts of Interpretation performed in a day, a week, a year, could add up to something socially and educationally significant. But can this be proved?

It helps to recognise that the insights that Interpreters are keen to offer are not isolated, self-contained or different from truths provided by other means. The messages of Interpretation are not incompatible with education given at school. Much of the factual content of Interpretation is gleaned from books, which are all out there and accessible in libraries. Hundreds of magazines on every sort of subject are on sale every day, and presumably they find buyers. Newspapers and their magazines carry numberless articles; television offers documentaries, as well as news on all sorts of topics. CD-ROM and the World Wide Web provide databases into which anyone with the necessary equipment may tap. Adult education classes provide opportunities for specialist study. Societies and charities circulate their own magazines and journals to subscribers with particular interests. All these are offering information that may help interpret or explain the world we live in.

Among this welter of information, Interpretation's special contribution is three-fold. First, it tries to give all information a context, to establish its relation to the real world we know, putting the local into the context of the regional, the earth within the universe. Secondly, its information is provided in terms that demonstrate the how and why of things. Thirdly, it seeks always to relate new information to human experience. Looked at like this, Interpretation – in its widest sense – can be seen, if not quite as a philosophy, at least as an attitude towards our environment. For an enquiring mind, it can serve as a life-time model of exploration, a system for accumulating wisdom.

One field in which institutions and media have combined to teach a whole generation has been nature conservation. It would be interesting to study the way in which so much progress was made, between (say) 1960 and 1990, in popularising concepts of wildlife and environmental conservation. Nature conservation organisations worked hard, with the support of the mass media, to urge man's responsibility for the welfare of our planet and all that lives on it. Public awareness was raised, public understanding enhanced – with results that sent shockwaves into politics, business, school curricula, even domestic kitchens. Interpretation was

Do not put too much reliance on visitors' books. 'Lovely', 'Very good', 'Keep up the good work' are comments that tell you very little. Few people will take the trouble to write, 'It was okay until I started reading the panel about geology, and then it got so technical that I didn't understand it,' but they might tell you in conversation. The visitors' book is often, I suspect, regarded by visitors as the management's method of fishing for compliments – those who are good-natured play along, while serious critics just boycott it.

involved in this process, and it worked. What were its mechanisms? It would be valuable to study how much it contributed to all this.

HOW DO PEOPLE DEVELOP ENTHUSIASMS?

A random survey that I have been conducting is intended to shed light on how enthusiasts are first bitten by their hobby, and what it means to them. This may have something significant to show Interpreters who take their mission seriously. Responses to the printed questionnaire have come from afficionados of subjects as varied as aircraft, bird-watching, butterflies, botany, canals, film, football, gardening, historic gardens, land management, landscape, motorcycling, music, photography, self-improvement, singing, skiing and tennis.

Provisional results of the survey

Interest began before eleventh birthday:	41 per cent
Interest began between the ages of 11 and 18:	41 per cent
Interest attributed to home influences:	36 per cent
Interest attributed to school or university:	27 per cent
Interest attributed to experiences away from home, including family excursions and holidays:	45 per cent
Social aspects important factors in the continuance of the interest:	59 per cent
Attempts made to communicate the interest to others:	55 per cent
Interest has influenced political or philosophical outlook:	50 per cent

The totals reflect some multiple influences.

Two significant things have emerged so far. The first is how many of these self-declared enthusiasts (82 per cent) initially became interested in childhood or adolescence; and the second is how large a proportion of them claim that their interest originated away from home, even if in the company of their parents. The aim was originally to try to shed light on how the activities of Interpreters might stimulate life-long interest in a subject. Many assessments of Interpretive provision have enquired how thoroughly providers have helped Visitors follow up the messages offered, which suggests that ongoing interest is something Interpreters are aiming to encourage. It seems from this survey that vivid and intellectually or emotionally stimulating experiences, followed up by opportunities to become actively involved, may be of much greater impact than communication through the printed word.

ASSESSMENT BY ONE'S PEERS

A different, unstructured kind of assessment is never-ending – the assessment of Interpretation by other Interpreters. Interpreters visit one another's presentations to make personal judgements, and to get ideas of what is successful practice and what is not. It sharpens up the practitioner's critical faculties, and is fed back into his own work. It can be ritualised in the form of award schemes. Because these are, to a certain extent, competitive, it is important that the assessing should be as impartial as possible – no easy thing if a team of ten assessors has to cover four or five submissions each, and then merge their judgements to come up with a unified 'league table'.

The Society for the Interpretation of Britain's Heritage has been running the Interpret Britain Award scheme since 1984 – under various names, according to whether, or by whom, the scheme is currently sponsored.[2] Concern to ensure a level playing field led, in early days, to a very long list of criteria, which each judge or assessor had to apply, and a computerised 'weighting system' for the results. The difficulties were that many of the questions could be interpreted ambiguously, some seemed to overlap, and points were difficult to award in any truly systematic way. Over the years, the list was revised once or twice to try to mitigate these problems and to help the judges in their interpretation of the questions, but with 44 questions the checklist was too long.

Then there was a reaction against the system: 'Surely we all know good Interpretation when we see it? We can trust our instincts,' was the new approach. An optional alternative set of 10 questions was introduced and the weighting system was jettisoned. Today, the experience of the judges and a joint discussion of every report form the basis of consistency in the marking. The scheme has a constant supply of fresh entries, and is very well administered; doubtless, it could still be refined and improved.

Would it be possible to devise a universally appropriate, but reasonably simple, set of criteria which any of us may apply to any Interpretation we come across? We have to recognise that good interpretation requires a well-planned INTERPRETATIONAL context in which to operate. That means that we would need to assess not only the skill with which messages are selected and communicated to the public, but entrepreneurial and administrative competence as well.

It has been argued that since car parks, signing, safety precautions and cleanliness are not actually interpretation, they are irrelevant to any assessment of it – the Visitors, however, will not agree. Interpretation schemes that may be good in some ways can forfeit much of their effectiveness by being hard to find through poor signing, having poorly surfaced footpaths if outdoors, or being badly lit if indoors. They may be too expensive, shut at weekends,

2. The scheme was first proposed by a member of the Society, Alan Machin.

or staffed by people who are not equipped to answer questions. Light bulbs or apparatus may be constantly faulty; gate catches may be broken; there may be sweet wrappers and drink cans lying among the displays, or broken glass in the car park. Leaflet dispensers may be jammed if mechanical, or empty if not. Promotion may be inadequate, or misleading, or may omit vital information.

Good Interpretation has to accept responsibility for good management. Training courses for Interpreters include the subjects of adminstrative skills and care of visitors. Since visitors' receptivity may depend on welcome, ambience and presentation, these matters are intimately bound up in the interpretation process. They must somehow be included in any assessment.

AN ASSESSMENT SCHEME FOR ALL SEASONS

I propose here a scheme of assessment that divides the elements of the Interpretation process into five stages, for each of which we can award marks.

- **Planning**: the concept, the principle, the interpretive plan.
- **Scripting**: the story-line and how it is told.
- **Design**: how the message is presented.
- **Visitor care**: how user-friendly the set-up is.
- **Management**: organisation, efficiency and attitudes.

These are general enough to be applied to almost any Interpretation project. Below, they are subdivided with specific questions.

Planning

1. How well does the strategy, the general method, suit the circumstances?

The circumstances comprise the nature of the Feature and its context, the nature of the Visitors, and the nature of the messages to be communicated. It is possible, remember, for the intensity of the interpretation to be either inadequate or overdone.

2. How conscientiously is the value of the Feature respected, and its conservation enhanced, by this scheme of interpretation?

If Interpretation has a conservation ethic, then the very least it must do is ensure that its provision does no harm to the Feature. It is better still if it actually contributes to the care or survival of the Feature in some way. Such contributions may be indirect as well as direct.

3. How sensibly are financial and human resources applied to this scheme of interpretation?

Promoters are free, of course, to spend their own money as they like. But an independent observer may reasonably feel that the educational and conservation objectives might be achieved more effectively by a different deployment of resources.

4. To what degree has the interpretation a sound, clear, individual theme and message?
The importance of themes has been discussed in chapter 7.

5. To what extent does the scheme show evidence of the successful application of imagination and originality?
Look for imaginative solutions to problems and original thinking, but note the word 'successful' here. There is no need to penalise simple schemes if they show good conventional practice.

The answers to these questions should reveal the quality of the Interpretive Planning.

Scripting
1. How easily understandable is the text or message?
Is it ever obscure or hard to follow?

2. How sound and accurate is the factual information?
This is not always easy to assess, for information is often specific to the Feature, or specialised in some other way. On the other hand, this matter is very important to any thorough assessment. Misinformation is a fault in Interpretation – though some instances may be trivial, others may positively mislead.

3. How relevant and significant are the information and the interpretation?
This is the chance to consider whether the interpretation says too little or too much, and whether the information supplied is calculated to enlighten or not. Is it people-based? Does it tell how and why? Does it explain what the Visitor actually experiences?

4. How much do the Visitors find themselves involved in the interpretation?
Involvement needs to be a little more than merely being present, seeing and hearing. It implies interaction – physical, emotional or intellectual – but consider critically whether any physical interaction has a useful intellectual component.

5. How well does the script manage to avoid errors in the use of words, spelling, grammar, syntax and punctuation?
If we stumble in speech it may not matter too much so long as we are informative or entertaining. But prepared scripts should be presented with correct use of language.

6. How well chosen and well varied are the media (form, technologies and techniques) for conveying the particular information and messages?

Note that simple media may be better than high-tech to convey some points. Some information may be better presented by a map or cartoon than by text; some in film or video rather than still pictures (and vice versa); some in line drawings rather than photographs. The medium should be chosen because it is best suited to the message (see chapter 9).

Design

1. How appropriate to the situation is the ambience or atmosphere of the presentation?

Does it help put the Visitor in a receptive mood? This may be applied not only to buildings, but to outdoor sites and even to the design and style of publications. Design must be appropriate both to the place and the occasion.

2. How physically easy is it to use or follow the system of interpretation?

Systems may be easy or hard on the eye, the ears, the hands, the feet. This is a good moment to consider the accessibility of the scheme to those with disabilities as well as the able-bodied.

3. How attractive – pleasant to look at or to listen to – is the presentation of the interpretation?

This is relevant not only to the graphic design, but to the general layout and appearance of rooms, structures and signs, even to the outfit of the guides.

4. How well do any graphics, layout and other aspects of the design help to explain and interpret?

Do they support and enhance the verbal interpretation?

5. How good and appropriate is the technical quality of graphics, photographs, mounting, audio and other material?

Specifications should not be unnecessarily extravagant, but is the standard of hardware (screens, etc.) adequate?

6. How thoroughly have proofs been read and the layout checked to avoid misprints, wrong captions, etc.?

This is a matter of taking care in presentation. There will be equivalents in visual media and even in live presentations.

Visitor care

1. How visitor-friendly is the set-up?

Is the system welcoming – in a genuine sense? It should be convenient, and planned to make things easy and pleasant for the user.

2. How suitable and well looked after are ancillary facilities such as parking, lavatories, sales counter?

The word 'suitable' is chosen here because the quality of car parking or lavatories will often have to match the nature of the site. You cannot expect a local authority to provide special parking for access to all rights of way, though guide literature that recommends walk routes should advise on this. Nor should visitors expect that every place of interest should be provided with lavatories, sales counters, refreshments and litter bins.

3. How much 'value for money' does the Visitor get?

It may seem unfair to judge Interpretation where it is offered free. But if a site is advertised as interesting, the visitor should not travel there to find that the presentation is hopelessly poor, even if he does not have to pay.

4. How adequate are the opportunities to follow up the subject or aspects of it?

If a Feature and/or its Interpretation has succeeded in arousing visitors' interest, it can be frustrating for them to have no idea where further information, or other comparable Features, may be found.

Management

1. How efficiently is the system run, and is it in full working order?

This can obviously refer to mechanical, electric or electronic equipment in displays. But guides who turn up late, lights that are not working and supplies of leaflets that have run out or whose information is out of date must all get low marks.

2. How conscientious is the management about training and instructing its staff?

'Front-of-house' staff – those who meet the public – need to be well briefed. 'I don't know, I'm only part-time,' is not a helpful reply to any question.

3. To what extent is the management concerned with evaluating the Interpretation offered, or seeking feedback from visitors?

The answer to this is not always evident, though some establishments make a point of publicly inviting suggestions and criticisms.

4. How suitable are the level and methods of publicity and promotion, and how good, honest and helpful are they?

For some Interpretation schemes, such as outdoor panels, their own location and appearance are their sole advertisement. They, in turn, may be the sole promotion for the Feature they interpret. The vulnerability or inaccessibility of a Feature may be a very proper constraint on its promotion: it is suitability and appropriateness that should be assessed.

The marking system

The marking system should be one that enables comparisons to be made across the different elements in the scheme. Experts recommend that the number of scores possible for each question should be an odd number, so that one can identify the central, neutral score; and either five or seven, to achieve a sufficient range of scores but not so many that they get allocated rather randomly. The diagram (below) shows these two with their central points; in each case the lowest score is 0.

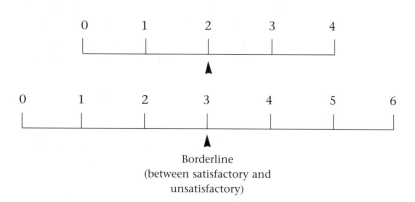

Borderline
(between satisfactory and
unsatisfactory)

To make it even clearer what each score represents in terms of quality, the 7-point sequence could be defined as follows:

6 = Perfect, could not be
      bettered
5 = Excellent
4 = Quite good
3 = Satisfactory but nothing
      special
2 = Weak, less than satisfactory
1 = Bad
0 = Utterly worthless.

Simple formulas for translating scores into percentages are suggested at the end of appendix B, which also lists the question headings.

Do not, at first, try this evaluation method on your own work because it is very hard to be sufficiently detached, but try it on the next piece of Interpretation that you encounter. An overall score of 100 per cent should mean 'perfect, could not be bettered'; and a score of 0 per cent 'utterly worthless'. But a good Interpretation Scheme should show some balance across the whole scoring – less than 50 per cent, say, in any one section should brand a scheme as poor, however well it does in other sections. A scheme can hardly be good if it is misconceived, unintelligible, uncomfortable to use, disrespectful of visitors or badly managed.

Girding on the panoply
Professionalism and training

15

Professionalism has its unacceptable as well as its praiseworthy faces. There is the jealous professionalism that deliberately tries to keep others out of the know; the arrogant professionalism that treats clients as mud; the cliqueish professionalism that is measured by its members' virtuosity in the use of jargon, and the self-protective professionalism that covers up its own weaknesses or errors.

But there is, of course, good professionalism, and even amateurs may aim at it. It means knowing the job; always being thorough and conscientious; taking pride in the quality of one's work, and being businesslike. It ought perhaps also to mean showing generosity, rather than jealousy, towards colleagues. No one is perfect, but good intentions are a sound start.

Interpreters come in many shapes, and we might classify them into four categories. First, there are those few full-time practitioners who are in a position to call themselves 'professional Interpreters', people whose duties or activities can be defined primarily in terms of Interpretation. Their job titles vary – Interpretation Officer, Education Officer, even (with unfortunate ambiguity) Information Officer. Interpretation consultants mostly fall into this category, too.

Secondly, part-time interpreters, whose job description requires or implies that some part of their time is to be spent in Interpretation. These will include park rangers, wardens of nature reserves, many teachers – especially those who take their students on field trips – some museum staff, perhaps some planners responsible for Interpretation projects. Thirdly, those who find themselves practising or contributing to interpretation even though it may not be an essential requirement of their job. They may be farmers, designers, illustrators, audio-visual or computer specialists, archaeologists or coach drivers, to name a few. And, fourthly, those in management posts with some responsibility for interpretation, but who do not practise it themselves.

It is interesting that few of those holding office in the Society for the Interpretation of Britain's Heritage (SIBH) have been in the first category: they may have been professionals who interpreted, but were not necessarily professional interpreters. The explanation is largely that the first category has never been a large one – not surprisingly, since the concept of Interpretation has been with us only for about one generation. This situation is changing: first, because Interpretation has become accepted as an essential element in heritage or environmental management; and secondly, because its functions have become more generally recognised and its standards have generally improved. More and more posts are advertised specifying Interpretation as a required skill; and more and more training establishments are including Interpretation in their courses (see appendix D).

THE SOCIETY FOR THE INTERPRETATION OF BRITAIN'S HERITAGE (SIBH)

The SIBH is the only independent specialist membership organisation in the country which is open to all those associated with Interpretation. It seeks to raise standards in Interpretation practice generally; to provide a forum for those who work in this field; and to serve as a representative body for Interpreters in negotiation or deliberation with other bodies (in education, tourism, training or museums, for instance). It represents Britain nationally among international membership societies, and is involved in the activities of Heritage Interpretation International. SIBH publishes its own journal, *Interpretation*, and administers a programme of weekend and day courses, workshops and conferences. Its Interpret Britain (and, recently, Interpret Ireland) Award Schemes attract dozens of entries every year, and are doing much to raise standards.

SIBH has recently restructured its system to make full membership dependent on qualification: aspiring members must prove that they have specified amounts of experience, and their applications must be sponsored, vetted and approved by existing members. Satisfactory completion of courses in interpretation is another factor that will be taken into account. Whether full membership (MSIBH) can strictly be regarded as a professional qualification is debatable. Who recognises it? What external body may monitor it? There is at present no external body competent to assess the quality of training courses.

So does full membership carry any more authority than the kind of qualifications one can get, for example, in alternative medicine? This will depend largely upon the developing reputation of SIBH itself; certainly, it has quite a long way to go before membership is seen as essential by the bulk of interpreters themselves. At the time of going to press, a little over half the Society's membership of 620 are non-voting organisations,[1] and about a further quarter consist of non-voting affiliate and student members.

Thus something under a quarter have voting rights, of whom a substantial majority are foundation members, whose qualifications are taken on trust.[2] By comparison, in 1989 there were some 1,200

1. This presumably represents a number of people with an interest in Interpretation who do not feel any need to contribute to its direction, but want to be kept informed about what is going on.

2. The present author falls into this category.

people in Britain working in Interpretation full time, and as many as 17,400 others whose work included Interpretation part of the time.[3] Today there may well be more. The continuing rise in overall membership of the Society is, perhaps, an indication that development (both professional and amateur) and improvement in standards are soundly based. It is to be hoped that SIBH will devise a system encouraging the participation of amateurs without implying that they are in any way second class.

The proper advice to novice interpreters must be to join the SIBH. This will ensure that they receive an informative journal three times a year, occasional newsletters, and details of conferences or workshops all over the country on a variety of topics. A Directory is issued, comprising the list of members, with further entries on specialists and consultants with relevant expertise. While not comprehensive, it is the only such national list available, and is much used by organisations in search of professional help.

Interpreters in many other countries have their own membership organisations. Interpreters with international perspectives may also join Heritage Interpretation International (see appendix D), which links Interpreters across the globe. An International Heritage Congress is held in alternate years, doing the rounds of various continents, but participation in this does not come cheap.

3. Calculation by the former Centre for Environmental Interpretation, Manchester.

15:1 Interpreters never stop learning

Many Interpreters find themselves working in professional isolation, often alone among fellow workers whose specialities are very different. It is a refreshing experience to be able to get together regularly with other Interpreters to discuss problems, to learn of new ideas and to visit and discuss schemes. Occasional conferences, workshops or excursions are a good tonic for stimulating enthusiasm and sharpening interpretational wits, and are essential for the development of Interpretation itself. It is unfortunate that in recent years economic restraints have made it less easy for employers to send staff for this kind of training.

The 'listening post' (right) was thought up by staff of the Countryside Commission and developed and manufactured by Reditronics. The post enclosed a small speaker fed by an off-site sound tape player. The visitor just had to plug in an acoustic earpiece to hear the sound – a spoken commentary on the Feature in front of him. The earpiece was disposable, available for a few pence to the visitor, who could if he wished keep it for the next listening post he encountered. Listening posts have now been replaced by more sophisticated audio systems.

Members of the SIBH trying out a 'listening post' at the industrial settlement of Ironbridge in Shropshire.

THE PROFESSION AND THE PUBLIC

Anybody can set up as an Interpreter, just as anyone can try to be a writer.[4] For many years certain bodies have been appointing interpreters, sometimes with considerable success. They have been selected from teachers, media people, museum display specialists, journalists, art school graduates, or those with specialist knowledge in areas such as wildlife or architecture who have already demonstrated an ability to communicate. The best qualification is evidence of successful work already accomplished. This means that it is not easy for a novice to get into the mainstream, but there are enough small jobs to be done for establishments with minimal funds for a number of would-be professionals to find a chance to try their hand, even if the financial rewards are at first not high.

How a prospective client can get in touch with such a novice is hard to advise. One way is to spot a piece of work you like and enquire who did it (it may have been a beginner); another would be to consult the SIBH for a recommendation; yet another might be to approach a well-established Interpreter or Interpretation consultancy, and ask if they know any aspiring practitioners who might do something for an extra-modest fee. Meanwhile, it is only too easy to get the public to accept shoddy work. Interpretation is not the only occupation that includes practitioners with insufficient perception and experience to know what is good and what is not.

An organisation with plans for an Interpretation scheme may decide that it has all the skills it wants within its own ranks. If that is really so, it is very lucky. Recently, I thought the scripting of display panels in the visitor centre of a cathedral was a model of conciseness and clarity. I asked someone on duty who had written it, expecting to hear that it was a professional author. 'It was my husband,' came the answer, 'He's a solicitor.' Sometimes conscientious amateur Interpretation is so well done and so appropriate (matching the nature of the project, reflecting the budget, involving the local community) that professional Interpretation could hardly better it. Some people are naturally skilled communicators – but even those with an instinctive understanding of what Interpretation is about can always refine their skills through training.

It is, however, more common that amateur input shows at least some signs of weakness – too much text or text that is too obscure, poor English or poor design, bad photographs or inadequate drawings. Good professional consultants should be willing to work alongside amateurs – that is entirely in the spirit of community input into Interpretation. But they need to be strong enough to tell their clients firmly if they believe certain work is not up to standard. This is not always easy, especially if the contribution in question comes from one of the client's friends or relatives.

4. The present author was appointed many years ago to set up an Interpretation project, despite having had no specific training in Interpretation – at that time, there was none to be had.

EMPLOYMENT IN INTERPRETATION

Interpretation is not at present a big employer. Its growth may depend partly on the emergence of an economy that can afford the provision of well-presented informal education, and partly on a growing recognition of Interpretation's value to society. However convinced practitioners may be of the importance of their own work, society still seems to regard it as something of a luxury – desirable, perhaps, but not affordable; so it is with adult education and the arts when times are hard.

Full-time Interpretation work exists mainly in two kinds. First, there are posts in organisations that employ one or two Interpreters within much larger workforces – a national park, for instance, or a wildlife trust. In such contexts competition for posts will be fierce, and they will usually be given to the experienced candidate with a proven track record. They are advertised in appropriate journals and newspapers; more and more often in such notices the term 'interpretation' appears alongside 'education' and 'information'. Clearly, the humbler the post, the less likely it is that experienced practitioners will apply for it, and the better the chance for some-one newly qualified, or even the comparative novice. Project officers may be sought for two- or three-year contracts – these give a chance for beginners, even if without much security. However, the number of such short-term opportunities seems to fluctuate with the economy and current fashion.

The second main category is consultancy. Some promoters of interpretation schemes will always require experienced outside advice for planning and guidance. At present, consultancies range from those whose basis is tourism, management, promotion or design to those with Interpretation as their essence (these are usually smaller). Prospective employees may write to such businesses in the hope of finding a niche, but most such consultancies have few staff and, when they are recruiting, secondary skills may be almost as important as experience in Interpretation. But there is no harm in trying.

A third field of opportunity is gradually opening up for more experienced Interpreters – training. New courses appear most years, reflecting not so much the requirements of Interpretation itself as the anxiety of education establishments to attract new students. Another small element in this phenomenon may be the desperation of young people to find a way on to a course, even if employment prospects are uncertain. But tutors have to be recruited from somewhere. Most people currently active in training Interpreters have not been practitioners themselves, but will have found their way in through teaching or some other related discipline. Eventually, experienced Interpreters may find that they are welcome in full-time training posts, rather than just being called on occasionally as visiting experts.

A branch of the Council for the
Protection of Rural England
accepted an offer from an A-level
Communication Studies student
to prepare a slide-tape
programme about its work.
An experienced broadcaster
was willing to record the
commentary, and the result
was a very successful, and
professional, promotional aid.

A sensible strategy for anyone interested in working as an Interpreter would be to earn a reputation for the ability to communicate within some other speciality. Forestry, archaeology, museums,
wildlife conservation and planning are just a few of the industries
in which communication with the public is becoming ever more
important. Specialist qualifications within such fields, with a qualification in Interpretation added, may prove a combination of skills
that will be in demand; proof of successful practice in Interpretation is, of course, an even better recommendation.

Trained or untrained, the chief problem for the novice may be
to find a first outlet for his or her talent, and achieve a first Interpretation project of his own which can be included on a curriculum vitae. A good plan might be to approach a local (rather than
national) voluntary organisation, and ask whether they would like
voluntary help with the production of publicity material or a promotional display. It is important to build up a portfolio of one's
work to show to prospective employers.

CONSULTANTS AND CLIENTS

The growing need for advice on local Interpretation schemes and
the development of consultancies to meet it have not been accompanied by any standard practice for procedures in contracting. In
some respects, this flexibility is to be welcomed, though occasionally it can result in distress. A prime problem is the nature of the
contract between the client (the Promoter) and the consultant.
Interpretation and its preparation stages are not always understood
by the client; nor can the consultant foresee with any accuracy
how much time and effort may be needed for site research, interviews and consultations, scripting and finding illustrations. How
many meetings will be required, how many times will scripts be
reviewed or commented on, how quickly will the client respond to
queries? The client sometimes assures the consultant that research,
illustrative material or text will be provided; it turns out to be of
poor quality or never materialises at all. It is unwise to promise an
early completion date in the light of all these unknowns.

Consultants may be asked to provide financial estimates at too
early a stage. Trustworthy estimates can be given only on the basis
of fairly precise specifications, including the time that the tasks are
likely to take. This may depend as much on the client as on the
consultant; while estimates of cost for producing, say, a booklet or
a display will have to depend upon decisions about style and materials. If the provision of text or illustrations is involved, there can
be confusion over copyright (see chapter 12). It is best to discuss
the matter first, then to write a statement for formal agreement by
both parties.

Many organisations – particularly those spending public money,
such as local government or certain charities – are required to seek

three or more estimates. Inevitably, a consultant may sometimes feel pretty sure that his or her estimate, prepared at some personal inconvenience and expense, is being sought purely so that the client may conform to its own rules, when a choice has perhaps already been made. Courtesy requires that commissioning organisations should always acknowledge tenders or estimates: this is not always done.

Planning the work

It is often useful to consider and to cost a job in three stages. The advantage for the client is that he can proceed step by step, and need feel no obligation to continue or to to complete; he pays only for one stage at a time, and knows how far that will take him and how much it will cost. The advantage for the consultant is that if for any reason the scheme comes to a premature end, he wastes no time and knows that he will be paid for work done. If the scheme proceeds, both parties should soon feel that they trust one another.

Phase A: a preliminary on-site discussion with the client, followed within a week by a brief report from the consultant with proposals on how to proceed, and the estimated cost of preparing an Interpretive Plan, however simple. This phase should be remunerated by a fee or expenses agreed in advance.

Phase B: work on the Interpretive Plan, consisting of the elements agreed in phase A. These may or may not include design specifications and a draft script, but will certainly include estimated costs for the programme itself.

If the client requires it, there may have to be a phase B2, a modification of the Plan to incorporate adjustments, but this should be avoidable if phase B is conducted with proper consultation.

Phase C: the implementation of the programme.

Payment

Work on some projects may last many months; for a long drawn-out scheme procedures for payment should be arranged at an early stage. Parties should agree a system of interim payments, with itemised invoices at intervals of, say, four or six weeks. Consultants should give warning immediately if for any reason they suspect that the project may not proceed according to schedule or budget.

Estimates should always mention VAT where relevant. If the consultant is not registered for VAT, the client should consider arranging for bought-in materials – such as photographic prints or display screens – to be invoiced direct by the supplier rather than through the consultant's account, so that the VAT can be reclaimed.

Contracts

Some clients prefer, or are obliged by their company rules, to prepare detailed formal contracts. They are entitled to do so, but consultants are equally entitled to negotiate their own terms; a contract is two-sided. It need not be over-formalised. A discussion between client and consultant may lead to a letter from one or the other, summarising what was agreed verbally. The second party will write and agree the contents of the letter, or perhaps request some modification. An exchange of letters agreeing to the text will then have the legal standing of a contract. This can work well between parties that trust one another. Consultants should not sign contracts without careful scrutiny; nor should clients over-look the fact that consultants may have their own views.

PUBLICATIONS

It is an interesting question whether or not the growth of Interpretation in Britain has been supported by adequate literature. There have been some good articles in *Interpretation Journal* (SIBH) and *Environmental Interpretation* (Manchester's Centre for Environmental Interpretation), which merged in late 1995 into *Interpretation* (published since 1997 by SIBH alone). But the range is limited; much is merely descriptive, and a certain amount has been rather drily academic. Intelligent analyses of aspects of Interpretation, with practical conclusions drawn from them, have been lacking.

This may be partly because Interpreters tend to be practical and creative people rather than trained academics. Academics, on the other hand, tend not to be Interpreters; and they can be over-detached (observant without being sympathetic) and poor communicators. Let us hope that before long there will be more analysts of Interpretation who know the subject from within, use sound academic method, and have the gift of clear exposition.

TRAINING

Staff at national parks and museums have had in-service training for many years, much of it devoted to practical skills – public speaking, use of audio-visual equipment, lettering for signs and notices. Full-time courses offering training in Interpretation as a vocational approach to a career are comparatively recent in Britain, and there is no coordinating body, no agreed syllabuses and no competent monitoring of standards. National Vocational Qualifications (NVQs) and Scottish Vocational Qualifications (SVQs), which are based on notional levels of achievement in specific skills, provide an element of standardisation. Trainers will work towards these so long as they are required by the tourist industry, but not all Interpretation is commissioned for the tourist industry as such. And the skills identified in the NVQ system are in any case not all that is required to produce good Interpretation.

Interpretation is as much an art as a craft, requiring imagination and experiment. The tools it uses and the contexts in which it is applied are constantly evolving: practices that are sound today may be old-fashioned or inappropriate next year. What does not change is the human condition: each new generation, approximately three times in every century, has to learn afresh how the world works if it is to gain the wisdom necessary to manage the world properly during its own brief tenancy. Thus the essential motivation for Interpretation is unchanging, as are the qualities needed in a good Interpreter.

Training in certain qualities is of even greater importance than teaching the mechanics of the communication aids in use at any one time. Such qualities are listed below, along with suggestions for training exercises, most of which have been tested. It is important to remember that, for successful training in all these qualities, the right candidates must be chosen. Other occupations face this matter of selection with varying degrees of success. There are many terrified teachers, unfulfilled clergymen and uninspired architects. They may survive and even manage to earn a living, but their work will be disappointing to their public and probably to themselves. It is not easy for a tutor trying to fill a course to turn away potential students at interview, but many may not find themselves comfortable in Interpretation.

Sympathy

This is the ability to put yourself not just in other people's shoes, but in their very minds and hearts – to play back, as it were, on your own internal machinery the tape that records their experiences. We need to try to imagine what it is like to be uninterested in wildlife; to be unable to read a map; to be bored with facts; to visit an attraction just because you were dragged there by someone else or wanted shelter from the rain; to read a paragraph right through, and still not get the point.

Sympathy may be a quality that some are destined never to acquire, but certainly it can be enhanced by insights into individual, group and educational psychology. This is not a matter of memorising textbooks, but of observing and analysing one's own feelings and those of others with whom one is studying, under skilled and sensitive leadership. Human experience is common to all, and is capable of observation and discussion.

How people feel, think and act can be explored further by structuring situations in which members of the public, having experienced some specific interpretation, can discuss the experience with the students. Any such training exercise will require careful planning in detail in order to maximise its usefulness. If exercises like this are repeated, students will discover that the lessons they think they have learned one day may have to be unlearned the next. The bewildering variety of public response will itself be appreciated – and might help interpreters to be less dogmatic and more perceptive.

15:2 Studying to understand the Visitor

This group of students, on an Interpretation course as part of a Manpower Services Commission training project in the 1980s, are visiting Angiddy in Gwent, South Wales, where the remains of a small rural iron foundry have been partially uncovered and made accessible to the public. The site is explained by a series of Interpretation panels.

An essential element in training students has to be visiting interpreted sites to see what others have done. This is not just so that good ideas can be copied. More importantly, the student acts as a Visitor and 'uses' the Interpretation. This is the best way to consider why certain features seem to be successful, and others less so; and why the interpretation has been handled in one way and not another.

Undeniably, the same piece of Interpretation can strike visitors very differently: some may find it helpful, others may not. The reasons for these different reactions must be explored and debated, and every person's point of view taken seriously. One's own opinion should never be considered superior to another's – we are all, to a certain extent, ignorant as well as intelligent. We need our ignorance to be understood and our intelligence respected; the Interpreter who does not recognise that each Visitor's reactions are valid is limiting his or her capacity to Interpret better.

Intelligence

More than just not being stupid, this means a reluctance to accept things from teachers on trust. It means an insistence on testing, by our own observation and experience, everything we are told, and doing things in certain ways because we have worked them out to be the best.

Whether intelligence is a result of nature or nurture is a moot point. However much we have, it can undoubtedly be exercised to keep it lively. Simulation exercises may play a part in this. For training purposes, it is not difficult to reduce Interpretive Planning to a kind of team card game. In a couple of hours you can demonstrate a process that, in reality, might take a couple of months. It can be made as complicated as you dare – after all, life is like that. But it is still only simulation, and some simulation exercises may turn out to be little more than tests of simulated intelligence.

The next stage is to tackle an exercise that is almost real – that is, with real parameters that students may explore and research, a real situation, a real site and real people. The only unrealities will be, perhaps, working in teams; a highly condensed schedule, with the necessary cutting of corners; and the fact that the Plan will never actually be translated into action. What might otherwise be a two-month task may in this way be reduced to a long weekend. But this is only preparation – a full-time Interpretation course must require each student to write a genuine Interpretive Plan that is intended to be carried through to implementation.

Students must learn to look at their own and other people's work objectively. They must learn to criticise intelligently and constructively, and not to mind when the process is applied to themselves. It is important to try to understand what lies behind a particular criticism, what the real objection is – and then to consider honestly whether it might have been avoided. One has to learn, too, how to respond graciously to critics, acknowledging truth, but prepared to defend one's position until it is shown to be less than perfect.

Enthusiasm

Contrast the attitude of the weary museum attendant ('It's not my job to answer questions') with that of wildlife presenters like David Attenborough or David Bellamy. There is specialist enthusiasm and polymath enthusiasm. Perhaps the Interpreter needs a touch of both – his own in-depth pet subject, together with an ability to get excited about spiders, steam engines, pingos and broken pots.

Enthusiasm being infectious, the best way to transmit it is by exposing people to it. Students should be introduced to enthusiastic experts, on the experts' home territory. Walk through a summer wood with an entomologist; let a farmer demonstrate his new muck-spreader; explore a quarry with a geologist, a town with an architectural historian. Students should be encouraged to spend time exercising their own hobby horses, to become comparative experts in their own fields, requiring research (the techniques of which will have to be taught) and hard work.

Clear thinking

Clarity of thought is needed not only for clear communication, but also to sort out what are the significant things to bring to people's attention. The Interpreter's raw material is a jumble of facts, a rag-bag of research, a miscellany of information. Very clear thinking is required to put aside, discriminatingly, ninety per cent of it.

It cannot be inculcated by lecturing, but may be developed by debate, especially of the hair-splitting rather than the partisan type. The object of such debate is not to crush, but to outwit. A strong element of good-natured humour is desirable, and the kind of delight in a good game that allows one to express admiration of one's opponent. Debating is not currently a sport with a great following, but it has many of the qualities of a good television game show or court scene, and could be dressed up as either if this would help.

It is good exercise to précis one's own and other people's writing; to reduce a book to a chapter, a chapter to a paragraph, a paragraph to a sentence, a sentence to headline. Discuss why one headline is more appropriate than another. Spot the connections between apparently unrelated phenomena. Why are pine trees often associated with gorse and heather? Why are animal feedstuff firms often sited alongside rivers, or old inns near river crossings? Why does East Anglia have so many round-towered churches, or the Loire valley so many fine châteaux?

Clear expression

The good interpreter must have the skill to grasp what experts mean, and to express it afresh in readily intelligible words or images. No piece of text, arrangement of illustrations, diagrams on a page or a display panel should need to be scanned twice in order to get the sense.

Look at examples of clear writing and obscure writing, and try to see what actually makes one clear, the other obscure. Do the same with displays, criticising the use of illustrations, diagrams, maps – do they add to understanding or not? If not, what, if any, is their useful function? Listen carefully to why another person finds something obscure, if you find it clear. Practise public speaking. Start, if students are shy, with each of them reading aloud a paragraph or two of an interesting or amusing book. Proceed with each person bringing and showing some object that they like, and speaking for half a minute on why they like it, or telling a story from their own experience. Get them to write a short explanatory description of a place, process or phenomenon that they are familiar with, and then to read it aloud, slowly and clearly, to the rest of the group. Use a video camera to experiment with presentational speaking: explain some feature on location, and play the results back. Practise composing single paragraphs, explaining some simple fact or process, then see if fellow students can improve on it, and discuss the results.

Creative imagination, or imaginative creativity

This is imagination that can solve problems. It is a quality found in some really good architects (how to make malthouse ovens into a coffee bar without obscuring the original function of the building); some really good schoolteachers (helping children to understand the role of the House of Commons by staging their own simple debates), and some really good cartoonists (how to illustrate graphically a transaction in canal shares).

Practise spotting the best elements in other people's Interpretation work – the original, the ingenious, the effective. Note also what is weak in other people's work, and devise better ways of presenting it. Tutors may set an interpretive exercise with artificially imposed constraints: discuss new, different strategies for accomplishing it. Apply lateral thinking. Experiment with a brainstorming session. Devise new approaches, test them, assess them coolly, noting their merits and disadvantages; then adapt and refine them.

Get students to devise a new table game or interactive feature (not necessarily on computer) to communicate some specific idea (for example, concerning pollution, building materials or ecology), using no written text except simple instructions. Work gradually from small-scale interpretive exercises to larger and more complex ones.

The suggestions made here are not meant to imply that techniques of communication and other practical matters are irrelevant. But these are so much easier to identify and to teach; they form the staple content of most existing courses and are often excellently taught. Trainers are not likely to overlook them.

A number of 'support' topics will be possible in full-time Interpretation courses. The most important are probably aspects of psychology, especially those of learning (cognition) and personal and group behaviour. Psychologists who have already applied their knowledge to Interpretation will be the appropriate people to devise modules in conjunction with training establishments.

Media and communication should also be studied; again, it will require experts to help prepare suitable modules for training. Media studies could include a consideration of the principles and practices of advertising. Other relevant skills include journalism, media production, adult education, consumer research and statistics. All students also need to consider conservation – of wildlife and countryside, buildings and artefacts – for this is fundamental to Interpretation.

Any course intended to train all-round Interpreters will have to include management and team leadership. Many Interpreters find that they need to be self-sufficient administrators and accountants. Practical ability in photography, audio-visual production and basic

It may not look like it, but this is a training exercise. Students of the Masters Diploma post-graduate course in Heritage Interpretation at St Mary's University College, Strawberry Hill, Twickenham, are asked, as part of the Interpretation module, to assemble a collection of items to express an idea that interests them. Here, a student has put together a display of objects associated with sleep – dressing gown, slippers, bedtime drinks, teddy bear, stoneware and rubber hot water bottles, and a warming pan.

This kind of exercise is not a lesson in display techniques, but in choosing and juxtaposing objects in such a way that they communicate something significant to other people. Fellow students will comment on and discuss the display; in this case, they might well argue whether bed-warming devices from three different eras – brass warming pan, stoneware hot water bottle and rubber bottle – give an extra dimension to the presentation, or weaken its otherwise late twentieth-century directness. The idea could give rise to a display showing, alongside one another, bedroom settings of several different centuries, with accessories appropriate to each one.

Exercises and analysis, discussion and criticism must be at the heart of Interpretation training. Exercises will experiment with a variety of media, and will develop in sophistication as training progresses.

design principles would not come amiss. And who today can do without computer skills? All these should be studied not just in their own right, but in relation to the practice of Interpretation.

Clearly, comprehensive training for Interpretation deserves at least a one-year, full-time course. Better still would be a three-year degree course that included additional major modules in local history and ecology, interwoven with Interpretation studies and examined as major component parts of the whole course.

Training at lower levels and by shorter courses has been done for many years, often as part of in-service training. Its weaknesses have, I think, been due to the inevitably piecemeal tackling of discrete subjects – for example, 'Interpreting Old Buildings', 'An Introduction to Audio-Visuals', 'Setting Up a Nature Trail'. Short courses – whether one-day, weekend or even one-week – can be very inspiring, and can provide initial insights into a variety of subjects and skills; but the students may then be sent forth with minimal back-up and support. Perhaps this pattern is the best that conditions of employment and finance can allow; but it is likely to leave gaps in the knowledge and experience of individuals. This is compounded by the fact that so many Interpreters work in isolation, even if they are surrounded by colleagues with other specialities and responsibilities.

All knowledge and skills have to begin somewhere. The principle behind the national system of NVQs and SVQs is that skills and training can be graded from basic levels to advanced. This is not too difficult for a subject like woodwork, in which the simpler tasks gradually advance to the more complicated, and in which a quick glance from an expert will suffice to see if a job is correctly done. It is harder to apply to a multi-faceted art like Interpretation. Any employer who takes on staff on the basis of the simpler NVQs in Interpretation should encourage them in their efforts to acquire higher grades. How much of a guarantee even a high grade will be of a person's practical competence as an Interpreter, not to mention their perception and imagination, will remain to be seen. Even a university degree cannot ensure a person's suitability for a particular job.

The slight anomaly remains that while the employers of Interpreters are primarily concerned with matters such as conservation or archaeology, tourism or management, Interpretation is in essence an independent educational activity. Education is something that specialists in other subjects are not necessarily skilled to practise or to assess. In my own experience of designing and examining courses in Interpretation, by far the most frustrating task was setting questions to which the examining body required, in advance, a list of 'correct' answers. Not surprisingly, any qualification achieved on this basis will be of minimal value in indicating a person's qualities, actual or potential, as an Interpreter.

16 World without end
Interpretation and the future

Interpretation cannot fail to have a future – of some kind. In its basic, casual forms it has always existed wherever man has lived. We are not concerned in this chapter with predictions so much as with hopes. It would be unwise to guess what the various forms of Interpretation will look like in a decade or two, but it will certainly be what Interpreters make it, as they respond to whatever needs and opportunities an evolving society presents.

WHERE INTERPRETATION SHOULD SIT

One direction that formal, self-conscious Interpretation might advantageously take is to establish and strengthen its associations with education and conservation. Tilden's pioneer analysis of Interpretation was that it was 'an educational activity' – but how little it has been noticed, let alone approved, by educationists!

Adult education, for all its qualities of voluntariness, semiformality and participation, falls within the recognised pattern of educational provision; so do youth and community work, with similar qualities though a very different clientèle and different techniques. Environmental Interpretation could be seen as a system that fills the last educational hiatus – informal education for adults.

The United Nations, at least, regards this as important. In 1974 UNESCO coined the title Global Perspective to describe a policy of global education, intended, among other things, to promote 'understanding and respect for all peoples, their cultures, civilisations, values and ways of life, including domestic ethnic cultures and cultures of other nations.' A similar concept in Britain is Development Education, which has among its aims 'to increase understanding of the economic, social, political and environmental forces which shape all of our lives', and 'to develop the skills, attitudes and values which enable people to work together to bring about change and take control of their own lives.'[1] The Workers' Educational Association has taken up the idea and is encouraging its regions to discuss how they may be involved.

The stress here may be upon the enabling of people, but behind it seems to be an educational ethic very similar to that which

1. As stated by the National Association of Development Education Centres.

motivates Interpretation. Interpretation performs this enabling function (though not always consciously) by encouraging us to look at our world – including the human elements in it – perceptively and critically, in the hope that increased understanding of the way the world works may generate the wisdom to manage it fairly and well. Global Education and Interpretation are compatible – indeed, they could be seen as mutually reinforcing. Both are consciously educational, though Interpretation would do well to enhance its reputation in the world of education by expounding its principles and methods more clearly and convincingly, and insisting more urgently on its informal educational role.

Interpretation also needs to emphasise its essential conservation ethos, and to cooperate with others concerned in the promotion of conservation. Conservationists are not all the same. There are those whose main aim is to proclaim the principle of the sound husbandry of our planet – a principle that is widely accepted today politically, even though specific measures remain open to debate; and there are those with rather narrower vision who, perhaps through frustration, see their role as direct action rather than dialogue and explanation. Two of the key principles of Interpretation are explanation and trying to appreciate all sides of a matter, so it can more easily identify with, and assist, the former.

Interpretation's relations with tourism and entertainment are less straightforward. In recent years, the balance of Interpretation has largely been dictated by money. When the Carnegie United Kingdom Trust sponsored Interpretation, it was able to insist, with considerable success, that educational criteria should be applied even in the informal context of tourism, and the philosophies of education and conservation remained paramount. Since Interpretation has become recognised as a potential tourist attraction in its own right, the philosophies of the economy-driven tourism industry have often taken over.

One small thing that tourism-motivated schemes could do to soften their mercenary image would be to recognise explicitly – when drafting aims and objectives for what they call 'interpretation' projects – that interpretation has its own educational aims, and a role in the overall scheme of looking after our world. It is more than just a devious way to entice people to spend more in local shops and restaurants. Tourism is, of course, entitled to think up its own ways of attracting paying visitors – so long as it does not exploit or patronise the visitor or imperil the basic resources of the natural and man-made heritage. Tourism will continue to do whatever it believes to be in its own interests, however much conscientious conservationists and scrupulous Interpreters may complain. The problem for orthodox Interpretation is whether or not it should be seen consorting with meretricious pseudo-interpretation. I use that disparaging phrase in order to show that it is the shoddier so-called heritage attractions that are to be regretted – there is also much genuine interpretation to be found in the field of tourism, to which orthodox Interpreters have been proud to contribute. If interpretation wants to be taken seriously by education and conservation, it needs to safeguard its own integrity by constant concern for standards and principles.

THINKING INTERPRETIVELY

The ideas underlying Interpretation can be adopted by anyone as a personal code for studying the way the world works. Anyone can exercise the following principles and practices, which are built in to the Interpretation method.

1. Observing and enquiring
2. Comparing, looking for similarities, analogies and interconnections.
3. Discerning differences
4. Asking why and how
5. Seeking to understand man's interaction with his environment
6. Seeking underlying principles
7. Trying to understand opposite points of view
8. Working out best compromises to achieve conservation
9. Translating understanding into politics[2]
10. Managing personal affairs in accordance with conservation principles.

The Interpreter's ideal world would be one in which every person became an interpreter – that is, shared his or her insights with others – with the result that all society adopted the habit of thinking interpretively, and developed a shared understanding and thus a shared wisdom. Parents would encourage their children to observe and to ask why and how, would plan for them to get about and to enjoy, talk about and understand a variety of experiences; formal education would employ many of the methods of Interpretation, and thus perhaps make schooling more relevant and more interesting; academics would keep at least one foot firmly on the ground, and would continually take pains to explain how their studies relate to man's management of the world. Whenever a committee met, its discussions would be based on wide and sympathetic understanding, rather than shallow perceptions and narrow interests. This may be a dream – but it helps to have a target, even if the rapid turnover of human generations makes its perfect achievement impossible. The development of Interpretation will be twofold, involving new contexts as well as new techniques.

NEW TECHNIQUES

Many of us who are professionally concerned with interpretation can become irrationally preoccupied with the latest technology. We have to remind ourselves that, whatever the lure of novelty,

2. Used here in its original sense of the way human societies manage themselves.

on-site Interpretation done face to face will never become obsolete nor, so long as it is well done, old-fashioned. Articulate enthusiasts explaining their pet speciality – a phenomenon, a history or a skill – on their home ground can hold the interest of their audience and share the excitement of discovery in just the same way that their ancestors did when they demonstrated how to exploit the habits of a species of fish in order to catch it, or the properties of flint by shaping it into a tool. Interpreters recognise that face-to-face communication provides a quality of Interpretation second to none.

Neither should the Interpreter's scorn for 'book-on-a-wall' communication be taken to imply that the age of graphics is past, but it does remind us that communicating by the written word needs to be done with understanding, imagination and skill. We are a long way away from the time when two-dimensional graphics become obsolete. There is no shame in using the panel, guide leaflet or indoor display technique wherever it is deemed suitable, and so long as the choice and presentation of words and images are skilled and appropriate.

As for other techniques, let them be used whenever they, too, are thought appropriate. The sole valid motive for choosing a particular technique (apart from considerations of cost) must be the informed conviction that it will, under the prevailing circumstances, do its job better than any other. So there will always be a place for all communication methods, from the latest to the most ancient – virtual reality, touch screens, video, slides, photography, printing, handwriting, one-to-one talk. All were innovations once.

Innovation in Interpretation is not so much a matter of new media, but the more imaginative use of what we have already got. What makes Interpretation occasionally boring is uninspired copycat work – which is why this book has not offered Interpretation-by-numbers. This is not to disparage technique, and previous chapters have tried to show how vitally important it is to communicate with skill and sensitivity. But there is scope for developing true, educational Interpretation in contexts beyond conventional tourism.

GIVE INTERPRETATION MORE SCOPE

The mass media should be encouraged to take on board the concept of Interpretation as meeting an educational need. Many television programmes have done this superbly well. Other providers, especially within the press, have not always recognised how scrupulously conscientious one has to be to Interpret truly and effectively. Interpreters should seek opportunities to share and discuss their principles with sympathetic editors and producers in press, television, radio and other publishing.

Already educational videos are on sale for home use, including many aimed at potential tourists. CD-ROMs carry information, both encyclopedic and specialised – on music, wildlife and geography, for instance – in an intrinsically attractive form. Can the spirit of Interpretation insinuate itself into this field, offering titles that are inspirational as well as informational? Could we see more documentaries, whether marketed as television programmes or videos, deliberately produced to 'interpret' – that is, consciously base their insights on how we experience places and situations?

Attractively presented information aimed at the home sometimes is and sometimes is not interpretive. Strictly speaking, this will depend largely on whether the information supplied explains the user's actual experience. Some Interpreters would no doubt exclude such domestic media from their catalogue of interpretive possibilities because they do not reach the user 'on site'. To a certain extent this may be fair – but who would argue that to watch a well-produced film about the wildlife of South America cannot contribute to a person's understanding of the world? Does the *National Geographic* fail to enlighten because it treats of places that the reader will almost certainly never visit? It is more realistic to accept that understanding what other countries are like, and why, provides a context for the appraisal of those parts of the world we do know. Such placing in context is a cardinal feature in the interpretive method. What matters is whether the information is provided in a way that stimulates comparisons and understanding, or merely offered as a curiosity.

The effectiveness of information in the process of enlightening can be seen in Trivial Pursuit™ – a method of making a game out of facts that became an obsession for many and helped encourage the cult of the quiz. In some respects, this can only be good, but it deals almost exclusively in matters of what and when rather than why and how. Members of enthusiastic quiz teams will memorise the Wimbledon, Derby and football cup winners of many decades in the hope of scoring an extra point at the next competition. It would require an ingenious advocate to convince a jury that such knowledge leads to any significant increase in understanding of the world, though a subtle change in the framing of quiz questions could make the whole exercise more interpretational.

There must be a wider scope for educational games: the seasonal market for board games and card games is enormous. Many are on the toyshop shelves already, but how many have benefited from the input of an experienced interpreter? Computer games might be designed to enlighten entertainingly rather than merely test speed of reaction and digital dexterity.

Books are potential allies in Environmental Interpretation. A person who reads a guide book before going on holiday is preparing himself to appreciate what he is going to see. A person who enjoys a fortnight in Crete so much that as soon as he gets back he goes to the library to get a book about it is seeking interpretation of the experience he has so recently enjoyed. Whether reading a book is an interpretive exercise depends on the extent to which the reader can relate what he reads to his own experience – and that will depend partly on the book and partly on the reader. A skilled writer who wants his book to be interpretive will know what to do – he will ensure that it is inherently interesting; that it stimulates vivid images in the reader's mind, and that it offers explanations of what he describes in terms that the reader will recognise. Just as clarity of text and thoughtful layout, design and illustration are vital to the effectiveness of interpretive displays and panels, so they are, in their own way, to an interpretive book.

For years we have been able to buy posters and wall-sheets. This essentially simple method of communicating with members of the public – the young person, perhaps, who puts it on his bedroom wall and sees it every day of the week for many months – is rarely used to interpret. Some of those that are meant to be educational will be crammed with little pictures to help identify wildfowl, or portray the process whereby milk gets from the cow to the breakfast table, and require almost as much study as a textbook; yet the poster may be placed on a wall where the small print is virtually illegible. A truly interpretive poster or wall-sheet should communicate its message with much more punch. The pattern of the design can play a significant part, so that however much detail can be read close up, the poster as a whole still conveys a meaning even when just glanced at from ten feet away. The important thing is for the designer and scriptwriter to envisage the actual circumstances in which the medium has to perform, and what it is capable of achieving under those circumstances.

Newspapers and magazines find their way into most homes. Occasionally articles will be intended to explain or interpret, but surprisingly not very often. It could be that publishers have never considered that interpretive articles might be popular. It will be up to Interpreters who enjoy journalism to see if they can fill this gap. Local papers often have articles on local history or wildlife, and these could be made more interpretational. Some run series of local rambles or walk routes – these often tell us no more than how to find the way, and fail to explain the features that will be encountered; this is an opportunity wasted. Glossy county magazines, three-quarters filled with advertisements for fashionable clothes and expensive restaurants, could be a market for well-written and illustrated interpretive articles on local history and the countryside.

Some local radio and regional television studios have devoted brief moments to matters of local wildlife, history or landscape. The scope for this, and its benefits, is almost boundless.

COMMUNITY PROJECTS

Beyond our front doors, but still near to home, are community projects. It would be good to think that more of this kind of happening, with interpretational content, might be initiated by local people to whom the concept of Interpretation is important. Such projects could take the form of games (treasure hunts with a historical slant, perhaps); conservation work (your local equivalent of 'scouring the White Horse'); study or survey (making a photographic record of the whole community's buildings, roads or landscape, for instance, or local history research based on an evening class), or art (anything from a historical pageant to a photographic exhibition with a topographical theme). An imaginative community might be able to provide some such event as often as once every two or three years. Professional Interpreters who specialise in this kind of approach could advise and help.

INFORMAL EDUCATION

Youth organisations could build interpretive activities into their programmes. Their national headquarters, which advise and monitor their work, might consider getting professional Interpreters to advise how to present Interpretation in forms that would appeal to young people, according to their age groups. This would be a practical way of fulfilling, in part, the avowed educational aims of the Youth Service. However, progressively severer cuts in education budgets over many years have made the appointment of expert advisers on this kind of thing an unaffordable luxury. Perhaps in the future such initiatives may become possible once more.

Adult education – manifested in the activities of local government evening classes, the Workers' Educational Association and extra-mural departments of universities – might do well to adopt the principles of Interpretation more thoroughly. This means relating teaching, whatever the subject, more deliberately to students' experiences, and maximising opportunities for structuring new experiences, inside or outside the classroom, that will generate understanding when explained. Those studying languages should have the opportunity to converse with native speakers in their own homes; for the study of history there should be visits out; and for other subjects whatever an imaginative and ingenious tutor can devise. The trouble is that the offices that administer adult education are not all sufficiently flexible – a tutor who wants to modify the pattern of a course in order to enhance its educational quality may unintentionally be made to feel that he or she is something of a nuisance to the administrators. On the other hand, administrators with vision probably wish that they could inject more initiative and imagination into their tutors.

Adult clubs and societies could pursue similar ideas. Many societies meet – over lunch, or in the evening – to listen to a visiting

Top: Wharf warehouse building at Aberteifi (Cardigan), converted for use as a community and visitor centre.

Right: dual-language Interpretive display at Hanes Aberteifi, in Welsh and English.

Hanes Aberteifi (Welsh for Cardigan's History) is 'a Cardigan-based community venture concerned with raising awareness of the culture, history and natural environment of Cardigan and its surrounding area.' Its official aims (under headings of conservation, information, education and attraction) refer specifically to 'focusing community and visitor interest in the conservation of Cardigan's built and natural heritage and environment' and the need 'to inform and inspire local people and visitors to value the history and environment of Cardigan'. There are many aspects to its work, including monthly meetings and special events (in particular, an annual Medieval Day). A headquarters and visitor centre has been newly converted from a historic warehouse on a wharf on the river Teifi.

The nature of this project neatly demonstrates the interdependence of conservation, interpretation, education and tourism. Even better, its basis in the local community ensures that it is driven by local enthusiasm rather than by commercial or sectional interests (though the books will have to balance). Everyone may become involved: all will learn in the process.

Hanes Aberteifi's display screens demonstrate one of the problems of bilingual interpretation. All text has to be given in Welsh and English, so that a display may appear at first sight to be wordy. But you only need to read half of it! The lower sections of the panels in the foreground carry material specially for children.

speaker, and they manage not to run out of ideas. But well-presented interpretation of some aspect of their local historical or natural environment might be not just fascinating, but influential. It will be important to invite speakers not just because they have a reputation as experts, but because they are known for interpretational ability. The two qualities are not always found together.

There must be countless other opportunities to vary the contexts in which Interpretation is offered. I have already alluded to viewing platforms with explanatory panels alongside urban archaeological digs – why not a simple interpretive statement to explain and give interest to lesser digs such as the laying of drains or cables? Often these provide the only opportunity people have to see what sort of surface geology their home town rests on.

A student of mine once prepared an interpretive plan for a local golf course. Done in cooperation with the club, it was intended to draw the attention of golfers to the historical or wildlife value of certain features near the greens. Public houses and country clubs might do more to promote interest and loyalty among their habitués by telling them a little about the building, the street or the village. Churches would do well in their guide literature or displays to tell more of the story of their civil parish, as a supplement to what can be rather dull details of ecclesiastical architecture. If it were not for the risk of vandalism, we might wish that certain roadside lay-bys with views of countryside, distant village or interesting buildings would carry interpretive panels.

Some junk mail – even household bills – might be made more acceptable with a touch of interpretive matter on them. This should not, of course, consist of a dry lecture – it could be simply an interesting or explanatory paragraph, or an expressive photograph or cartoon. Such an addition need not in itself be promotional – its purpose could be to lessen, not add to, the sense of injury such unsolicited items often bring.

In a sense, much Interpretation is itself unsolicited. All of us who care for our environment will wince at the thought of Interpretation popping up, especially in its more permanent manifestations, at every turn. To lessen this risk, we might urge that most new interpretation schemes should be short-term, even ephemeral, so that Interpretation's face is constantly changing. Of the financial resources poured into interpretation, perhaps a higher proportion should be spent on smaller, locally generated, inexpensive projects.

SHARING INTERPRETATION SKILLS

It would be good to see Environmental Interpreters who work in the traditional contexts of museums or national parks, stately homes or nature reserves, discussing their work and their strategies with colleagues in the media or youth work, in teaching or sport,

Among the fascinating byways of interpretation must be included the table mats that once confronted visitors to Little Chef diners in Britain. There were about six versions, each featuring an illustration of one of the earlier restaurants in the chain, with a paragraph about the historical and geographical context. If they have not been incinerated they will be collectors' pieces one day, and might even find their way into a future Museum of Interpretation.

A few years ago, a double-decker bus half-fell down a deep subsidence hole in a Norwich street. Besides being topical and relevant, what fun it would have been to produce an instant temporary interpretive panel, expounding this unexpected interconnection between twentieth-century public transport, local chalk geology and medieval mining!

in conservation or politics. There may be more common ground between interpretively minded individuals in such apparently diverse fields than between the generality of persons working within any one field.

Any significant expansion of the practice of Interpretation would require two things: first, a growing general awareness of the concept of Interpretation among the general public; and secondly, opportunities for its principles and techniques to be more widely expounded and discussed. A development programme of this kind would need the authority of a body such as Common Ground or SIBH (see appendix D) and probably charitable funding. Those who might be interested are conservationists (amateurs just as much as professionals); Friends organisations (set up to support local cathedrals, churches, hospitals, etc.); amenity societies; local government; schoolteachers; community workers; youth workers; field study centres; smaller museums; archaeologists; adult education lecturers; tour operators; journalists; church workers; charities; charitable clubs (Round Table, Inner Wheel, Rotary, Lions, etc.), and any businesses (from farmers to chocolate manufacturers) interested in public education. Government departments concerned with education and environment (and, indeed, others) should be persuaded to take Interpretation, by whatever name, seriously.

AN OUTLOOK ON LIFE AND THE WORLD

If readers take seriously the concept of interpretation that this book has tried to expound, and approve the list of principles and practices recommended for the aspiring interpreter in chapter 13, I hope they will agree that these principles could almost form a training for life. If they can be taught in a manner inspired by the ethos of Interpretation (personal discovery, intellectual integrity, respect for others, respect for the natural world and constant concern for right decisions based on conscientiously pondering the facts), then I believe that Interpretation can be more than an occasional activity or function. It could become a way of looking at the world, almost a philosophy.

It is significant that Bruce Babbit, US Secretary of the Interior, wrote recently in *National Geographic*:

> Our national parks are important because they are a gateway to the conservation ethic. In these our most precious sites, we can engage people in a discussion of natural conditions, and of our place in relation to them.[3]

Interpretation is an exercise in explaining our world, as much to ourselves as to others. But its methods are universally valid, and its scope almost boundless. We can readily recognise that it is excellently designed for a localised and limited educational use; but before long we shall find that this excellence is also available for

---

Torfaen Borough Council in Gwent submitted a children's playground in Pontypool for an Interpret Britain Award. The items in the playground – swings, slides and so on – incorporated design features that reflected the landmarks and traditions of the town, such as the railway and canal, local industry and the Rugby football club. Parents who sat watching their children play could read worksheets interpreting this symbolism.

The London Underground has for some years sought to alleviate the boredom of travellers with posters of poems offering food for thought. Perhaps a similar series of interpretive 'believe it or nots' would serve the same purpose.

---

3. Bruce Babbit, introduction, 'Our National Parks', *National Geographic*, vol. 186, no. 4 (October 1994).

In the past two or three decades village signs have become the fashion in East Anglia, and the idea is spreading across Britain. Often craftsman-made of wood or metal, they serve both to identify the heart of a village or small town, and to proclaim its story. Some are erected by parish councils, others by branches of the Women's Institute or by amenity societies like those affiliated to the Council for the Preservation of Rural England.

In every case, they reflect local pride, and reinforce local concern for the appearance of the village as well as an interest in its past. Many villages have competed successfully in competitions for best kept villages; while others may have their own local history societies.

Another function is interpretation: though few signs carry verbal explanation, they serve to remind locals as well as indicate to visitors what gives a particular town or village its character.

This sign (left) is in the former market town of Wymondham, Norfolk, which is rich in medieval houses. On top is perched a replica of the town's fine abbey church, with its two vast towers built in rivalry by the monks and the townspeople not long before the Reformation; while on the shaft is portrayed the town's former industry of wood-turning.

applications less local, less limited, and that the discussion of natural conditions can be extended to cover more than geology and wildlife. Since Freeman Tilden's vision of interpreting the wilderness areas of the USA, we have learnt to apply Interpretation to man-made landscapes and to cities, towns and villages, even the industrial activities of man. But we also have social environments to consider, and cultural environments, and economic and political environments. These, too, make best sense when the principles of Interpretation are applied to them.

The Interpretational way of thinking that is already fundamental to conservation (whether concerned with wildlife, countryside, heritage or museums) needs to be applied wherever decisions have to be made – planning decisions, political decisions, family decisions. All relevant factors need to be investigated, all resources identified and assessed: material and non-material, financial, cultural, historic and social. Whether such an approach needs actually to be labelled 'Interpretational' is not as important as whether or not the principles behind it are sound and practicable.

The future of Interpretation training

The previous chapter offered a number of practical suggestions for certain subject matter and training methods. It did not, however, explore very far the possibility of making the study of Interpretation itself more widely and generally attractive and accessible. There are now vocational courses in the subject, but just as not everyone interested in ancient Egypt wants to become a professional Egyptologist, nor everyone who enjoys the study of politics intends to be a full-time politician, so Interpretation may fascinate people who do not plan to make it their vocation. Courses in communication studies or human psychology, books on how to make friends or self-education have substantial followings among the general public. Phrases such as 'reading the landscape', 'nature detective' and 'upstairs, downstairs' imply a general fascination with matters of local history, wildlife and human relationships. It could be worth offering people an opportunity to study the principles of Interpretation as something relevant to themselves as individuals and to society as whole. The problem is how to introduce them, when to most people the term 'Interpretation' seems esoteric and the concept remains strange. The process may have to be part of a general promotion of Interpretation as an art or a philosophy, which may best be achieved by first making the topic respectable in education circles.

'Them and us' or 'we together'?

Some might argue that Interpretation as we know it is so called only because the word defines that specific us-to-them communication by which 'we who like to think that we know the language of the wilderness can tell the visitor what the wilderness has to say to those who will listen.' Historically and semantically, however, the term has always also suggested the individual's capacity for personal, subjective understanding: 'I interpret Salvador Dali this way' or 'I interpret Fred's actions to mean so-and-so.' And how rightly we interpret Dali or Fred may depend on how practised we are in consciously and subconsciously searching for and synthesising explanations – learning how the world works. The game is the same, whatever the name.

The aim of Interpretation will, I hope, always be not to create a docile public that accepts Interpreters' statements and doctrines as ultimate authority, but a public that learns to interpret for itself, a public that really understands and grows wise. Nothing would delight a genuine Interpreter more than that those whom he has served should think more clearly, become wiser, and be better communicators than he is himself.

Appendix A

The evolution of conservation in Britain

The setting up of the National Trust in 1895[1] must be reckoned a crucial landmark: it made a reality of ideas that had been fermenting quietly ever since the growing appreciation of landscape and architecture became confronted with the deleterious effects on our towns and countryside of the Industrial Revolution and the nineteenth-century population explosion. The National Trust for Places of Historic Interest or Natural Beauty operates in England, Wales and Northern Ireland; a separate National Trust for Scotland was established in 1931. Acquisition and preservation, rather than conservation, were the original intent; but gradually, as the principles of conservation became better understood and gained more widespread support, the National Trusts became conservation organisations.

Britain has long amused the world by its untidy but effective pattern of enthusiast voluntary organisations. Like so many of the country's movements and institutions – education, medical care and garden cities, for example – conservation was pioneered by amateurs and volunteers, with government following reluctantly as public opinion (or at least the voting classes) seemed to demand. As late as 1938, a group of influential writers and scholars felt it necessary to put together some two dozen hard-hitting chapters, effectively addressed to Britain's politicians, on the condition of the country's towns, fine houses and countryside: the title of their book was *Britain and the Beast*.[2] The 'Beast' was industrialisation, unscrupulous development and the kind of materialism that rates financial profit above beauty.

It was not until 1949, more than fifty years after the National Trust began, that parliament approved the National Parks Act. With hindsight, this can be recognised as an element in the great social self-assessment of Britain, which began during the Second World War and resulted in a programme of general restructuring during the following decade. The National Parks Commission set up the National Parks of the Lake District, Snowdonia, Dartmoor, Peak District and six others. The objectives could not be quite the same as those that had guided the National Parks in the USA. Most of the American Parks had been declared decades earlier, and many

1. It is noteworthy that the Commons, Open Spaces and Footpaths Preservation Society (concerned primarily with access) had been founded as early as 1865.

2. Clough Williams-Ellis, ed., *Britain and the Beast*, J. M. Dent and Sons, London, 1938. Contributors included J. M. Keynes, E. M. Forster, C. E. M. Joad, Clough Williams-Ellis, A. G. Street, Patrick Abercrombie, G. M. Trevelyan, John Gloag, Sir William Beach Thomas, S. P. B. Mais and R. M. Lockley. The book was prefaced by a series of supporting 'messages' from celebrated personages including David Lloyd George, Sir Kingsley Wood, Lord Baden-Powell, Sir Stafford Cripps, J. B. Priestley, Prof. Julian Huxley, two earls and a marquis who between them represented the National Trust, the Council for the Preservation of Rural England and the Travel Association.

were much, much bigger – some were newly discovered tracts of land never occupied by the colonisers. From the start, they were intended to be preserved as wilderness. The Parks in Britain had always been owned, lived in and farmed, and their resources commercially exploited, throughout history. What is more, British Parks are potentially within a day's travel from anywhere in the island.

Today there are twelve National Parks or near equivalents; one of the latest is The Broads which, in contrast to its upland companions, is comprised of a system of lowland rivers and their valleys which all converge to enter the sea through the same estuary on the coast of East Anglia. In Britain the county and district equivalents of National Parks, many owned by local councils, are known as Country Parks. They may be considered as about three-quarters down the scale between National Parks and most Municipal Parks, both in size and in pattern of use.

In institutionalised form (individuals had always looked after the wildlife on their own estates), Nature Conservation started in Britain with occasional local committees that acquired or leased land for reserves. The Farne Islands, Northumberland, were managed from the first decade of the twentieth century by an association of naturalists, until eventually ownership was transferred to the National Trust. The Hon. N. C. Rothschild bought Woodwalton Fen, Cambridgeshire, in 1910 in order to safeguard it. Two years later, with three others, he set up the Society for the Promotion of Nature Reserves (SPNR), intended not so much to acquire land for nature conservation as to encourage other bodies to do so. The Norfolk Naturalists' Trust was formed in 1923 by Sidney Long and his friends in order to secure the Cley Marshes, on the north Norfolk coast, as a reserve. The next county naturalists' trust to be established was that for Yorkshire, founded in 1946. By about 1965 virtually every part of Britain was covered by a county or regional trust for nature conservation. Today most of them are called Wildlife Trusts, and are united under the umbrella of the Royal Society for Nature Conservation (the former SPNR).[3] Together they own or manage nearly 2,000 nature reserves. The Royal Society for the Protection of Birds, founded in 1889,[4] is today the largest of the voluntary conservation organisations in Britain, with about 130 reserves, and a current membership of one million.

One by one (often the newer ones first), the independent nature conservation organisations recognised that, since their growth and survival were going to depend largely on voluntary donations, their future security would require ever wider public support. They started to polish their images, they took trouble to explain their work in simple terms, and they began to welcome visitors. Soon, almost without knowing it, they were engaging in Interpretation.

The Forestry Commission, set up in 1919 primarily to meet the nation's long-term timber needs, was the first government-

3. It now prefers to be known, rather ambiguously, as The Wildlife Trusts.

4. Chiefly in order to campaign against the then fashionable use of birds' plumage in women's hats.

226 Appendix A
The evolution of
conservation in Britain

sponsored agency to hold land on any large scale; in the 1930s it developed the idea of National Forest Parks. The Commission's regard for amenity and nature conservation has grown gradually since. Many people were pleasantly surprised when it embraced Interpretation, once the concept was articulated in Britain in the 1960s. Forest Enterprise is the current title of the Division of the Commission that manages and interprets its own forests.

The National Parks Commission was renamed the Countryside Commission for England and Wales in 1968, when it was given additional responsibilities for conservation of, and access to, the countryside in general. A similar Countryside Commission for Scotland was established at the same time.

The Nature Conservancy was created by royal charter in 1949 to be the official advisory and research body on nature conservation. The Natural Environment Research Council (NERC), created in 1965, took over its research responsibilities, while the Conservancy continued as a department with the task of co-ordinating nature conservation throughout the country. They were both responsible for the designation of National Nature Reserves (NNRs) and Sites of Special Scientific Interest (SSSIs). Later, the Nature Conservancy was renamed Nature Conservancy Council; more recently, it became English Nature. Its powers – and, some say, its efficacy – have been somewhat reduced.

ANCIENT AND HISTORIC MONUMENTS

William Morris's Society for the Preservation of Ancient Buildings was formed in 1877, with Morris as Secretary. Like many similar bodies (including the National Trust), it began as an élitist organisation, though it had the interests of the general public at heart. It worked alongside the younger National Trust, and encouraged the latter in its very first purchase, the timber-framed Clergy House at Alfriston, Sussex.

Official government interest in the conservation of buildings and ancient monuments followed campaigns in the nineteenth century by a far-sighted naturalist and conservationist MP, Sir John Lubbock; later Lord Avebury, he took his title from the great stone circle in Wiltshire. This monument owed much to Lubbock for its preservation from building development. He persisted in haranguing parliament on such matters until the Ancient Monuments Protection Act was passed in 1882.

From 1908, historical monuments in Britain were being methodically studied and recorded by the Royal Commission on Historical Monuments, though by the end of the Second World War surveys of only eight of Britain's counties had been published. Various post-war Town and Country Planning Acts gradually advanced the cause of listing and protecting historic buildings, while certain historic properties were directly administered and maintained by the Ministry of Works. That ministry was eventually subsumed by the Department of the Environment, until in 1984 many of its responsibilities were merged with the Royal Commission, which became The Historic Buildings and Monuments Commission for England, later given the short title English Heritage. England may also feel grateful for the existence of the Council for the Preservation of Rural England and the Civic Trust, with their associated local amenity societies concerned respectively with the countryside and the town. These provide a milieu for local conservationists to work for the better management of their own districts, with an input into local planning processes. The Historic Gardens Society was founded in 1955, and specialist conservation groups continue to arise: the Public Monuments and Sculpture Association began in 1991.

The historic role of museums in looking after collections is well documented; many, both large or small, are also housed in listed buildings. Charles Darwin's home and its grounds, Down House, Greater London, are now in the care of the British Museum (Natural History), and are to be re-opened to the public as a Darwin Museum, under the management of English Heritage.

General concern for the environment was greatly stirred in the 1960s. Influential books in that decade included Rachel Carson's *Silent Spring* (1963), Jean Dorst's *Avant que nature meure* (1965) and Garth Christian's *Tomorrow's Countryside* (1966); the less well-known *Landscape in Distress* (1965) by Lionel Brett sounded a similar message. The first National Nature Week was held in 1963, and a second in 1966. There can be little doubt that the Countryside in 1970 conferences of that period, and the coordinated European Conservation Year of 1970, driven largely by expert concern, made a powerful contribution to public understanding and stimulated grass-roots activity. Friends of the Earth and Greenpeace (both established in Britain in 1971) have been energetically popularising environmental conservation ever since, effectively influencing – or at least challenging – the attitudes not only of the general populace, but also of industry and politics across the world.

The story of conservation in Britain has been more complex and sometimes more traumatic than this brief summary suggests. Politics and personalities have hindered almost as often as advanced the cause; but Britain, like many other countries, has made noticeable progress in its efforts to integrate conservation into national life. Perhaps reluctantly, politicians have recognised that there are votes in it.

Appendix B

A checklist for Interpretive Planning

The items in this list are explained in chapter 13; anyone intending to use this checklist should first become familiar with that chapter. Although the list has, I hope, a logical sequence, the tasks do not necessarily have to be tackled strictly in this order, nor need every Interpretive Plan present its findings and proposals according to this pattern.

Introductory
1. Identify the site or feature, and its location, ownership and present management.
2. Tell how the site or feature comes to be the subject of the proposed interpretation.

Social and political
3. Determine the underlying motive for suggesting an interpretive scheme at this place.
4. Predict local reactions – political, official, individual, public, etc.
5. Investigate the pattern of tourism locally, and predict visitor pattern/use for this site/feature.
6. Predict the types of potential users, and their attitudes, expectations and behaviour – the expected visitor profile.

Strategic
7. Define official aims and objectives.
8. Assess the nature, quality and conservational needs of the site or feature to be interpreted.
9. Note any external constraints on management and Interpretation.
10. Note any constraints imposed by the Promoter/ Proprietor.
11. Assess the Promoter's/Proprietor's resources – manpower, skills, experience, materials, premises, finance, storage, etc.
12. Note the relationship between the new project and any existing scheme of Interpretation administered by the same Promoter/Proprietor.
13. Propose an outline strategy based on or consistent with all other factors envisaged in this checklist.

Academic
14. Research the site or feature, and record the findings.
15. Catalogue the documentary sources used and/or available.
16. Study the context (geographical, historical, cultural) of the site or feature.
17. Draw out the messages of the site/feature and express them in simple, single-sentence form.
18. Select possible main themes for the Interpretation.

Communicational
19. Select appropriate media to communicate the theme, messages and stories.
20. Draft provisional script (including suggestions for illustrative material) for the Interpretation.
21. Consider general ideas for design and style.

Administrative
22. Consider and suggest how the proposed scheme will be administered.
23. Assess the staff time and skills required.
24. Consider the need for, and recommend in detail, any necessary supporting provision.
25. Estimate ongoing maintenance requirements.

Financial
26. Estimate the capital costs.
27. Consider sources of capital finance, if relevant.
28. Estimate the running costs.
29. Estimate any income to be generated by the scheme itself.
30. Estimate the likely costs of eventual replacement of Interpretation material.

Procedural
31. Consider the need for any further consultations.
32. Propose a time schedule and phasing.

Appendix C

A simple scheme for assessing Interpretation

Having carefully read the explanatory notes in chapter 14, award marks out of 6 for each of the 25 criteria listed below, according to this scale:

6 = Perfect, could not be bettered
5 = Excellent
4 = Quite good
3 = Satisfactory but nothing special
2 = Weak, less than satisfactory
1 = Bad
0 = Utterly worthless.

A PLANNING: the concept, the principle, the interpretive plan

A1 How well does the strategy, the general method, suit the circumstances?
A2 How conscientiously is the value of the Feature respected, and its conservation enhanced, by this scheme of interpretation?
A3 How sensibly are financial and human resources applied to this scheme of interpretation?
A4 To what degree has the interpretation a sound, clear, individual theme and message?
A5 To what extent does the scheme show evidence of the successful application of imagination and originality?

B SCRIPTING: the story-line and how it is told

B1 How easily understandable is the text or message?
B2 How sound and accurate is the factual information?
B3 How relevant and significant are the information and the interpretation?
B4 How much do visitors find themselves involved in the interpretation?
B5 How well does the script manage to avoid errors in the use of words, spelling, grammar, syntax and punctuation?
B6 How well chosen and well varied are the media for conveying the particular information and messages?

C DESIGN: how the message is dressed for presentation

C1 How appropriate to the situation is the ambience or atmosphere of the presentation?
C2 How physically easy is it to use or follow the system of interpretation?
C3 How attractive – pleasant to look at or to listen to – is the presentation of the interpretation?
C4 How well do any graphics, layout and other aspects of the design help to explain and interpret?
C5 How good and appropriate is the technical quality of graphics, photographs, mounting, audio and other material?
C6 How thoroughly have proofs been read and the layout checked to avoid misprints, wrong captions, etc.?

D VISITOR CARE: how visitors feel they are treated

D1 How visitor-friendly is the set-up?
D2 How suitable and well looked after are ancillary facilities such as parking, lavatories, sales counter?
D3 How much 'value for money' does the Visitor get?
D4 How adequate are the opportunities to follow up the subject or aspects of it?

E MANAGEMENT: organisation and attitudes

E1 How efficiently is the system run, and is it in full working order?
E2 How conscientious is the management about training and instructing its staff?
E3 To what extent is the management concerned with evaluating the Interpretation offered, or seeking feedback from visitors?
E4 How suitable are the level and methods of publicity and promotion, and how good, honest and helpful are they?

When every criterion has been used

If you have given appropriate scores based on each of these 25 criteria, omitting none as not applicable, you can turn the total score into a percentage (i.e. a score out of 100) by multiplying it by two thirds (.666).

If some criteria are not applicable

If you are assessing a project to which some of the questions do not apply, use the formula:

$$S \div Q \times 50 \div 3 \quad (or \ S \div Q \times 16.666)$$

where S is the sum of the marks awarded, and Q is the number of questions, or criteria, used.

This same formula can also, if required, be used to calculate a percentage score for each major group of criteria separately.

Once reduced to percentages according to these formulas, the score of any interpretive scheme, whether or not some criteria are treated as not applicable, may be compared with any other – though the greater the number of questions deemed inapplicable, the less strictly fair the comparison will be.

It would also be possible (though probably not worthwhile for such a subjective method of assessment) to devise refinements by which certain criteria were given greater or less weighting according to opinion about their relative importance. Reasonable weighting is already built in to this system, in that the maximum marks that can be earned in each section are:

- scripting and design: 36 marks each
- planning: 30 marks
- visitor care and management: 24 marks each.

Any scheme that scores less than 50 per cent of possible marks *in any one* of the five sections should be regarded as essentially unsatisfactory, even if its total percentage is higher.

Appendix D
Training, professional and other organisations

I hope this list will not only be useful for reference, but also serve to demonstrate how wide a range of organisations are actually or potentially concerned with Environmental Interpretation. It has been difficult to decide what organisations *not* to include: I hope that all the major bodies with an essential concern for Interpretation are listed here, and apologise to any others that may be disappointed.

Readers will be aware that organisations, their titles, addresses, publications and so on, may be impermanent – as the third entry below demonstrates. Information in this appendix was as accurate as it could be made before going to press; it is likely that there have been changes since.

MAIN INTERPRETATION BODIES

Society for the Interpretation of Britain's Heritage (SIBH)

The Membership Co-ordinator of SIBH may be contacted at P.O. Box 6541, Warley, West Midlands B65 0AP, tel. or fax 0121-559 2022.

Since this address may not be a permanent one, enquiries addressed to John Iddon, Organiser for the Society's Interpret Britain Award Scheme, at St Mary's University College, Strawberry Hill, Twickenham TW1 4SX, will be passed to the appropriate officer. Or visit the Society's web site at http://www.quinion.demon.co.uk/sibh.

SIBH (alternatively known by its brief title Interpret Britain) was founded in 1975, and is the only general membership organisation for Interpreters in Britain. It runs conferences and courses, and publishes the journal *Interpretation* three times a year. It also publishes the *Interpretation Directory* (see appendix E); and administers the annual Interpret Britain and Interpret Ireland Awards (see end of this appendix).

Heritage Interpretation International (HII)

Box 7451 NECSC, Edmonton, Alberta, Canada TFE 6K1

The International body that links national Interpretation organisations; in recent years it has coordinated a series of international Interpretation Congresses.

Centre for Environmental Interpretation (CEI)

Until 1997 a unit of Manchester Metropolitan University, with an office attached to the The University of Edinburgh. It was closed down unexpectedly in 1997, and at the time this book goes to press, it is still uncertain which of its many valuable functions may be taken on by other organisations or institutions.

CEI was established in 1980 with grant aid from the Carnegie United Kingdom Trust as a national centre to promote good practice in Interpretation. Its aim was to 'develop the concept of Interpretation and to place it within the context of natural and built resource management, economic development, recreation and tourism practice and environmental education.'

CEI ran training courses in interpretation, undertook consultancy work, kept what must have been the most comprehensive library in Britain relating to Interpretation, and distributed its own and other publications on the subject.

TRAINING IN INTERPRETATION OR FOR INTERPRETERS

There is not space to list all organisations that offer occasional short courses in aspects of Interpretation; but SIBH will be aware of most of them, and may be able to help enquirers; while the Countryside Commission (see below) publishes a reasonably priced *Countryside Education and Training Directory* (ref. CCP363).

Birkbeck College (University of London)
Centre for Extra-Mural Studies, 26 Russell Square, London WC1B 5DQ (tel. 0171-631 6654)
Offers diploma and MSc courses in Heritage Interpretation and Environmental Education.

Capel Manor (Horticultural and Environmental Centre)
Countryside Training Unit, Bullsmoor Lane, Enfield, Middlesex EN1 4RQ (tel. 01992 763849)
Has for many years been running short courses on aspects of Interpretation.

Insite (Consultancy for Management and Training)
9–23 St Leonards Crag, Edinburgh EH8 9SP (tel. 0131-667 1246)
A leading agency in the training of heritage and tourism on-site staff; among other opportunities it offers National Certificate courses.

Institute of Travel and Tourism
113 Victoria Street, St Albans, Hertfordshire AL1 3TJ (tel. 01727 854395)
Offers, among other services, training in visitor identification, visitor care and staff relations with visitors, and other matters relevant to the management side of Interpretation.

Ironbridge Institute (University of Birmingham)
Ironbridge Gorge Museum, Ironbridge, Telford, Shropshire TF8 7AW (tel. 01952 432751)
Has been running training courses in the management and interpretation of heritage sites since 1981, including Masters and Diploma courses, and CPD.

Losehill Hall
Peak National Park Centre, Castleton, Derbyshire S20 2WB (tel. 01433 620373)
The training centre of the Peak District National Park, which offers a regular programme of shorter courses on subjects related to Interpretation and Environmental Management, as well as leisure courses with an interpretive content.

Museums Training Institute
Kershaw House, 55 Well Street, Bradford, West Yorkshire BD1 5PS (tel. 01274 391056)
Concerned to encourage the highest possible standards in the work of museum staff, by researching into, and promoting, best training methods. Interpretation is recognised as a necessary skill for museum staff.

Oxford Brookes University
Headington, Oxford OX3 0BP (tel. 01295 710554)
The School of Planning offers units in Interpretation and related matters appropriate to planning, urban design and architecture at undergraduate and graduate levels.

St Mary's University College
Strawberry Hill, Twickenham, Middlesex TW1 4SX (tel. 0181-240 4078)
Offers MA and postgraduate courses in Heritage Management and Interpretation, as well as a series of one-day conferences on heritage and interpretation topics. The Heritage Interpretation Centre also offers on-site training for staff in guiding, customer care and Interpretation.

Snowdonia National Park Study Centre
Plas Tan-y-Bwlch, Maentwrog, Blaenau Ffestiniog, Gwynedd LL41 3YU (tel. 01766 590324)
Offers short course on many subjects connected with environmental and conservation matters, including interpretation.

Society for the Interpretation of Britain's Heritage
For contact addresses, see page 231
Runs a number of day or weekend conferences on specific themes each year, at which non-members are welcome.

Note also that CEI and SIBH were involved in working with TICK, the travel services 'lead body', in establishing content and standards for National Vocational Qualifications (NVQs) in 'travel services (commentaries and interpretation for tourism)'.

NATIONAL ORGANISATIONS THAT INTERPRET THEIR OWN PROPERTIES

British Waterways
Melbury House, Melbury Terrace, London NW1 6JX (tel. 01923 226422)
Responsibility for education and interpretation within BW is now mostly devolved to the various Waterway Offices responsible for the administration of particular lengths of waterway. A list of addresses can be obtained from BW Melbury House headquarters.

Cadw (Welsh Historic Monuments)

Crown Building, Cathay Park, Cardiff CF1 3NQ
  (tel. 01222 500200)

The Welsh equivalent of English Heritage and Historic Scotland, Cadw's mission is 'to protect, conserve and to promote an appreciation of the built heritage of Wales.' There are 131 monuments in its direct care, and it has general planning responsibilities for all Wales's archaeological sites and historic buildings. Its colourful brochure devotes two full pages to the topic of 'Presenting the Past – How Cadw interprets and displays sites for public interest and enjoyment.' Heritage in Wales is Cadw's membership scheme.

Countryside Council for Wales (Cyngor Cefn Gwlad Cymru)

Plas Penrhos, Ffordd Penrhos, Bangor,
  Gwynedd LL57 2LQ (tel. 01248 370444)

The Government's statutory adviser on countryside and nature conservation in Wales, with responsibilities that can be compared with (but are not identical to) those of English Nature and the Countryside Commission in England, or Scottish Natural Heritage in Scotland. The Council directly manages and interprets National Nature Reserves in Wales. One stated objective is to 'increase people's understanding and appreciation of the countryside, its wildlife and habitats.' The set-up includes a Countryside Management and Interpretation Group.

English Heritage

Headquarters: Fortress House, 23 Savile Row,
  London W1X 2HE

Visitor and Interpretation section: Keysign House,
  429 Oxford Street, London W1R 2HD
  (tel. 0171-973 3461)

The Government's official adviser on all heritage conservation matters, which itself manages over 400 sites. Its Visitor and Interpretation section is progressive, both in matters of research on visitor profiles and patterns, and the provision of a wide range of Interpretation, including 'living history'. It has a membership scheme (currently about 360,000), and a quarterly magazine *Heritage Today*.

English Nature

Headquarters, Northminster House, Peterborough,
  Cambridgeshire PE1 1UA (tel. 01733 340345)
  (Publicity and Grants: tel. 01733 455000)

Derived from the former Nature Conservancy Council, English Nature is responsible for the designation of SSSIs, and the management of many of the UK's 250 National Nature Reserves, 164 of which are located in England. Of these, English Nature owns 46, and parts of 30 others. Most Interpretation of national and other nature reserves is now initiated at local level. For information, contact Publicity and Grants at the above address.

Forestry Commission

231 Corstophine Road, Edinburgh EH12 7AT
  (tel. 0131-334 0303)

Active for many years in the Interpretation of its forest properties, by means of the provision of forest parks, visitor centres, walk routes, live guiding, publications and so on. Local enquiries may be made to the Commission's local offices as shown in telephone directories. Of the Commission's present two major divisions, the Forest Authority and Forest Enterprise, it is the latter that is concerned with the management of the Commission's own timber business and access to, and interpretation of, its own properties.

Historic Scotland

20 Brandon Street, Edinburgh EH3 5RA
  (tel. 0131-668 8600)

A government agency resulting from a 1991 restructuring of the former Historic Buildings and Monuments Commission, with over 330 monuments in its care. Its aims comprise conservation, public access and education ('to encourage knowledge about Scotland's built heritage'). A recent annual report refers to customer surveys, new exhibitions, battle re-enactments, story-telling and a free CD-ROM audio tour for visitors to Edinburgh Castle. Historic Scotland 'values its relationship with the Friends of Historic Scotland.'

National Trust

36 Queen Anne's Gate, London SW1H 9AS
  (tel. 0171-222 9251)

Britain's biggest land-owning charity, founded in 1895 to preserve places of historic interest or natural beauty in England, Wales and Northern Ireland. The Trust provides Interpretation at its properties by a wide range of means, from signing to guided tours, from interpretive displays to living history.

While the managers or wardens are responsible for the Interpretation of their own properties, the Trust has a central Interpretation and Design Office.

National Trust for Scotland

5 Charlotte Square, Edinburgh EH2 4DU
(tel. 0131-226 5922)

Does for Scotland what the National Trust does for England and Wales, acquiring and maintaining (and interpreting) historic and countryside properties for the purposes of conservation and the enjoyment of the general public. The Trust has an Education Department, and also runs courses of an interpretational nature.

Nuclear power stations

(Magnox, Nuclear Electric, British Nuclear Fuels)

There are lavishly presented high-tech displays in free-admission visitor centres at most of Britain's nuclear power stations, managed by one or more of the companies within the nuclear power industry. Look up the name of the power station in the local telephone directory, and ring for further details.

Royal Society for the Protection of Birds (RSPB)

The Lodge, Sandy, Bedfordshire SG19 2DL
(tel. 01767 680551)

With just over one million members, this is the largest conservation membership organisation in Britain, owning some 130 nature reserves, many interpreted by visitor centres, information boards and literature; it publishes a magazine, *Birds*, three times a year. It also produces books, videos and other interpretive material.

Scottish Natural Heritage

12 Hope Terrace, Edinburgh EH9 2AS
(tel. 0131-447 4784)

The Scottish equivalent, though with a slightly different range of responsibilities, of English Nature and Countryside Commission combined. Its advisory services (which include specialist expertise in Interpretation) are based at The Battleby Centre, Redgorton, Perth (see entry in next section, page 235).

Scottish Wildlife Trust

8 Dublin Street, Edinburgh EH1 3PR
(tel. 0131-557 1525)

This fulfils the same role for Scotland as the County Wildlife Trusts do for England and Wales.

The Woodland Trust

Autumn Park, Dysart Road, Grantham, Lincolnshire NG31 6LL (tel. 01476 581111)

Acquires and manages woodland, and wherever possible encourages public access to its properties. A general guide to all the properties is available, but on-site interpretation is not at present a priority.

NATIONAL AND REGIONAL PROMOTERS AND SUPPORTERS OF INTERPRETATION ACTIVITIES

Area Museum Councils

Details obtainable from the Committee of Area Museum Councils, 141 Cheltenham Road, Cirencester, Gloucestershire GL7 2JF (tel. 01285 640428)

There are ten Area Museum Councils (for Scotland, Northern Ireland, Wales and seven regions of England), independent charitable bodies that provide a wide range of services to their members, including advice and information about displays and education. The English Councils are part funded by the Museums and Galleries Commission; the others by the government's territorial departments.

Common Ground

Seven Dials Warehouse, 44 Earlham Street, London WC2H 9LA (tel. 0171-379 3109)

Devises, coordinates and provides advice for specific community projects and events intended to stimulate appreciation, understanding and care of people's own localities. Imaginative ideas include the widely popular and praiseworthy Parish Maps scheme. A range of publications is available.

Countryside Commission (for England and Wales)

John Dower House, Crescent Place, Cheltenham, Gloucestershire GL50 3RA (tel. 01242 521381)

Established in 1968, one of the few government-sponsored organisations that has not changed its name in recent years, though it has been restructured. Formerly among the initiators of

Interpretation projects and publisher of many Interpretive Plans and Handbooks on Interpretation, it is now less active in this field, though it still offers grants for countryside interpretation projects.

A *Publications Catalogue* has much material of interest to Interpreters, including an 'Advice manual for the preparation of a Community Forest plan'; a variety of educational material; and National Nature Trail guide leaflets. A few of the Commission's former publications relating to the practice of Interpretation are still available. The Commission recommends contacting Regional Offices concerning any local projects; addresses given in *Publications Catalogue* or try public libraries or telephone directories. Information about publications can be obtained from the Commission's Recreation and Access Branch.

Countryside Commission for Scotland
See under Scottish Natural Heritage.

Department of the Environment
Eland House, Bressenden Place, London SW1E 5DV (tel. 0171-276 0900)

Tollgate House, Houlton Street, Bristol BS2 9DJ (tel. 0117-987 8000)

Among the many divisions of this government ministry are Rural Development (London address); and Countryside (including Nature Conservation), European Wildlife (including British), and Global Wildlife (Bristol address).

English Tourist Board
Thames Tower, Black's Road, London W6 9EL (tel. 0181-846 9000)

The body to which the independent English regional boards are affiliated (see Tourist Boards, below). For most practical purposes it is best to deal direct with the regional boards.

Museums and Galleries Commission
16 Queen Anne's Gate, London SW1H 9AA (tel. 0171-233 4200)

Incorporated under Royal Charter and funded by the Office of Arts and Libraries, it advises the government on museums and art galleries, and funds the seven English Area Museum Councils, plus purchase schemes, training and other services. The Commission's *Publications List* includes material relating to access for the

disabled, creative approaches to education in museums and methods of carrying out visitor surveys.

Northern Ireland Tourist Board
St Anne's Court, 59 North Street, Belfast, Northern Ireland BT1 1NB (tel. 01232 231221)

Scottish Natural Heritage
(Communications Directorate) Battleby, Redgorton, Perth PH1 3EW (tel. 01738 27921)

Formed by a merger in 1992 of the Nature Conservancy Council for Scotland and the Countryside Commission for Scotland. The Communications Directorate is responsible for education, training, interpretation, design and publications. SNH's aims include 'to foster understanding and facilitate the enjoyment of the natural heritage of Scotland.' It issues an extensive *Publications Catalogue* with many items directly interpretive; resource material for teachers and students; and a free six-monthly newsletter of interpretation in Scotland, *Communicating the Message* (see appendix E).

Scottish Tourist Board
23 Ravelston Terrace, Edinburgh EH4 3EU (tel. 0131-332 2433)

Tourism Concern
Stapleton House, 277–281 Holloway Road, London N7 8HN (tel. 0171-753 3330)

Devoted to devising and promoting ways of reducing the damaging ecological, social and economic effects of tourism. Publishes the journal *In Focus*, and *Beyond the Green Horizon; Sustainable Tourism: Moving from Theory to Practice*, and *Trading Places: Tourism as Trade*.

Tourist Boards (regional)
Interested in, and support, Interpretation insofar as it enhances tourism in their own areas. Names and addresses of the English regional tourist boards can be found in the reference sections of most public libraries, or from the English Tourist Board (see above). Wales, Scotland and Northern Ireland have their own Tourist Boards (see under their own names).

Wales Tourist Board
Brunel House, 2 Fitzalan Road, Cardiff CF2 1UY (tel. 01222 499909)

Amenity Societies

Many of these will be affiliated either to CPRE or
Civic Trust (see next section). Many of these local
societies arrange talks and slide shows,
publications, exhibitions, guided walks, local
community projects, etc. Some larger ones have
their own visitor centres or heritage museums.

County, District and Parish Councils

Local government administers and interprets a range
of facilities including country parks, nature
reserves, historic buildings, museums and so on;
and supports such initiatives as Parish Maps,
interpretation panels and 'Pocket nature reserves'.

Libraries

As a local information resource equipped with books,
specialist magazines, information technology and
space for temporary displays, a library is
potentially in the game of Interpretation. The
extent to which its services become
interpretational may depend largely on the vision
(and available time) of library staff. (See also
Department of National Heritage.)

Museums

Virtually all museums interpret their collections, some
with very great skill, some with less. Many have
their own Education and/or Interpretation
Officers. Some of the national museums have been
among the pioneers of interpretation in recent
years, and have published excellent material on
the subject. Seek addresses of local museums via
Tourist Information Centres, or in telephone
directories or Yellow Pages.

National Parks

Britain's ten national parks, together with The Broads
and The New Forest, are managed to provide
access for the general public, and each provides
interpretation in a variety of forms. Lists of the
parks should be available in the reference sections
of most libraries or from the Countryside
Commission (see above).

Water Companies

Some, at least, conscientiously provide interpretation
of features such as reservoirs, in some cases
providing visitor centres. Seek addresses of
companies in telephone directories or libraries.

Wildlife Trusts (County)

Exist to conserve wildlife and wildlife habitats. Many
provide interpretation at suitable sites; some have
Education and/or Interpretation Officers. Details
of local Wildlife Trusts, and probably lists of all
the Trusts, should be available in the reference
section of most libraries; or from The Wildlife
Trusts (see next section).

NOTE: the annual guides issued by the regional
tourist boards give extensive details of visitor
attractions, many of which are interpreted on
site in one way or another.

ORGANISATIONS THAT REPRESENT OR ADVISE INTERPRETERS OR HERITAGE PROPRIETORS

Association of Independent Museums

Secretary: c/o London Transport Museum, 39
Wellington Street, Covent Garden,
London WC2E 7BB (tel. 0171-379 6344)
Publishes a bi-monthly Bulletin *AIM*, in which aspects
of Interpretation are dealt with from time to time;
and organises specialist seminars, often in
association with other bodies.

Association of Scottish Visitor Attractions (ASVA)

Suite 6, Admiral House, 29–30 Maritime Street, Leith,
Edinburgh EH6 6SE (tel. 0131-555 2551)
A membership organisation that aims to improve the
quality and viability of visitor attractions in
Scotland. Advice and assistance is available on
Interpretation as well as other operational matters.

Civic Trust

17 Carlton House Terrace, London SW1Y 5AW
(tel. 0171 930 0914)
Founded in 1957, it encourages the protection and
improvement of the urban environment, and
advises and supports the 1,000 and more amenity
societies on its register. It has been forward in
encouraging urban interpretation. The Trust issues
a newsletter, *Civic Forum*, and can supply a list of
its other publications. There are associated
regional civic trusts for the North-East of England,
Scotland, and Wales.

Council for the Preservation of Rural England
Warwick House, 25 Buckingham Palace Road, London SW1W 0PP (tel. 0171-976 6433)
Essentially a pressure or ginger group, since its inception in 1926 it has campaigned to protect the best qualities of the English countryside. Its membership of over 45,000 is to be found mainly in its local branches, at county, town and village levels. Since its motivation consists of the personal concern of individuals, and its political effectiveness on profound understanding of the English countryside, Interpretation is inevitably involved, and it is appropriate that its current president is not only a countryman but a media person. The Council issues a long publications list including items relevant to interpretation, and a newsletter/magazine, *CPRE Voice*.

Countryside Management Association
CMA Administration, Drury Lane, Knutsford, Cheshire WA16 6HB
A membership organisation not only for wardens and rangers, but for all countryside management field staff. Has a busy training programmme (courses are open to anyone involved in or interested in countryside management); and publishes *Ranger Magazine* and weekly job vacancy newssheet.

Museums Association
42 Clerkenwell Close, London EC1R 0PA (tel. 0171-608 2933)
A membership organisation that represents and informs museums run by statutory authorities (independent museums are linked by the Association of Independent Museums; see above). Offers training courses and seminars; and publishes the excellent monthly magazine, *Museums Journal*, and a technical magazine, *Museum Practice*, which often deal with matters of interpretation or visitor care.

Royal Society for Nature Conservation
See under Wildlife Trusts below.

Society for the Preservation of Ancient Buildings
37 Spital Square, London ED1 6DY (tel. 0171-377 1644)
In addition to providing technical advice for professionals, runs courses for owners of old properties.

Scottish Countryside Rangers Association
P.O. Box 37, Stirling FK8 2BL
Offers training (including in Interpretation), and publishes a quarterly journal.

Town and Country Planning Association
17 Carlton House Terrace, London SW1Y 5AS (tel. 0171 930 8903)
No longer publishes the *Bulletin of Environmental Education*, but its monthly *Town and Country Planning Journal* from time to time includes articles on relevant aspects of Interpretation.

The Wildlife Trusts
(Operating name of Royal Society for Nature Conservation)
The Green, Nettleham, Lincoln LN2 2NR (tel. 01522 544400)
The umbrella body that links the 47 county wildlife trusts, whose names and addresses can be obtained from this address. Currently preparing guidelines on Interpretation for use by the member trusts (see Wildlife Trusts, County, under Localised Providers, above).

Youth Hostels Association
Trevelyan House, 8 St Stephen's Hill, St Albans, Hertfordshire AL1 2DY (tel. 01727 55215)
For many years designated certain of its hostels as field study hostels, with special facilities for studying local natural and historical features. This is no longer the case, but all hostels have the opportunity to provide for their visitors some kind of Interpretation of their areas.

BODIES CONCERNED WITH THE PROMOTION OF EDUCATION, AND THUS (ACTUALLY OR POTENTIALLY) OF INTERPRETATION AS AN EDUCATIONAL ACTIVITY

Adult Education Centres
To be found in every county, administered mainly by county councils, universities or the Workers' Education Association (see appropriate headings below; for local centres, consult local libraries).

Council for Environmental Education (CEE or CoEnEd)
University of Reading School of Education, London Road, Reading RG1 5AQ (tel. 0118-975 6061)

CEE is a 'forum' organisation whose stated aims include: to influence and develop policy at all levels as it relates to environmental education; and to influence, develop and spread good practice in environmental education. It publishes 'reviews, briefings, news sheets and resource sheets on issues and developments', and runs seminars, conferences and other events. It concerns itself with informal youth work as well as formal education.

County Councils (Education Departments)

Due to changes in government policy and reduction of funding there have have been fewer county specialist education advisors in recent years. If things change for the better, advisors – whatever their speciality – aware of the principles and skills of Environmental Interpretation should be appointed.

Department for Education and Employment

Sanctuary Buildings, Great Smith Street, London SW1P 3BT (tel. 0171-925 5000)
Government department ultimately responsible for the content and quality of teaching at all levels within formal and informal sectors of education, including Adult Education and the statutory Youth and Community Service. The Department includes Directorates for Employment and Lifetime Learning, and for Further and Higher Education and Youth Training. Administration, policy and standards are largely in the hands of some 22 Non-Departmental Public Bodies and Agencies Associated with the Department. Some of these are:

Further Education Funding Council
(remit not confined solely to funding)
Cheylesmore House, Quinton Road,
  Coventry CV1 2WT (tel. 01203 863000)

National Council for Vocational Qualifications
222 Euston Road, London NW1 2BZ
  (tel. 0171-387 9898)

School Curriculum and Assessment Authority
Newcombe House, 45 Notting Hill Gate,
  London W11 3JB (tel. 0171-229 1234)

Teacher Training Agency
13th Floor, Portland House, Stag Place,
  London SW1E 5BH (tel. 0171-925 3700)

Department of National Heritage

2–4 Cockspur Street, London SW1Y 5DH
  (tel. 0171-211 6000)
Two of the groups within the department are Heritage and Tourism; and Libraries, Galleries and Museums. The concept of libraries as information resources implies that they may encourage members of the public to study. Government could persuade Libraries to understand, practise and promote Interpretation (see also Libraries under Localised Providers, page 236).

Field Study Centres

Self-organising centres, mostly to be found in rural or coastal areas, under varied management, though many have had to close down through lack of funding in recent years. Among the best known of the survivors are the 11 excellent ones run by the Field Studies Council (see below).

Field Studies Council (FSC)

Preston Montford, Montford Bridge, Shrewsbury, Shropshire SY4 1HW (tel. 01743 850674)
An independent charity, it is 'committed to helping people explore, learn about and understand their environment'; the first of 11 centres was opened in 1946. Issues an exciting annual brochure offering over 500 courses.

Friends of the Earth (FoE)

26–28 Underwood Street, London N1 7JQ
  (tel. 0171-490 1555)
Should need no introduction to readers; active not only scientifically and politically, but also in 'explaining our world' to the general public, whether in global or local terms. FoE's magazine *Earth Matters* is published quarterly.

Heritage Education Trust

Pickwick, Vicarage Hill, Badby, Daventry,
  Northamptonshire NN11 3AP (tel. 01327 77943)
Seeks to promote high standards of educational use of all historic buildings, their contents and surroundings. Administers two annual awards, the Sandford Award and the Reed Award, which are made to properties that have exhibited 'excellence in their service to schools'.

Libraries

See under Localised Providers, page 236.

National Institute of Adult Continuing Education (NIACE)

21 De Montfort Street, Leicester LE1 7GE
(tel. 0116-204 4200)
NIACE Cymru: WJEC, 245 Western Avenue,
Cardiff CF5 2YX (tel. 0122-226 5001)

A registered charity that 'represents the interests of all adult learners and those who work with them to local and national authorities in the UK and . . . is a partner in the Campaign for Lifelong Learning.' Recent publications include *Museums and the Education of Adults*, *Voluntary Organisations*, and *Adult Learning, Critical Intelligence and Social Change*. Undertakes research, runs conferences and seminars, and publishes the journals *Adult Learning* and *Studies in the Education of Adults*, and an annual reference *Yearbook*.

Northern Ireland Adult Education Association

c/o 42 Northland Road, Londonderry,
Northern Ireland BT48 7JL

The equivalent of NIACE in Northern Ireland.

Oral History Society

Department of Sociology, University of Essex,
Colchester CO4 3SQ (tel. 01206 873333)

Promotes and supports the use of sound or video recording to preserve people's memories and impressions, for use as an archive and in other ways (including Interpretation). Publishes a journal twice a year, and runs conferences and training courses. Members come from a wide variety of backgrounds.

Scottish Community Education Council

Rosebery House, 9 Haymarket Terrace,
Edinburgh EH12 5EZ (tel. 0131-313 2488)

The Scottish equivalent of NIACE.

Scottish Environmental Education Council

University of Stirling, Stirling FK9 4LA
(tel. 01786 467868)

An independent voluntary organisation, established in 1977. Its brochure quotes the words of a former Secretary of Scotland: 'In turning to a more sustainable management of our world we must raise awareness, change aspirations and enable people to understand the issues.' Its lively *Scottish Environmental Education News* ('seen') shows that its work is imaginatively interpretational in spirit (although the word 'interpretation' does not feature in one recent issue). It also promotes international youth conservation exchange.

Scottish Field Studies Association

Kindrogan Field Centre, Enochdhu, Blairgowrie,
Perthshire PH10 7PG (tel. 0125 081286)

Runs just this one Field Studies Centre, and aims to 'create among both adult and younger members of the general public a greater understanding of all aspects of the Scottish countryside.'

Teacher Training Colleges

The principles of environmental interpretation in its widest sense should be demonstrated and taught at these institutions. Listed in *The Education Year Book*, available in most major public libraries. The Teacher Training Agency is the relevant government-sponsored body.

University Extra-Mural Departments

Whether or not the term 'interpretation' is familiar in these circles, some of the best teaching in such departments is interpretational.

Voluntary Youth Organisations

Good youth work has an interpretational element in it: the concept should be developed within the youth work context, and relevant training offered both to professional and part-time youth leaders. Lists of local youth organisations are available from County Council Education Departments, in local libraries, and (incompletely) in Yellow Pages.

Workers' Educational Association (WEA)

17 Victoria Park Square, London E2 9PB
(tel. 0181-983 1515)

With 13 regional offices, it exists 'to interest men and women in their own continued education and to promote education for all sections of the community,' and through its local branches runs evening, day and weekend courses in a wide variety of subjects, and residential summer schools at home and abroad. It issues a regular newsletter, *Feedback*, and a variety of teaching materials. Comments under University Extra-Mural Departments (above) apply.

The Museums and Heritage Show

Organiser's Office: The Town House, Leigh,
 Worcester, WR6 5LA (tel. 01886 833505)

The only entirely commercial organisation to feature
 in this list, included because it provides a unique
 service in the form of annual rallying points for
 all those engaged in Interpretation and heritage
 management, at whatever level and in whatever
 sphere, in London and Edinburgh.

The Show has in recent years been held in London for
 two consecutive days in late March. A number of
 the stands are concerned with such things as
 display systems, audio-visual equipment, design
 and interpretation technology, etc. Relevant
 seminars also take place on these occasions.

A comparable event organised by the same office, but
 on a somewhat smaller scale, is The Scottish
 Museums and Attractions Show (known as
 SMASh). Up to now it has been held in alternate
 (even) years, in autumn, in Edinburgh.

An international show, with exhibitors from abroad,
 is also expected to become a regular, perhaps
 biennial, event – so far, held in London.
 Particulars of all these may be obtained from the
 address given above.

Interpretation Award Schemes

Interpret Britain Awards and Interpret Ireland Awards

Award Schemes Organiser, John Iddon, St Mary's
 University College, Strawberry Hill, Twickenham,
 Middlesex TW1 45X (tel. 0181-240 4000)

Inaugurated and administered by SIBH, these schemes
 are intended to 'recognise and publicise
 outstanding practice in the provision of
 interpretive facilities.' Entry is open to 'any
 organisation or individual in the public, private or
 voluntary sectors interpreting a theme, place, site,
 collection or facility, for the benefit of the general
 public.' Details and application forms are available
 each spring on request from the Award Schemes
 Organiser.

Appendix E
Recommended reading

This list is not intended to be a bibliography. It suggests a selection of books, booklets or articles that seem relevant to the themes of this book, and deliberately suggests some reading that would not usually appear in Interpretation book lists.

GENERAL INTRODUCTIONS TO INTERPRETATION

Aldridge, Don. *Site Interpretation: A Practical Guide* (Scottish Tourist Board, 1993, 56pp)
Included in this section because although it is largely about interpretive signs or panels, the author constantly stresses why good Interpreters do (or do not do) certain things. Principles of Interpretation are always to the fore, even in the midst of practicalities.

Aldridge, Don. *Guide to Countryside Interpretation, Part 1: Principles of Countryside Interpretation and Interpretive Planning* (HMSO for Countryside Commission for Scotland and The Countryside Commission, 1975, 40pp)
The first British exposition of the subject. Practical, basic, a little dated because so much has happened in British interpretation and in development of media in the (nearly) quarter of a century since. Now out of print.

Ham, Sam. *Environmental Interpretation: A Practical Guide for People with Big Ideas and Small Budgets* (North American Press, Golden, Colorado, 1992, 450pp)
A full, competent, up-to-date but by no means inexpensive book, covering why, when, what, where and how. Almost the only all-round book on the practice of Interpretation so far, and very wise and realistic.

Jenkins, J. Geraint. *Getting Yesterday Right: Interpreting the Heritage of Wales* (University of Wales Press, 1992, 207pp)

The former Curator of the Welsh Folk Museum at St Fagan's, Cardiff, and first Chairman of SIBH explores the problems of interpreting regional character without distortion and stereotyping.

Lewis, William. *Interpreting for Park Visitors* (Eastern Acorn Press, USA, 1981, 159pp)
Very much based on practice in USA National Parks, and addressed to park rangers, front-line Interpreters. Good advice that can easily be applied more widely.

Percival, Arthur. *Understanding Our Surroundings* (Civic Trust, London, 1979, 138pp)
The first British book devoted to suggestions for urban interpretation. Influential in the Civic Trust's promotion of visitor centres, but now inevitably dated, especially the section on financing! Out of print.

Tilden, Freeman. *Interpreting our Heritage* (Chapel Hill, University of North Carolina Press, 1957, 110pp)
The Interpreter's Bible – the pioneer exposition of the 'principles and practices for visitor services in parks, museums and historic places'. A little dated in terms of practices, but eternally valid as to principles. Many times reprinted, and still available.

BOOKS, BOOKLETS OR ARTICLES RELATING TO SPECIALIST ASPECTS OF INTERPRETATION

Interpretation of buildings

Keith, Crispin. *A Teacher's Guide to Using Listed Buildings* (English Heritage, 1991, 36pp)
Addressed to schoolteachers, but just as relevant to any Interpreter. Excellent examples of how education/interpetation can be made to stimulate observation and thought.

Communication theory

Gill, D. and B. Adams. *ABC of Communication Studies* (Macmillan Education, 1989; Nelson, 1992, 167pp)
An A-level handbook, with articles in alphabetical order, with suggestions for further reading.

O'Sullivan, T., J. Hartley, D. Saunders and J. Fiske. *Key Concepts in Communication* (Routledge, 1983, reprinted, 270pp)
In alphabetical encyclopedia form, defining the terminology at the same time as expounding the principles.

Earth education

Van Matre, Steve. *Sunship Earth* (Acclimatization Experiences Institute, Illinois, 1979)

Education theory

Jarvis, Peter. *Adult and Continuing Education: Theory and Practice* (Routledge, 1983)
Looks as if it has come straight from the typewriter, and so none too reader-friendly; but thorough, practical and with good chapter-by-chapter recommended reading lists. Interpretation as we know it is not specifically recognised.

Evaluating Interpretation

O'Riordan, Timothy, Christopher Wood and Ann Sheldrake. *Landscapes for Tomorrow* (Yorkshire Dales National Park Committee, 1992, 64pp)
An interesting and unusual report of an interesting and unusual exercise that combined evaluation with public participation and practical interpretation.

Prince, David R. *Evaluating Interpretation* (CEI Occasional Paper no. 1, 1982, 25pp typescript)
Dipped a tentative toe into the subject, which was a very new idea to most British Interpreters at the time. With hindsight, based on a rather limited vision of Interpretational methods; conclusions not a great help.

Prince, David R. *Countryside Interpretation: a Cognitive Evaluation* (CEI, 1982, 17pp typescript)
Some interesting data based on careful assessment of visitor learning (or remembering), and some sobering conclusions about what facts people seem able to recall after a visit to a display.

Taylor, Graham, ed. *Evaluation of Interpretation* (SIBH, 1982, 27pp typescript)
Report on a conference held in December 1981. Still of interest, though nothing very profound.

Interpreters – professional or amateur?

Breakell, Bill. 'Professional Eyes?', *Interpretation Journal*, no. 53 (Summer 1993)
A brief but heartfelt and original plea to beware of the dangers of 'over-professionalising' Interpretation.

Interpretive planning

Carter, James, ed. *A Sense of Place: an Interpretive Planning Handbook* (Tourism and the Environment Initiative, Inverness 1997)
This practical and colourfuly illustrated manual describes the steps involved in planning Interpretation, and includes guidance on working in consultation with local community groups.

Veverka, John. *Interpretive Master Planning* (Faken Press, Montana, 162pp)
A very thorough exposition of the why and how of Interpretive planning.

Media studies

Price, Stuart. *Media Studies* (Pitman, 1993, 438pp)
Perhaps unexpectedly, almost every chapter of this book turns out to have something relevant to say to the professional Interpreter.

Museums and Interpretation

Durbin, Gail. *Studying the Victorians at the Victoria and Albert Museum – a Handbook for Teachers* (Victoria and Albert Museum, 1994, 48pp)
Besides its primary object of briefing teachers on how to make the best of a visit to the Museum, it demonstrates that true Interpretation is alive and well in Museum education, and could be in schools, too.

Hooper-Greenhill, Eilean, ed. *Initiatives in Museum Education* (Department of Museum Studies, University of Leicester, 1989, 32pp)
13 articles, including 'Learning about the natural environment'; 'Evaluating learning from historical objects'; 'Reaching the community: modern art and the new audience'; 'Pre-vocational education and museums'; and 'Managing museums for learning'.

Miles, Roger S. et al. *The Design of Educational Exhibits* (Unwin Hyman, 1982, 1988, 198pp)
Highly professional study of the principles and practice of display design, and full of practical examples. Interesting chapters treating educational psychology, access for disabled, and evaluation of design effectiveness.

Zetterberg, Hans L. *Museums and Adult Education* (Evelyn, Adams and Mackay, for the International Council of Museums, 1968, 89pp)
This book is evidence that the museum world was aware early of the need for interpretation and for a systematic academic as well as practical approach to it. Contains international bibliography that should be of value to students of the development of museum education and interpretation.

Oral history
Evans, George Ewart. *Spoken History* (Faber and Faber, 1987, 255pp)
The author's last book, summarising his life's work as a pioneer of oral history. Chapters 'The Interview' and 'Conclusion' are especially relevant to interpreters.
Perks, Robert. *Oral History: Talking about the Past* (The Historical Association, 1996, 44pp)
A practical beginner's handbook, including a section on 'how oral history can be used . . . ranging from publications and exhibitions to teaching materials'.

Parish maps
Clifford, Sue and Angela King, eds. *From place to PLACE; maps and Parish Maps* (Common Ground, 1996)
Celebrates the success of the Parish Maps scheme.
Mayfield, Beatrice and Sue Clifford. *Parish Maps* (Common Ground, n.d., 24pp)
Booklet, illustrated in colour, explaining the concept of Parish Maps, illustrating several examples, and giving helpful advice to anyone thinking of taking up the idea.

Psychology
Berne, Eric. *Games People Play* (USA, 1964; Deutsch, 1966; Penguin 1968 and reprints)
— *What Do You Say After You Say Hello?* (City National Bank, USA, 1972; Deutsch 1974; Corgi, 1975 and reprints)
Popular and entertaining introductions to Transactional Analysis.
Lee, Terence. 'Some thoughts on informing, revealing and persuading', *Interpretation Journal*, no. 47, 1991
Includes a simple exposition of the concept of *schemata*. Cognition theory applied to Interpretation.
See also under **Education theory**

Sense of place
Clifford, Sue and Angela King, eds. *Local Distinctiveness: Place, Particularity and Identity* (Common Ground, 1993)

Subject research
Hey, David, ed. *The Oxford Companion to Local and Family History* (Oxford University Press, 1996)
Entries of various lengths, including essays on landscape history, industry and trade, and architectural styles. Appendix lists all Record Offices in Britain.
Iredale, David. *Enjoying Archives: What They Are; Where to Find Them; How to Use Them* (David and Charles, 1973, 264pp)
Plenty of examples and case studies.
Richardson, John. *The Local Historian's Encyclopedia* (Historical Publications, 1986, recent updated editions)
Terms defined, archives explained, sources listed, bibliographies.
See also **Oral history** and, for picture libraries, an up-to-date edition of *The Writers' and Artists' Yearbook* (A. & C. Black)

Tourism and Interpretation
O'Toole, Fintan. 'The Emperor's Map makes us tourists in our own Land', *Interpretation Journal*, no. 51 (Winter 1992; reprinted from *The Irish Times*)
A salutary reminder of the just resentment that can be aroused by poor tourism or interpretation planning. See also Derek Baylis's response in *Interpretation Journal*, no. 52)

Tourism, sustainable
Shirley Eber, ed., for Tourism Concern. *Beyond the Green Horizon* (WWF UK, 1992)
'A discussion paper on principles for sustainable tourism', with detailed case studies and bibliography – though, surprisingly, little mention of public education or interpretation.

Visitor centre design
Beazley, Elisabeth. *The Countryside on View* (Constable, 1971, 207pp)
Very sensible, practical advice, most of it still relevant after a quarter of a century, though the appendices on materials are quite out of date.

NOTE: the CEI's *Bulletin*, over the period 1985–95, consisted of themed issues each containing articles on various aspects of a single relevant specialist topic. These included heritage centres, audio-visuals, living history, access and interpretation for the disabled, visitor centres, urban interpretation, evaluating interpretation, writing skills, outdoor panels and signs, interpretive publications, self-guided trails, training, exhibitions, arts in interpretation, tourism and the travel, industry, interpreting for children and interpretation in Scotland.

The journal *Interpretation*, a joint production since 1996 of SIBH and CEI, is at present also themed (see **Current periodical publications** below).

The long series of the SIBH's newsletter *Interpretation* (1975–83) and its successor *Interpretation Journal* (1984–95) contained a number of reports and articles that illuminate the development of Interpretation in Britain. An index is being prepared, and complete sets of the 57 issues are held for reference by SIBH.

CURRENT PERIODICAL PUBLICATIONS RELATING TO INTERPRETATION

Communicating the message
Scottish Natural Heritage, Battleby, Redgorton, Perth PH1 3EW
A simple but first-class 12-page magazine for Interpreters and proprietors, relevant far beyond the shores of Scotland!

Interpretation
Enquiries to SIBH
The thrice-yearly journal formerly published jointly by the CEI and SIBH and now by SIBH alone, issued free to paid-up members of SIBH. Issues have included themes of multicultural issues; enabling access; visitor centres; multimedia, carrying capacity and outdoor panels.

International Journal of Heritage Studies
Editorial and Distribution: EFAE, Earl Richards Road North, Exeter, EX2 6AS
Quarterly academic publication which aims to deal with a wide range of topics in various disciplines relating to what is now often known as 'heritage', though here the term is interpreted widely – 'from the aesthetic object conserved in a museum to the wildlife conserved within a nature reserve, and from a cathedral to a canyon.' One of the eight disciplines cited as targets for the journal is 'Interpretation and Communication'.

InterpEdge
Enquiries c/o Touchstone, Cruachan, Tayinloan, Tarbert, Argyll PA29 6XF (tel. 01583 441208)
A thrice-yearly publication originating in the USA, very much addressed to practitioners of Interpretation, and highlighting new ideas, techniques and technologies.

Interpretation Directory
List of SIBH members and specialist interpreters (including general consultants, designers, copy-writers, researchers, model-makers, living history exponents, sign makers, etc.). Issued at two- or three-year intervals free to members.

Museums Journal
Publication of the Museums Association: frequently includes articles on aspects of presentation and interpretation.

PUBLISHING: GENERAL REFERENCE

The Writers' and Artists' Year Book (A. & C. Black, issued annually)
Contains lists of picture libraries and art studios; articles on copyright, picture research, proof-correcting.

BOOKS ON THE HISTORICAL BACKGROUND TO CONSERVATION

Allen, David Elliston. *The Naturalist in Britain: A Social History* (Allen Lane, 1976; Penguin Books, 1978)
Arvill, Robert [pseudonym]. *Man and Environment: Crisis and the Strategy of Choice* (Penguin Books, 1967, revised 1969)
Sheail, John. *Nature in Trust: The History of Nature Conservation in Britain* (Blackie, 1976)
Tilden, Freeman. *The National Parks: What they Mean to You and Me* (Alfred A. Knopf, New York 1951)
The first four chapters and the final envoi are relevantly philosophical; the chapters between describe and evaluate over fifty of the USA's National Parks and Monuments.

Williams-Ellis, Clough, ed. *Britain and the Beast*
(J. M. Dent, 1938)
Articles by celebrated persons on the plight of
Britain's towns and countryside.

Books that Interpret

Good examples of interesting and relevant content,
clear exposition, attractive presentation, and
design that helps the understanding, created on
Interpretation principles:

Bellamy, David et al. *Woodland Walks* (Hamlyn, 1982)
Colebourn, Phil and Bob Gibbons. *Britain's
Countryside Heritage* (Blandford, in association with
the National Trust, 1990)
Hoskins, W. G. and Christopher Taylor. *The Making of
the English Landscape* (Hodder & Stoughton, 1988)
Rackham, Oliver. *The Illustrated History of the
Countryside* (Weidenfeld and Nicolson, 1994)
There are, of course, many good films, videos and
CD-ROMs that Interpret, and whose methods
Interpreters may study with profit.

Bibliographies and booklists

Barclay, Derrick, ed. *Interpretation of the Environment –
a Bibliography* (Carnegie United Kingdom Trust,
1983, 52pp)
Useful still, though an update would be welcome.
A number of books and articles relating to
Interpretation carry their own bibliographies.

A novel about Interpretation

Masterman, J. C. *To Teach the Senators Wisdom*
(Hodder and Stoughton, 1952)
Perhaps the only novel describing the compilation
of a guidebook. Mainly for entertainment, but
contains some perceptive comments and
situations that Interpreters might care to note.

A book with a message

Aldridge, Don. *The Monster Book of Environmental
Education* (Geo Abstracts, 1981)
Beyond classification, consisting of hugely
amusing cartoon sequences that pack a savage
bite. Muddled thinking, pretension, copy-catting
and smugness in Environmental Interpretation are
scathingly exposed in what is rather like a
warning from a smiling but savage Old Testament
prophet – with perhaps a touch of Cassandra, too.

Picture credits

The author and publishers would like to thank the following for permission to reproduce illustrations. We have made every effort to contact and acknowledge copyright holders, but if any errors have been made we would be happy to correct them at a later printing.

page 3	Associated Press, London
page 6	James Carter, CEI, Manchester
page 35	Norfolk Museums Service
page 51	Sue White
page 66	Ray Manley
page 77, top	Norfolk Library Services
page 77, bottom	Martin Warren
page 95, both	Avril Pierssené
page 107	Mark Cleghorn
page 144	Eureka!, Halifax
page 146	Bristol Civic Trust
page 163	Environmental Management Group, Hertfordshire County Council
page 172	Insite Consultancy
page 181, all	Avril and Andrew Pierssené
page 188	Kennet and Avon Canal Trust
page 210	John Iddon, St Mary's University College, Twickenham
page 219, both	Hanes Aberteifi
page 222	Avril Pierssené
all other pictures	Andrew Pierssené

Index